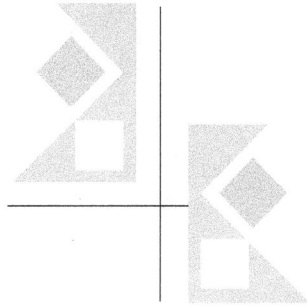

POVERTY, INEQUALITY, AND EVALUATION

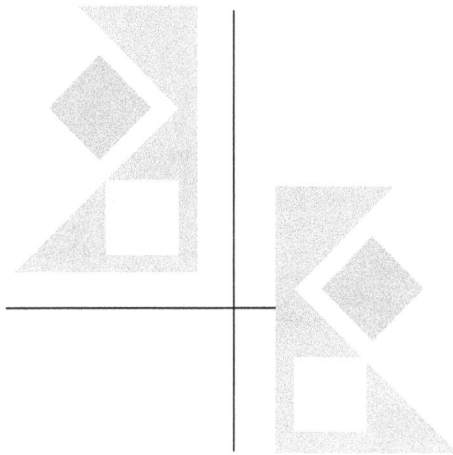

POVERTY, INEQUALITY, AND EVALUATION

Changing Perspectives

Ray C. Rist,
Frederic P. Martin, and
Ana Maria Fernandez,
Editors

WORLD BANK GROUP

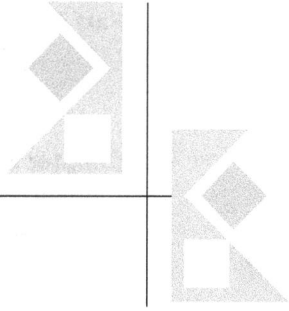

CONTENTS

Chapter 5. Addressing Inequality and Poverty:
An Evaluation of Community Empowerment in Jordan   73
Ann M. Doucette

Chapter 6. Determining the Results of a Social
Safety Net Program in St. Lucia   97
Paulette Nichols, Bobb Darnell, and Frederic Unterreiner

Chapter 7. HIV/AIDS Services Delivery, Overall Quality
of Care, and Satisfaction in Burkina Faso: Are Some
Patients Privileged?   121
Harounan Kazianga, Seni Kouanda, Laetitia N. Ouedraogo,
*   Elisa Rothenbuhler, Mead Over, and Damien de Walque*

Chapter 8. A Portfolio Approach to Evaluation:
Evaluations of Community-Based HIV/AIDS Responses   **139**
Rosalía Rodriguez-García

Part Three: Assessment and Design of Public Management
**   Systems That Reduce Poverty and Inequality**   **175**

Chapter 9. Evaluating How National Development Plans
Can Contribute to Poverty and Inequality Reduction:
The Cases of Cambodia and Costa Rica   **177**
Ana Maria Fernandez, Roberto Garcia-Lopez, Thavrak Tuon,
*   and Frederic P. Martin*

Figures

Maps

Photos

Tables

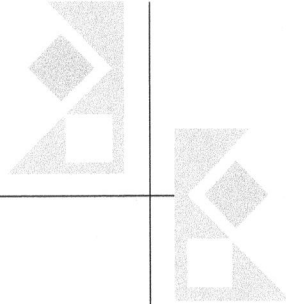

ABOUT THE EDITORS

Ray C. Rist completed his second term as president of the International Development Evaluation Association (IDEAS) in 2014. He is also a cofounder and codirector of the International Program for Development Evaluation Training (IPDET). Retired from the Independent Evaluation Group of the World Bank, he continues to advise organizations and governments throughout the world on how to design and build results-based monitoring and evaluation systems. His career includes senior appointments in the U.S. government, academic institutions, and the World Bank. He is the author or editor of 31 books and more than 150 articles. He serves on the boards of nine professional journals.

Frederic P. Martin is principal economist and copresident of the Institute for Development of Economics and Administration (IDEA International). He taught from 1987 until 2005 at Laval University, Canada, where he served as professor and chair for international development. He also served from 2010 until 2014 on the IDEAS board of directors. He has 34 years of experience in 42 countries of Africa, the Americas, Asia, and Europe, supporting governments in implementing results-based management, including improving monitoring and evaluation systems and building evaluation capacity. He is the author or coauthor of nearly 115 publications.

Ana Maria Fernandez has been senior economist at the Institute for Development of Economics and Administration (IDEA International) since 2010. Between 2003 and 2009, she worked as a professional in various public agencies in the government of Colombia, including the presidency, implementing results-based management practices and monitoring and evaluation systems. From 2010 to the present she has worked as a monitoring and evaluation specialist, strengthening public sector management practices in 14 countries of the Americas, Asia, and Europe. She is the coauthor of six publications.

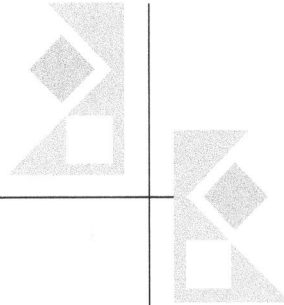

ABBREVIATIONS

A4R	assessment for results
AIDS	acquired immune deficiency syndrome
aOR	adjusted odds ratio
ART	antiretroviral treatment
CBO	community-based organization
CEP	Community Empowerment Program
CI	confidence interval
CSO	civil society organization
DFID	U. K. Department for International Development
DHS	Demographic and Health Survey
EPU	Economic Policy Unit
ERR	economic rate of return
EU	European Union
FBO	faith-based organization
FCG	family caregiver
FDI	foreign direct investment
FSW	female sex worker
FT	fair trade
GDP	gross domestic product
GTFP	Global Trade Finance Program
HBCT	home-based counseling and testing
HIV	human immunodeficiency virus
IDA	International Development Association (of the World Bank Group)
IDEA	Institute for Development in Economics and Administration
IDEAS	International Development Evaluation Association
IFC	International Finance Corporation (of the World Bank Group)

IEG	Independent Evaluation Group
IPDET	International Program for Development Evaluation Training
IPRSAP	Interim Poverty Reduction Strategy and Action Plan
JRF	Jordan River Foundation
KPI	key performance indicator
LFA	logical framework approach
M&E	monitoring and evaluation
MDG	Millennium Development Goal
MIDEPLAN	Ministry of National Planning and Economic Policy (Costa Rica)
MOST	Ministry of Social Transformation (St. Lucia)
MSC	most significant change
MSME	micro, small, and medium enterprise
MSM/Ts	men who have sex with men and transgender individuals
NDP	national development plan
NGO	nongovernmental organization
NSDP	National Strategic Development Plan
OAS	Organization of American States
OECD	Organisation for Economic Co-operation and Development
OR	odds ratio
PEPFAR	U.S. President's Emergency Plan for AIDS Relief
PLI	poverty line income
PLWHA	persons living with HIV/AIDS
PMD	Prime Minister's Department
PPP	public-private partnership
PSD	private sector development
PSI	People Living with HIV Stigma Index
RBM	results-based management
RCCDP	Rural Community Cluster Development Program
RCT	randomized control trial
SME	small and medium enterprise
SSDF	St. Lucia Social Development Fund
STI	sexually transmitted infection
UNAIDS	United Nations HIV/AIDS Program
UNESCO	United Nations Educational, Scientific, and Cultural Organization
UNICEF	United Nations Children's Fund
VCD	value chain development

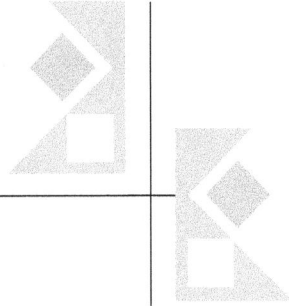

Introduction

Ray C. Rist

Poverty is about power, and the distribution of chronic poverty is about inequality.

—Tom Ling, chapter 12 of this book

The Premise

This book seeks to shift the conversation on the future of development needs away from a focus on poverty and toward a focus on inequality. Essentially, the contributors to this volume believe that the emphasis on poverty is caught in an intellectual and political cul de sac that fails to address the fundamental question of why people are poor or what can be done structurally and institutionally to reduce and eliminate poverty. The conversation needs to change. We need to focus on the structural issues of inequality—economic inequality, political inequality, and social inequality. Why is it that tens of millions of persons are without fresh water? Why is it

Ray Rist is with the International Program for Development Evaluation Training (IPDET).

that tens of millions are without food, medicine, education, or a political voice? The realities go far deeper than just being poor.

This book seeks to open up the conversation among development evaluators as to what we know about inequality, how we have assessed it, how we have evaluated it, and what our work tells us about how to address it head-on. However, the evaluation literature on inequality is extremely thin, unlike the evaluation literature on economics, where the topic of inequality is extensively analyzed and assessed. Few evaluators have specifically addressed inequality in their work. The citations in this book are overwhelmingly in reference to poverty, not inequality. The evaluation community has focused so much more on alleviating poverty than on alleviating inequality. Inequality is apparently an afterthought for most everyone in the development arena.

Inequality and the Evaluation Literature

This does not mean that there is no or little more general literature on inequality. The past seven to eight years, in particular, have brought forth a new and focused literature on inequality—particularly in the discipline of economics. For example, Joseph Stiglitz, winner of the Nobel Prize in Economics, has recently written a book entitled *The Price of Inequality: How Today's Divided Society Endangers Our Future* (Stiglitz 2013). Thomas Piketty has published his opus, *Capital in the Twenty-First Century* (Piketty 2014), and Chrystia Freeland has provided her critique, *Plutocrats: The Rise of the New Global Super-Rich and the Fall of Everyone Else* (Freeland 2012). These and many other books address the growth of inequality over the past decade. That the evaluation literature has had so little to offer to this discussion is disconcerting. But this book takes one step in a new direction.

Why has inequality become such an important topic in at least some of the social sciences? Consider this quote from Tom Ling in chapter 12 of this book:

> The argument is now well known. Between the 1990s and the 2010s, we have seen reductions in extreme poverty, severe acute malnutrition, and children with no access to schools. Only progress on one [Millennium Development Goal] (maternal mortality) remains well behind the target. However, despite these overall improvements, the people excluded from these gains are found in increasingly predictable locations. They are individuals who belong to groups that are discriminated against and excluded within their own societies. This discrimination may be on grounds of religion, ethnicity, gender, or disability. The poor are also likely to be chronically poor—rather than dipping in and out of poverty—and their poverty is variously described as deep seated, embedded, or deep rooted. Poverty is about power, and the distribution of chronic poverty is about inequality.

Part of the notion of "donor fatigue" that frequently appears in the development literature is that the amount of aid to developing countries is not even remotely capable of making a real dent in extreme poverty. As Taylor (2013, 14–15) notes,

Official development assistance (ODA) totaled $133.5 billion in 2011 with approximately 2.5 billion people living on less than $2 per day (OECD 2011). So, at current levels, if aid is regarded as directly delivering benefits/resources, aid could offer under $0.15 to each poor person per day. In the context of rising global food prices, as population pressures increase, this would barely make an impact on the majority of people's lives. Therefore, for aid to be effective, it has to stimulate wider change, and there is a need to leverage current levels of aid to produce greater outcomes. There has been an increasing recognition in recent years that this is not likely to happen through traditional delivery of "charity" (Pronk 2001; Rogerson 2010). Instead, donors have begun, discursively at least, to incorporate objectives of systemic change into a greater number of their programs in an increasing range of sectors.

Again, returning to Ling (chapter 12 of this book),

Consequently for the world's poorest to survive and thrive would require removing the inequalities that bind them. Without addressing systemic change, the benefits of economic growth will be sequestered by the already-rich, and jobless growth will mean that unemployed people—and often unemployed youth—will live in extreme poverty alongside a high-income elite. Programs may be improved by using mobile technology, improving cash transfers, achieving higher agricultural yields, or improving cold supply chains to deliver vaccines. But without transforming the binding constraints that reinforce the deep-seated causes of chronic poverty, substantial progress is unlikely. In turn, reducing inequalities in income, wealth, and social and cultural power requires achieving change in the systems or underlying causes of impoverishment.

Ling is one of the few evaluators calling attention to the causes and consequences of inequality. Another articulate voice on this matter is Robert Picciotto, whose chapter in this book essentially calls for a reformulation and a rethinking of evaluation in the development arena. In chapter 13, Picciotto notes,

The unprecedented 2008 financial crisis, its root causes, and its aftermath call for a thorough reconsideration of evaluation models and practices. Public perceptions have changed, and there is no turning back. Equality, long neglected as an explicit objective of public policy, has made a comeback. As a result, evaluators everywhere have to engage more critically and independently with the antecedents and effects of inequality in society.

His critique of evaluators is unrelenting:

Given that they are fee dependent, evaluators have been prone to frame their evaluations to meet the needs and concerns of program managers rather than those of citizens. They have found ample justification for their supine stance in the organizational management literature and utilization-focused evaluation textbooks. Yet evading or downplaying the summative dimension of evaluation in order to make evaluation findings palatable does not serve to make authority responsible or responsive to the public interest.

The implications of this transition within evaluation are the need to examine the processes and consequences of inequality more carefully and thoroughly. This means that evaluators will need to start addressing issues of social justice. They will also need to start looking to the social sciences for research on inequality and implications for public policy. In short, they will need to start looking critically at the vested interests in our societies that benefit from the status quo. Turning a blind eye to these interests and instead evaluating bed nets, water pumps, and cash transfers will leave the discipline where it is at present—increasingly irrelevant and unable to take on and address the global inequality challenge.

Postscript

The editors of this book wish to acknowledge publicly the intellectual innovation and willingness of IDEAS (International Development Evaluation Association) to take on this topic of evaluation and inequality. We know of no other evaluation association that has explicitly addressed this issue so frankly and so directly. This book grows out of this intellectual courage not to stay silent, not to focus simply on methods or on irrelevant distinctions between complicated and complex issues, but to address one of the most pressing issues of this early part of the 21st century.

Thank you, IDEAS!

References

Freeland, C. 2012. *Plutocrats: The Rise of the New Global Super-Rich and the Fall of Everyone Else.* New York: Penguin Books.

OECD (Organisation for Economic Co-operation and Development). 2011. "The Busan Partnership for Effective Development Co-operation." Development Assistance Committee, OECD, Paris.

Piketty, T. 2014. *Capital in the Twenty-First Century*. Cambridge, MA: Belknap Press.

Pronk, J. P. 2001. "Aid as a Catalyst." *Development and Change* 32 (4): 611–29.

Rogerson, A. 2010. "The Evolving Development Finance Architecture: A Short List of Problems and Opportunities for Action in Busan." Consultation paper for Seoul Workshop, OECD, Paris.

Stiglitz, J. 2013. *The Price of Inequality: How Today's Divided Society Endangers Our Future*. New York: W. W. Norton and Company.

Taylor, B. 2013. "Evidence-Based Policy and Systemic Change: Conflicting Trends?" Springfield Working Paper 1, Springfield Centre, Durham, U.K.

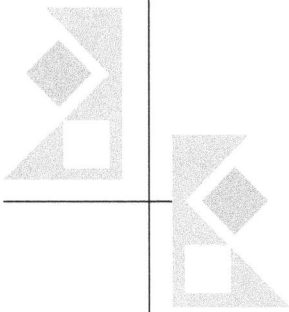

PART ONE: ANALYTICAL FRAMEWORK

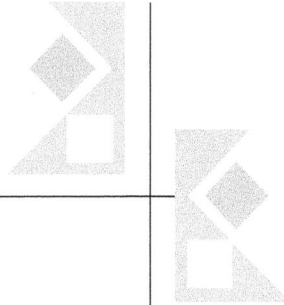

CHAPTER 1

Moving the Discussion from Poverty to Inequality: Implications for Evaluation

Paul Shaffer

Introduction: The Return of Inequality

> *To determine the laws which regulate this distribution [of the produce of the Earth] is the principal problem in Political Economy.* (Ricardo 2004 [1821], 1)

There is nothing new about inequality as an empirical phenomenon, object of inquiry, or topic of policy relevance. Still, the past few years have seen a marked shift in the attention afforded inequality in academic, policy, and applied development circles. This shift is evidenced by the publication of some important texts on the subject, including Thomas Piketty's *Capital in the Twenty-First Century* (Piketty 2014), Joseph Stiglitz's *The Price of Inequality* (Stiglitz 2012), and Branko Milanovic's *The Haves and*

Paul Shaffer is with the Department of International Development Studies and the Trent in Ghana Program at Trent University. He is grateful to Frederic Martin, whose comments significantly improved this chapter.

Have-Nots (Milanovic 2011). Important policy statements have come from the likes of U.S. President Obama, among others, who famously characterized inequality as the "defining challenge of our time" (White House 2013). In applied international development circles, the World Bank has moved forcefully in the direction of inequality in its "shared prosperity" approach, whereby the average income or consumption growth of the bottom 40 percent of the population is proposed as a core gauge of development progress (World Bank 2015). Similarly, 1 of the 17 recently proposed Sustainable Development Goals is to "reduce inequality within and among countries" (United Nations General Assembly 2014). There is little question that inequality has reemerged on the scene in a significant way.

In this regard, inequality poses a challenge to poverty as the dominant theme in international development circles. Prior to this "inequality renaissance," the centrality of poverty was evidenced by a series of high-profile and best-selling books on the subject, including Jeffrey Sachs's *The End of Poverty* (Sachs 2005), Paul Collier's *The Bottom Billion* (Collier 2007), and Abhijit Banerjee and Ester Duflo's *Poor Economics* (Banerjee and Duflo 2011). Applied research on the topic flourished in such publications as the World Bank's flagship *World Development Report 2000/2001* (World Bank 2001), the Chronic Poverty Research Centre's *Chronic Poverty Reports 2004–05* and *2008–09* (Chronic Poverty Research Centre 2005, 2009), and so forth. Operationally, poverty reduction took center stage as the first of eight Millennium Development Goals intended to guide overseas development assistance.

This chapter teases out the implications of the shift from poverty to inequality, arguing that the "inequality turn" (a) expands the dimensions of deprivation or social "bads" under consideration, (b) changes the focus of causal analysis from households and individuals to social structures and relationships, and (c) enlarges the range of policy instruments and programming options under review. The net effect is to expand the scope for evaluation, but also to increase its complexity and difficulty. These three changes are reviewed in the three sections that follow. Empirical examples are provided to illustrate certain of the issues addressed. A final section summarizes the discussion.

First it is necessary to be clear about how inequality and poverty are defined in this chapter. Poverty is about the lack or insufficiency of something of value for units of a population (or sample). It is widely acknowledged that poverty is multidimensional, so that "things of value" include physiological and social dimensions of deprivation (Shaffer 2008). The units in question are typically households or individuals. The core point is that poverty is about those who fall below an adequacy threshold, or poverty line, which in applied work is often set in terms of minimal levels of consumption expenditure or income. Of the many poverty measures, the industry standard is the Foster-Greer-Thorbecke class of indexes, which can account for the percentage of population, the gap, and the distribution below the poverty line (Ravallion 1994).

Unlike poverty, inequality is about the distribution of something of value across units of a population (or sample). As with poverty, objects of value may include all sorts of things, including Amartya Sen's notion of capabilities (Sen 1982), freedoms, life opportunities, income, and so forth. There are many measures of inequality, which differ in their aggregation properties, approaches to weighting components of the distribution, and so on (Cowell 2000).

For the present purposes, the core difference between the two concepts is that inequality is an inherently aggregate concept in a way that poverty is not. It makes sense to speak of an individual in poverty and not an individual in inequality.[1] Inequality is about the entire distribution, whereas poverty is about individuals below a threshold. As mentioned, causal analysis of inequality tends to shift the focus from individuals to social aggregates. The implications are discussed further in the section on causal analysis.

Expanding Dimensions of Deprivation or Social "Bads"

As discussed, inequality is about the distribution of things across a population, while poverty is about persons below an adequacy threshold. Overlapping concerns are raised by both concepts, although distinct aspects of deprivation, or social "bads," may be associated with each. More specifically, inequality tends to raise a much broader range of issues than is typically posed by poverty.

First, high (or rising) levels of inequality may conflict with our intuitions about distributive justice or the "just" distribution of things of value in society. For example, it is hard to square very high levels of inequality with Rawlsian accounts of justice, based on a hypothesized "just" distribution of primary goods, derived from behind the so-called veil of ignorance whereby one's place in the distribution is unknown. One of the core principles of justice, the difference principle, maintains that "social and economic inequalities are to be arranged so that they are to the greatest benefit of the least advantaged" (Rawls 1971).[2] High levels of inequality in the context of want are equally hard to reconcile with needs-based conceptions of justice, whose most famous exposition is from Marx (1977 [1875], 569): "From each according to his ability, to each according to his needs."

Consider also desert-based accounts of justice based on returns to effort or contribution (Miller 1976). One such variant is the neoclassical marginal productivity theory of distribution, whereby the derivation of the factoral distribution of income follows from the assumption that factors of production are paid their marginal product (Dobb 1973). From the perspective of distributional justice, however, several problems arise: (a) it is very hard to believe that the extremely high compensation packages received by top chief executive officers and persons employed in the financial sector or the historically low compensation offered in female-dominated professions, for example, have very much to do with marginal productivity (the violated assumption problem); (b) it is hard to justify vast differences in life opportunities between high- and low-income countries, even if they are due to productivity differences (the accident of birth problem); (c) there is no particular reason why economic valuation should trump social or normative valuation when assessing distributional outcomes as evidenced, for example, in very high returns (and associated marginal product) for munitions makers and casino operators, among others (the market valuation problem).

In addition to concerns of distributive justice, other social ills are associated with inequality, but not poverty per se, which include (a) fracturing society into distinct publics, (b) diminishing public resources for addressing problems, (c) making beggars of citizens (insofar as charity substitutes for entitlements), (d) fostering elitism and resentment, and (d) undermining democracy (Cunningham 2007). In terms of economic effects alone, Joseph Stiglitz (2012) has recently argued that high inequality creates or reflects (a) overleveraging and financial instability, (b) low levels of needed public investment, (c) rent seeking and excessive financialization, (d) perverse work incentives (through undue reliance on pecuniary rewards), and (e) consumerism. Clearly, the items on these lists cover issues that go beyond those typically associated with poverty. In this regard, the concepts of positional goods and horizontal inequality deserve special attention.

The idea of positional goods was originally proposed by Fred Hirsch to denote the increasingly social nature of consumption in the sense that "the satisfaction that individuals derive from goods and services depends in increasing measure not only on their own consumption but on consumption by others as well" (Hirsch 1976, 2). Robert Frank (2007) has extended this insight to show how rising inequality has increased the "positional good premium," with harmful effects for middle-class households. Specifically, he argues that the value associated with certain types of goods, such as homes, cars, higher education, and so forth, is derived largely from their effects as signaling mechanisms of relative standing or social rank. Rising inequality acts to increase the share of disposable income spent on positional goods by raising the bar of comparator households or individuals. Accordingly, proportionately more is spent on such goods, with no appreciable increase in satisfaction, as all are situated on a moving treadmill. However, real costs are associated with these higher outlays, including longer working hours, increased indebtedness, longer commutes, and growing sleep deprivation, among others.

A second example of social "bads" associated with inequality involves the relationship between conflict and horizontal inequalities— inequalities between "cultural" groups, based on ethnicity, race, gender, region, and so forth. It has been argued that conflict becomes more likely when access to economic, political, or social resources coincides with membership in such groups. Several empirical examples from the Global South appear to fit this explanatory framework (with the necessary qualifications), including Chiapas (Mexico), Fiji, Sri Lanka, Malaysia, and South Africa. Likewise, the analytical framework has explanatory power for populations in higher-income countries, as evidenced, for example, by recent conflicts involving African American communities in the United States and First Nations peoples in Canada. In these cases, conflict is likely related more closely to inequality than to poverty per se, although the latter is also relevant.

The most pervasive forms of horizontal inequalities in virtually all societies relate to gender. There are many dimensions of gender disadvantage that go beyond the dimensions of deprivation typically discussed in the context of poverty. A short list would include gender-based differences with respect to occupational choice, remuneration, labor force participation, decision-making authority, division of labor within the household, workload, access to resources such as land and credit, physical security, domestic violence, and so forth. Many of these types of issues do not receive adequate treatment when analyzing gender differences from a poverty perspective alone (Jackson 1996).

This expansion of the dimensions of deprivation, or social "bads," matters for evaluation because it bears directly on the gauge used to assess the performance of development policies or programs. De Silva and Gunetilleke's (2008) evaluation of a resettlement scheme following a highway development project in Sri Lanka provides an example. The standard indicators used in the evaluation were related to poverty and included measures of payment allowances, replacement of agricultural land, physical quality of housing, and access to basic utilities. In general, these indicators presented a favorable assessment of the resettlement process.

However, perceptions of participants in the resettlement scheme painted a different picture:

> Shared ownership of lands among families, the informal social networks where housework such as child care is often shared, and open access to assets within the extended family are characteristics of these villages which the STDP [Southern Transport Development Project] has caused to be suddenly severed.... Despite making resettlement decisions that allowed them to maintain their social networks, the whole process of relocation and the change it stimulates has an impact on social well-being. A major articulated loss is the loss of the traditional/ancestral village and the lifestyle that goes with it.

The sense of unease expressed by participants relates much more closely to social isolation and growing inequality than to poverty. The core point is that, while the evaluative metric always "matters" in poverty-focused evaluations, the metric "matters more" when dimensions of deprivation and social "bads" expand in the shift from poverty to inequality.

Shifting Causal Analysis to Social Structures and Relationships

> Processes of accumulation bring about the reproduction of poverty. The wealth of some is causally linked to the crushing poverty of others. (Harris 2009, 220)

As discussed in the introduction to this chapter, poverty can be understood as an individual- or household-level phenomenon in a way that inequality cannot.[3] Various traditions of inquiry into poverty rely on this fact to base causal analysis on characteristics of poor households or communities. One example is the causal analysis of "poverty traps" offered in one of the most influential, and best-selling, monographs on poverty in recent years, Jeffrey Sachs's *The End of Poverty*: "Poor rural villages lack trucks, paved roads, power generators, irrigation channels. Human capital is very low, with hungry, disease-ridden, and illiterate villagers struggling for survival" (Sachs 2005, 56). Another example from anthropology is Oscar Lewis's "culture of poverty" thesis that poverty is perpetuated by harmful social, economic, and psychological traits of poor people, including "lack of impulse control, strong present-time orientation with relatively little ability to defer gratification and to plan for the future" (Lewis 1968, 192). Lewis does not argue that such factors are the underlying causes of poverty, which he attributes to the "culture of capitalism," but he does say that they have causal force.

The applied tradition of microeconomics, which provides the "gold standard" of poverty analysis in the Global South, offers another example.

Here, an expenditure function is estimated that represents the monetary value, or cost, of a given level of utility, appropriately adjusted for differences in household composition and prices (Deaton and Muellbauer 1980). Next, determinants of (low) expenditure, or poverty, are estimated econometrically using variables representing such factors as household composition, physical assets, human capital, region, community characteristics, and so forth. Such models may be interpreted as reduced-form estimates of the underlying relationships generating expenditure and only require that the included variables be exogenous (Glewwe 1991). A typical list of the determinants of poverty includes low levels of education, human capital, and productive assets, lack of access to credit and irrigation, remoteness, high dependency ratios, and so on. In applied poverty analysis, determinants of this sort are often given a causal interpretation (Haughton and Khandker 2009).

By contrast, inequality tends to shift causal analysis to social structures and relationships. The reason is that understanding the causes of inequality entails understanding how society is set up and who gets what. There is nothing automatic about the shift and, in fact, there is a strong individualist orientation of inequality analysis in applied microeconomics—in particular, the social welfare function tradition (Kanbur 2000, 2006). Still, causal analysis of inequality points in a more direct way to social structures and relationships in that it is about the determinants of the entire distribution.

There are various examples of such analysis, including the Marxian tradition of political economy, which explains inequality in terms of the underlying dynamics of capitalism or forms of social relationships that obtain in different modes of production (Harriss-White 2005). For example, in the Marxian tradition of agrarian political economy, analyses of rural differentiation have focused on processes inhibiting the accumulation of a surplus by the peasantry, including rent paid in labor, cash, and kind and surplus appropriation by landlords, employers, or the state in the form of wages, prices, usury, or taxation (Deere and de Janvry 1979). Contemporary examples of similar analysis figure prominently in the so-called "adverse incorporation" literature, whose core thesis is aptly summarized by the opening quotation of this section (Harris 2009; see also du Toit 2009; Green 2009; Mosse 2010).

Another example is the explanatory framework adopted by sociologist Charles Tilly (1998) to account for "durable inequality." Tilly focuses on the relationships between socially organized systems of distinction—that is, "categories"—that serve to perpetuate social differentiation over time. The causal mechanisms at play include (a) exploitation (exclusion of outsiders from the full value of their effort), (b) opportunity hoarding (monopoly control of valuable resources and networking opportunities), (c) emulation (the replication of social relations in different settings), and (d) adaption (the conduct of everyday transactions or activities that reinforce unequal social structures). Tilly uses the analytical framework to explain, inter alia, occupational segregation whereby certain types of jobs become attached to certain categories of persons who actively work to maintain their monopoly (through networking and hiring) and actively exclude others who attempt to break in. The key point is that the focus of causal analysis shifts from characteristics of the poor to social structures and relationships within society as a whole.

What are the implications for evaluation? Consider the following example of a collective action problem involving the management of irrigation systems (see Shaffer, forthcoming). A typical impact assessment in the randomized control trial (RCT) tradition, for example, would focus on the design of such systems, comparing, say, allocation, supervisory, monitoring, and enforcement mechanisms associated with better outcomes. Detailed ethnographic work from the Tamil plains region of India, relying on an analytical framework similar to that of Tilly, has shown how such analyses can be deeply misleading (Mosse 2006). In Mosse's study, the most successful instances of collective action were those in which management of irrigation systems served as a mechanism of caste domination and social control. Failure to understand this broader social structure within which micro-level mechanisms operate is misleading on two counts. First, it leads to faulty analyses of the determinants of "successful" water management insofar as the most important drivers are excluded from the causal field. Second, it may lead to perverse policy recommendations, such as support for water users associations, which may perpetuate the exercise of caste power and domination or fuel social conflict over control of such institutions. The point here is that social structure and relationships matter. Their relative absence from excessively micro-focused RCT-type analyses may be missing the forest for the trees, or worse.

A second implication for evaluation of the broadening of the causal framework is the imperative of integrating a wide range of concepts of causation and approaches to causal inference in the social sciences. The standard toolkit in applied economics, which includes RCTs and econometric modeling at the micro level, partial equilibrium models, and computable general equilibrium models to capture higher-order effects (Bourguignon and da Silva 2008), is too narrow. There are several possibilities, including combining counterfactual and mechanism-based approaches to causation in ways that allow for a richer explanation of outcomes and processes, integrating intersubjectively observable data and dialogical information from thought experiments to arrive at a fuller account of counterfactual causation, using narrative information to inform the specification of model and selection of instrumental variables, and so forth.[4] As argued by Cartwright (2007) and others, no one concept of causation or model of causal inference adequately captures the vast range of causal phenomena under review.

Widening Policy Instruments and Programming Options

Inequality is embedded in our social structure, and the search for a solution requires us to examine all aspects of our society. (Atkinson 2014, 620)

Along with a broadening of the causal framework associated with the shift from poverty to inequality, there is a corresponding broadening of the range of policy instruments and programming options under consideration. Causal analyses that focus on the characteristics of poor households or communities, such as those in Sachs's poverty traps, map closely onto interventions associated with such. For example, Sachs's Millennium Villages Project was predicated on investments in agricultural inputs, basic health, education, power, transport, communication services, safe drinking water and sanitation, and so forth. Such interventions are the standard micro elements in typical poverty reduction strategies.

Measures to address inequality, in contrast, may also focus on the top end of the distribution. Consider the following list of measures proposed by Stiglitz (2012) aimed at "curbing excesses at the top": (a) greater curbs on the financial sector, (b) stronger and more effectively enforced competition laws, (c) comprehensive reform of bankruptcy laws, (d) end of government giveaways in public assets or procurement, and (e) creation of an effective state tax system. Similarly, Atkinson (2014) suggests several options, including more progressive taxation, capital gains taxes, annual wealth taxes, inheritance taxation, guaranteed positive real interest rates on savings, and so on.

In addition, there are other policy instruments where the likely beneficiaries overlap only partially with poor people. For example, measures to address actual or potential conflict associated with horizontal inequalities may include antidiscrimination policies or affirmative action. Such policies may work to the advantage of better-off individuals within deprived groups and may exclude poor persons in relatively privileged groups, as well as others. Moreover, the intent of these policies—to forestall or reduce conflict and to redress historical wrongs—is simply different from that of reducing poverty.

A second example may involve support for small and medium enterprises. The size distribution of firms—in particular, the so-called "missing middle"—has implications for overall inequality. More specifically, firm size may bear on the labor intensity of production and, in the aggregate, on the employment elasticities of growth, the intra- and inter-sectoral dispersion of wages, as well as the overall absorption of labor in the secondary versus tertiary sectors. Mazumdar (2010) and Mazumdar and Sarkar (2012) have argued persuasively that the "missing middle" in firm size distribution is a major factor contributing to relatively higher inequality levels in India. Similar analyses relying on Organisation for Economic Co-operation and Development data have demonstrated a striking relationship between growth in firm size and increases in wage inequality (Mueller, Ouimet, and Simintzi 2015). Unlike policies to support micro-level enterprises, measures to support small and medium enterprises (SMEs) are more likely to have a direct impact on inequality, through their effect on the lower-middle of the distribution, than on poverty per se.

One implication for evaluation, as noted by other contributors to this volume, is the move upstream to evaluate the impact of policies, or structural features of the economy, on inequality. One example is Shaffer and Le's (2013) assessment of the impact on inequality of Vietnam's rightward skew in the firm size distribution or "missing" SMEs.[5] Their analysis concludes that the effects on inequality were quite minimal based on the following evidence: (a) overall consumption inequality, as measured by the Gini coefficient, has risen only slightly following reforms in Vietnam, (b) the dispersion of wages across size categories of firms in manufacturing is quite low by comparative standards and has fallen over time, (c) employment in manufacturing has grown quite rapidly since 2000, due in part to the fact that large firms appear to be more labor intensive than medium-size firms, and (d) the contribution of urban-based manufacturing (a proxy for large firms) to overall income inequality is small, according to a Gini decomposition exercise, because of its small share in household income. As argued in the section on the causation of inequality, this type of analysis redirects inquiry to structural features of the economy with a view to determining how much they matter in explaining inequality outcomes.

Conclusion

There is a strong case to be made for addressing inequality more systematically in the context of international development. Some of the arguments in favor of this "inequality turn" have been presented in this chapter. However, the shift from poverty to inequality is not seamless. It likely implies far-reaching changes to the field of inquiry and analytical approaches selected.

To reiterate, it implies (a) a widening of the dimensions of deprivation or social "bads" under consideration, (b) a change in the focus of causal analysis from households or individuals to social structures and relationships, and (c) an enlargement of the range of policy instruments and programming options under review.

Accordingly, it raises several challenges for evaluation. The widening of dimensions of deprivations or social "bads" makes the evaluative metric "matter more," in particular, in cases where policies or programs reduce poverty at the expense of inequality, as evidenced by the Sri Lankan resettlement project. The imperative of analyzing social structures and relationships to capture the drivers of change, as shown in the collective management of irrigation systems in India, implies the need for integrating a wide range of concepts of causation and approaches to causal inference in the social sciences. Finally, the widening of the policy and programming framework extends the field of evaluation work. The net effect of these three changes is to expand the scope for evaluation, but also to increase its complexity and difficulty.

Notes

1. It does, of course, make sense to talk about household inequality, as discussed later in the context of horizontal inequalities and gender.
2. In Rawls's theory, the first core principle of justice is the priority of liberty. In addition, the "difference principle" sits alongside the proviso that economic and social inequality must be arranged to ensure that offices and positions are open to everyone under conditions of fair equality of opportunity.
3. This discussion draws on Shaffer (2015b).
4. For theoretical discussion and empirical examples, see Shaffer (2013, 2015a).
5. In Vietnam, the contribution of large firms to total employment in manufacturing, at around 60 percent, is almost 10 percent higher than in any other country in a database covering 12 Asian countries (Mazumdar and Sarkar 2012).

References

Atkinson, A. 2014. "After Piketty." *British Journal of Sociology* 65 (4): 619–38.

Banerjee, A., and E. Duflo. 2011. *Poor Economics: A Radical Rethinking of the Way to Fight Global Poverty.* New York: Public Affairs.

Bourguignon, F., and L. da Silva, eds. 2008. *The Impact of Economic Policies on Poverty and Income Distribution.* Washington, DC: World Bank.

Cartwright, N. 2007. *Hunting Causes and Using Them: Approaches in Philosophy and Economics.* Cambridge, U.K.: Cambridge University Press.

Chronic Poverty Research Centre. 2005. *The Chronic Poverty Report 2004–05.* Manchester: CPRC Publications.

———. 2009. *The Chronic Poverty Report 2008–09.* Manchester: CPRC Publications.

Collier, P. 2007. *The Bottom Billion.* Oxford: Oxford University Press.

Cowell, F. 2000. "Measurement of Inequality." In *Handbook of Income Distribution,* vol. 1, edited by A. Atkinson and F. Bourguignon, 87–166. Amsterdam: Elsevier.

Cunningham, F. 2007. *What's Wrong with Inequality?* Ottawa: Canadian Centre for Policy Alternatives, November.

Deaton, A., and J. Muellbauer. 1980. *Economics and Consumer Behavior.* Cambridge, U.K.: Cambridge University Press.

Deere, C., and A. de Janvry. 1979. "A Conceptual Framework for the Empirical Analysis of Peasants." *American Journal of Agricultural Economics* 61 (4): 601–11.

de Silva, N., and N. Gunetilleke. 2008. "On Trying to Be Q-Squared: Merging Methods for a Technical Minded Client." *International Journal of Multiple Research Approaches* 2 (2): 252–65.

Dobb, M. 1973. *Theories of Value and Distribution since Adam Smith.* Cambridge, U.K.: Cambridge University Press.

du Toit, A. 2009. "Poverty Measurement Blues: Beyond 'Q-Squared' Approaches to Understanding Chronic Poverty in South Africa." In *Poverty Dynamics: Interdisciplinary Perspectives,* edited by T. Addison, D. Hulme, and R. Kanbur, 225–46. Oxford: Oxford University Press.

Frank, R. 2007. *Falling Behind: How Rising Inequality Harms the Middle Class.* Berkeley: University of California Press.

Glewwe, P. 1991. "Investigating the Determinants of Household Welfare in Côte d'Ivoire." *Journal of Development Economics* 35 (2): 211–16.

Green, M. 2009. "The Social Distribution of Sanctioned Harm: Thinking through Chronic Poverty, Durable Poverty, and Destitution." In *Poverty Dynamics: Interdisciplinary Perspectives,* edited by T. Addison, D. Hulme, and R. Kanbur, 309–27. Oxford: Oxford University Press.

Harris, J. 2009. "Bringing Politics Back into Poverty Analysis: Why Understandings of Social Relations Matter More for Policy on Chronic Poverty Than Measurement." In *Poverty Dynamics: Interdisciplinary Perspectives,* edited by T. Addison, D. Hulme, and R. Kanbur, 205–24. Oxford: Oxford University Press.

Harriss-White, B. 2005. "Poverty and Capitalism." QEH Working Paper Series 134, Department of International Development, Queen Elizabeth House, Oxford University, Oxford.

Haughton, J., and S. Khandker. 2009. *Handbook on Poverty and Inequality.* Washington, DC: World Bank.

Hirsch, F. 1976. *Social Limits to Growth.* Cambridge, MA: Harvard University Press.

Jackson, C. 1996. "Rescuing Gender from the Poverty Trap." *World Development* 21 (3): 489–504.

Kanbur, R. 2000. "Income Distribution and Development." In *Handbook of Income Distribution,* vol. 1, edited by A. Atkinson and F. Bourguignon, 791–841. Amsterdam: Elsevier.

———. 2006. "The Policy Significance of Inequality Decompositions." *Journal of Economic Inequality* 4 (3): 367–74.

Lewis, O. 1968. "The Culture of Poverty." In *On Understanding Poverty: Perspectives from the Social Sciences*, edited by D. Moynihan. New York: Basic Books.

Marx, K. 1977 [1875]. "Critique of the Gotha Program." In *Karl Marx Selected Writings*, edited by D. McLellan, 564–70. Oxford: Oxford University Press.

Mazumdar, D. 2010. "Decreasing Poverty and Inequality in India." In *Tackling Inequalities in Brazil, China, India, and South Africa*. Paris: OECD.

Mazumdar, D., and S. Sarkar, eds. 2012. *The Size Distribution of Manufacturing and Economic Growth: Studies in Asian Industrialisation*. London: Routledge.

Milanovic, B. 2011. *The Haves and Have-Nots*. New York: Basic Books.

Miller, D. 1976. *Social Justice*. Oxford: Clarendon Press.

Mosse, D. 2006. "Collective Action, Common Property, and Social Capital in South India: An Anthropological Commentary." *Economic Development and Cultural Change* 54 (3): 695–724.

———. 2010. "A Relational Approach to Durable Poverty, Inequality, and Power." *Journal of Development Studies* 46 (7): 1156–78.

Mueller, H., P. Ouimet, and E. Simintzi. 2015. "Wage Inequality and Firm Growth." LIS Working Paper 632, Luxemburg Income Study.

Piketty, T. 2014. *Capital in the Twenty-First Century*. Cambridge, MA: Harvard University Press.

Ravallion, M. 1994. *Poverty Comparisons: Fundamentals of Pure and Applied Economics*. Chur, Switzerland: Harwood Academic Publishers.

Rawls, J. 1971. *A Theory of Justice*. Cambridge, MA: Harvard University Press.

Ricardo, D. 2004 [1821]. *The Principles of Political Economy and Taxation*. 3d ed. London: J. M. Dent and Sons.

Sachs, J. 2005. *The End of Poverty*. New York: Penguin Press.

Sen, A. 1982. "Equality of What?" Reprinted in *Choice, Welfare, and Measurement*. Cambridge, MA: Harvard University Press, 1997.

Shaffer, P. 2008. "New Thinking on Poverty: Implications for Globalisation and Poverty Reduction Strategies." *Real World Economics Review* 47 (3): 192–231.

———. 2013. *Q-Squared: Combining Qualitative and Quantitative Approaches in Poverty Analysis*. Oxford: Oxford University Press.

———. 2015a. "Structured Causal Pluralism in Poverty Analysis: Implications for Poverty." *Journal of Economic Methodology* (March). doi: 10.1080/1350178X.2015.1021829.

———. 2015b. "Two Concepts of Causation: Implications for Poverty." *Development and Change* 46 (1): 148–66.

———. Forthcoming. "The World Development Report 2015: An Assessment." *Canadian Journal of Development Studies*.

Shaffer, P., and T. Le. 2013. "Pro-Poor Growth and Firm Size: Evidence from Vietnam." *Oxford Development Studies* 41 (1): 1–28.

Stiglitz, J. 2012. *The Price of Inequality*. New York: Penguin Books.

Tilly, C. 1998. *Durable Inequality*. Berkeley: University of California Press.

United Nations General Assembly. 2014. *Report of the Open Working Group of the General Assembly on Sustainable Development Goals*. A/68/970. New York, August 12. http://undocs.org/A/68/970.

White House. 2013. "Remarks by the President on Economic Mobility, December 4, 2013." Office of the Press Secretary, Washington, DC. https://www.whitehouse.gov/the-press-office/2013/12/04/remarks-president-economic-mobility.

World Bank. 2001. *World Development Report 2000/2001: Attacking Poverty*. New York: Oxford University Press.

——. 2015. *A Measured Approach to Ending Poverty and Boosting Shared Prosperity: Concepts, Data, and the Twin Goals*. Policy Research Report. Washington, DC: World Bank.

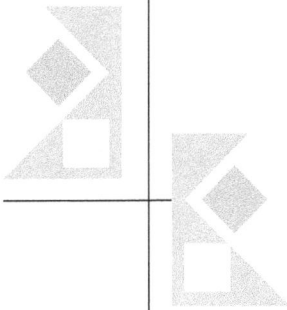

PART TWO: EMPIRICAL MEASUREMENT OF THE PERFORMANCE AND RESULTS OF POVERTY AND INEQUALITY REDUCTION PROGRAMS AND PROJECTS

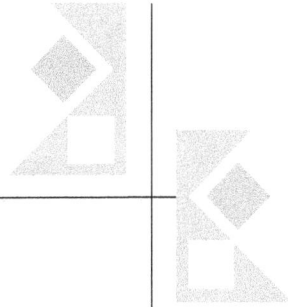

CHAPTER 2

Evaluations as Catalysts in Bridging Developmental Inequalities

Rashmi Agrawal and Banda V. L. N. Rao

Introduction

Development is by and large a relative concept. It implies a change (usually an improvement) in the economic, social, or cultural situation of a society, or segment of society, over what existed on a previous occasion or in comparison to another society or segment at the same time. The process of development, left to itself, is rarely equitable—it benefits those who control resources and trickles down only slowly to the socially and economically weaker segments of society, if it does not bypass them altogether. Differential development creates new inequalities or accentuates the pain of existing inequalities.

While inequalities can lead to social tensions and even violence, in a scenario of rapid globalization, inequality in one part of the world can also have an impact on relatively or seemingly egalitarian societies elsewhere.

Rashmi Agrawal is with India's National Institute of Labour Economics Research and Development, and Banda V. L. N. Rao is a consultant.

As Kirk (2012) has pointed out, "A growing body of research confirms that high levels of inequality in the distribution of income, power, and resources can slow poverty reduction, exacerbate social exclusion, and provoke political and economic instability. Even in rich countries, inequality is dysfunctional, as Kate Pickett and Richard Wilkinson [Pickett and Wilkinson 2009] so convincingly demonstrate with the mass of evidence presented in their influential book, *The Spirit Level*."

Development interventions, therefore, have to aim not only at raising the overall social and economic well-being of a nation but, more importantly, at containing economic and social disparities and exclusions at subnational levels, as these can threaten the very fabric of society. Even in a democratic free market economy, complete equality among all is an unattainable and unsustainable dream.

Distinct from equality, equity demands that all segments of society have equal access to opportunities of education and skills, employment and income, health and welfare, and various public services so that they can attain their full potential of personal, social, and economic development. Present-day inequalities are to a large extent the legacy and consequence of yesterday's unequal access to opportunities—in other words, lack of equity.

Equity considerations have been influencing the socioeconomic development policies and programs of governments in India and elsewhere. The Millennium Development Goals of the United Nations have given impetus to this shift (Ministry of Statistics and Programme Implementation 2012). The sustainable development agenda for the coming years will be more explicit in emphasizing social equity and gender equality. This implies that monitoring and evaluation of development interventions need to focus on the ability and effectiveness of such interventions in ensuring that the fruits of development percolate to all segments of society in such a manner that disparities are contained and gradually reduced. According to Bamberger and Segone (2011), such equity-focused evaluations have to provide "assessments of what works and what does not work to reduce inequity," and they need to highlight the "intended and unintended results for worst-off groups as well as the gaps between best-off, average, and worst-off groups," enabling authorities to incorporate the findings, recommendations, and lessons into the decision-making process in a timely manner.

This chapter discusses how evaluations function as a catalyst to bridge inequalities. It cites case studies from the development experience in India and argues that evaluations can play a proactive role in promoting sustainable, inclusive development if they are supported by an evaluation policy that promotes the use of evaluation findings.

Focus on Equity and Equality in India

The Constitution of India is based on the principles of equality and equal opportunities for all citizens (Ministry of Law and Justice 2007). It also recognizes the fact of unequal development between different segments of society and enables the state to make any special provisions that may be necessary for the advancement of socially and educationally backward classes of citizens and other disadvantaged groups. Various legislative instruments have been put in place to bring such groups into the mainstream of social development. Moreover, since its inception in 1951 development planning in India has aimed not only to achieve economic and social growth overall but also to address the interests of citizen groups that had been left behind in the past—women, the disabled, the economically backward classes, and minorities, among others. Special programs to promote the welfare and empowerment of such groups have had some positive results, but the country is still far from achieving the goal of equality in development. There is a growing feeling that the high rate of economic growth witnessed during the last decade has not benefited all segments of the population uniformly.

Strategic development planning in India has recently attached a greater sense of urgency to these inequalities than before. The last two Five-Year Plans (the Eleventh Plan 2007–12 and the Twelfth Plan 2012–17) recognized the glaring differentials in development among different segments of society (Planning Commission 2007, 2011). According to the Planning Commission (2011),

> Inclusive growth should result in lower incidence of poverty, broad-based and significant improvement in health outcomes, universal access for children to school, increased access to higher education, and improved standards of education, including skill development. It should also be reflected in better opportunities for both wage employment and livelihood and in improvement in provision of basic amenities like water, electricity, roads, sanitation, and housing. Particular attention needs to be paid to the needs of the SC [scheduled casts]/ST [scheduled tribes] and OBC [other backward classes] population. Women and children constitute a group which accounts for 70 percent of the population and deserves special attention in terms of the reach of relevant schemes in many sectors. Minorities and other excluded groups also need special programs to bring them into the mainstream.

Rapid economic growth in the last two decades has enabled massive public investments in the social sector that are expected to bring the benefits of education, health, employment, and incomes within reach of all segments of society (Ministry of Human Resource Development 1998, 2011; Ministry of Labour and Employment 2009). Flagship programs of national importance such as the Mahatma Gandhi National Rural Employment Act, the Mid-Day Meal Program for schools, Education for All (*Sarva Shiksha Abhiyan*), Right to Education, and Health for All are seeking to bring about inclusiveness in development. *Jan Dhan Yojana* (National Mission for Financial Inclusion) is intended to draw the multitudes of uncovered population into the mainstream of formal financial services. More recent schemes provide pension and accident insurance at nominal premiums, with the aim of covering all segments of society.

Evaluations and Equity Issues

Evaluations may address equity issues in three scenarios. In the first scenario, development programs may focus directly on achieving equity and reducing inequalities. In this case, the terms of reference should specify that the evaluation will assess impact in terms of equity and equality.

In the second scenario, programs may not focus directly on equity and equality issues (for example, a program for constructing a railway bridge through a village), but policy makers and program planners may be keen to know about the positive or adverse effects of the program. In this case, the terms of reference may not specify that the evaluation will assess these impacts. However, the evaluator has the responsibility to make the program planners and implementors aware of the importance of judging the program on the basis of its social consequences. The evaluator should design the evaluation to identify such impacts by consulting with stakeholders from all concerned segments of society, choosing appropriate survey respondents, choosing suitable survey protocols, and focusing on equity and equality issues.

In the third scenario, the evaluator has not planned in advance to assess social impacts. Even then, he or she would do well to analyze whatever information is gathered in the process of evaluation from the perspective of social impact and inform the program planners of the positive as well as the negative social consequences.

The role of evaluations in bridging inequalities also depends on the nature of evaluation undertaken. Ex ante evaluations, for example, indicate developmental differences as well as trends in development, which could suggest ameliorative interventions. Ex post evaluations throw light on the impact of interventions on inequalities among various social groups, with reference to a specified aspect of development. They also assess the outreach of interventions, whether the intended benefits have been achieved, whether there have been any unintended impacts, beneficial or otherwise, and whether such unintended impacts have reduced or accentuated existing inequalities. Such information could help planners to modify and amend existing policies or programs and to find more efficient methods of delivery. Social impact assessments identify differential impacts, if any, on various socioeconomic groups. For example, laying a highway through a village could adversely affect the livelihoods of the poor, while benefiting the relatively well-to-do.

Case Studies from India

This section presents case studies from Indian developmental experience to illustrate how evaluations have helped to focus attention on issues of equity and equality.

Evaluations, Policy Modifications, and Equity

Various development interventions have been conducted in India in the education and training sector. India is committed to achieving universal elementary education for all children, irrespective of caste, religion, gender, or geographic location, and several programs have been implemented to achieve this goal. The most ambitious of these is *Sarva Shiksha Abhiyan* (Education for All), which aims to provide all children 6 to 14 years of age with free, compulsory education through a multiprong approach that covers student enrollment, school infrastructure, teacher availability, and other crucial aspects. The National Program for Girls' Education was implemented at the elementary level in educationally backward blocks of the country.[1] The Mid-Day Meal Program was launched to enhance enrollment in school, retain children in school, and improve nutritional levels. Other schemes were implemented to bring minority communities, economically backward classes, and other disadvantaged groups into the mainstream of educational development. These initiatives were taken to address equity issues with regard to coverage of the population, accessibility of education, and flexibility in education. The interventions to achieve these goals were made to increase the number of schools, to expand enrollment, and to lower dropout rates, which were very high.

In the area of training, many people are out of the formal institutional network, and the skills of workers who were informally trained are often not recognized in the organized labor market. Efforts have been made to mainstream these workers by increasing the number of training institutions and providing flexible training opportunities so that workers can continue to perform their present activity while joining the formal system of skill development.

Evaluations conducted from time to time by government as well as by other organizations have indicated that the interventions are not enough. They have raised the issues of quantity as well as quality of education and indicated that informally trained workers have not been mainstreamed. Still, these interventions have led to major policy modifications. Government has adopted a National Policy on Education as well as a National Policy on Skill Development. The right to education has been made a fundamental right, and the Right to Education Act provides for the following:

- Establish neighborhood schools within three years
- Provide school infrastructure and teachers as per prescribed pupil-teacher ratio within three years
- Train untrained teachers
- Undertake specified interventions to improve quality

In the area of training, government has adopted the National Vocational Qualification Framework to facilitate testing and certification of informally trained persons so that their skills can be recognized in the labor market. Education and training are to be organized through public-private partnerships, which will enhance the relevance of the skills attained in the labor market and actively involve the private sector in training. This new policy, which is providing educational opportunities to all segments of society on a wider scale than before, is intended to bring about greater equity in education. However, the impact on equality is yet to be assessed, as these policy modifications are very recent.

Evaluations, Program Modifications, and Equality

Evaluations play a significant role in program modifications. The *Swaranjyanti Gram Swarozgar Yojana* (Rural Self-Employment Scheme) was launched to help rural families living below the poverty line to augment their incomes and to rise and stay above the poverty line. Under this scheme, beneficiaries received credit, training, and marketing support.

An evaluation indicated that there was a need to promote group self-employment because individual self-employment too often failed. Most of the ventures either were never started or closed down, as individuals were not confident enough to handle multiple business operations and individual credit was insufficient. The scheme did not cover enough women. The evaluation also found that a national body was needed to control the various operations under the scheme.

These evaluation results led to major modifications of the program. A self-help group approach was adopted, and a goal was set for at least 50 percent of the beneficiaries to be women. The National Rural Livelihood Mission was established, and a cluster approach was used to select activities for self-employment, supporting the selection of demand-based activities.

These efforts were found to have had an impact on inequality. Rural poverty fell from 41.8 percent in 2004–05 to 33.8 percent in 2009–10. The proportion of women in self-employment in rural areas rose from 69 percent in 2011–12 to 80 percent in 2012–13.

Evaluations and New Interventions

Evaluations can also lead to new interventions. The government has sought to promote equity through a system of subsidies. For example, a public distribution system (PDS) has been in place for a long time to supply essential foodgrains to the poor at subsidized prices. With a network of more than 460,000 fair-price shops, food items are distributed for more than Rs 300 billion annually to about 160 million families. India's PDS is the largest distribution network of its kind in the world.

However, evaluations conducted from time to time have indicated various lapses in this program. Benefits were not reaching the intended population, and similar loopholes were evident in many other subsidy schemes. These weaknesses led government to try direct cash transfers in which money equivalent to the subsidies is transferred to the bank accounts of poor families, eliminating dual pricing in the market. To support this process of direct cash transfers in a transparent manner, the *Jan Dhan Yojana* (National Mission for Financial Inclusion) was launched, opening new bank accounts for more than 125 million households.

Equity Interventions Leading to Lower Inequality

Various policies, programs, and legislative initiatives have practically wiped out the socioeconomic inequalities in certain spheres, such as gender inequalities in primary education. In several other areas, the dimensions of inequality have decreased, such as enrollment of girls in secondary and higher education, infant mortality, representation of women in local administrations and formal employment, and participation of socially and economically backward segments of society in education and employment. The poverty rate has fallen in both rural and urban areas from 45.3 to 29.8 percent overall (figure 2.1).

Figure 2.1   Poverty Rate in India, 1993–2010

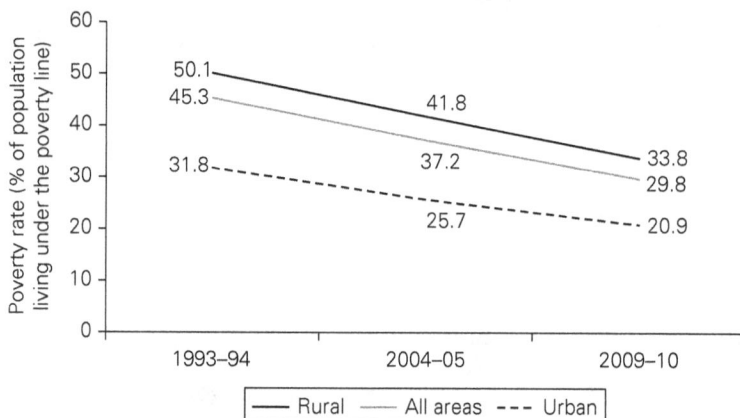

Source: Ministry of Finance 2013, 273.

Figure 2.2   Literacy Rate and Gender Gap in India, 1981–2011

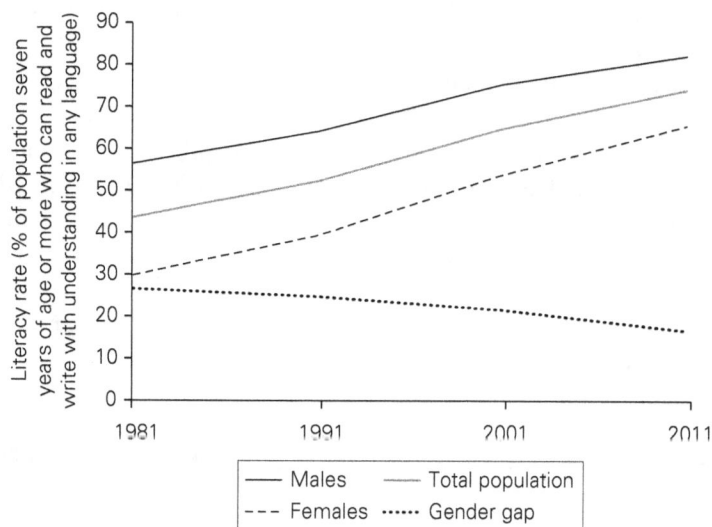

Source: Registrar General of India 2011.

According to the 2011 census, the overall literacy rate was 74 percent in 2011, but again there were gender, regional, and social disparities.[2] While 82 percent of males were literate, only 65 percent of females were literate. As shown in figure 2.2, the gender gap closed some between 1981 and 2011.

In higher education women are also catching up with men, and the gender gap is closing (figure 2.3).

Poverty, Inequality, and Evaluation

Figure 2.3 Enrollment in Higher Education in India, by Gender, 1950–2011

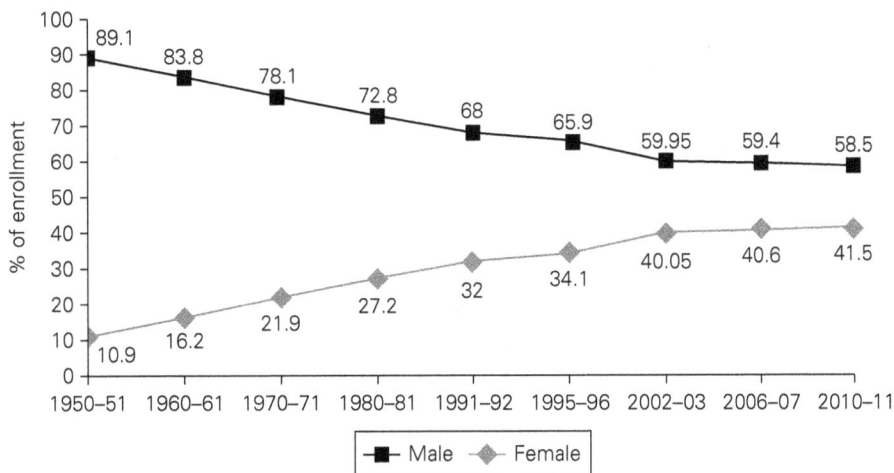

Source: University Grants Commission 2012.

Persistent Inequalities despite Improved Equity

Access to health services is uneven between urban and rural areas despite India's large network of rural public health institutions. Societal prejudices work adversely against females. The impact is clearly visible in the form of a declining child sex ratio, notwithstanding numerous legislative and other measures to arrest the trend (figure 2.4). According to the Registrar General of India (2011), "The child sex ratio for the age group of 0–6 years as per the 2011 Census (provisional) has dipped further to 914 girls as against 927 per 1,000 boys recorded in 2001 Census. This is the worst dip since 1947. This negative trend reaffirms the fact that the girl child is more at risk than ever before."

The inequalities shown in figure 2.4 are in some of the most important basic parameters. More detailed measures like the consumption patterns of the rich and poor, access to high-quality education, enrollment in higher education, acquisition of vocational skills, and access to and affordability of quality health services indicate even sharper differences between gender, social class, and rural and urban areas (table 2.1). Periodic evaluations of development policies and programs show that, while incomes at all levels have risen and quality of life has improved in absolute terms, relative differences persist in several areas of development. Social inclusion has not taken place to the extent desired, and certain

Figure 2.4   Overall and Child Sex Ratio in India, 1961–2011

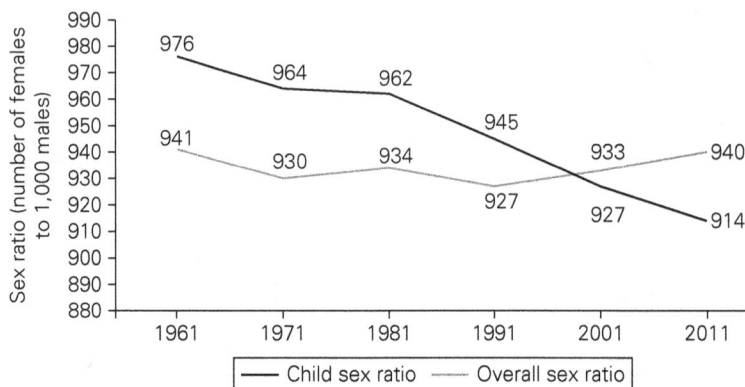

Source: Registrar General of India 2011.

Note: The child sex ratio is for children 0–6 years of age.

Table 2.1   Average Monthly Per Capita Expenditure in Rural and Urban Areas of India, by Social Group, 2009–10
rupees

Social group	Rural	Urban
Scheduled tribes	873	1,797
Scheduled castes	929	1,444
Other backward classes	1,036	1,679
Others	1,281	2,467
All	1,054	1,984

Source: National Sample Survey Organization 2011.

socioeconomic and cultural groups have not been fully integrated into the mainstream of development.

India's economy grew rapidly during the last two decades, with the growth in gross domestic product exceeding 8 percent in many years. Nonetheless, extreme poverty persists, with 29.8 percent of the population living below the poverty line in 2009–10. Among the poorest 10 percent of households, rural households have an average monthly per capita consumption expenditure of around Rs 453 (US$8) compared with Rs 599 (US$11) for urban households; the richest 10 percent spend 5.6 times more than the poor in rural areas and 9.8 times more in urban areas. Regional variations also persist, with average monthly expenditure in the state at

Table 2.2   Changes in Average Monthly Per Capita Expenditure of Various Social Groups Relative to the Total Population in Rural and Urban Areas of India, 1999–2000 to 2009–10

Social group	Rural areas			Urban areas		
	1999–2000	2004–05	2009–10	1999–2000	2004–05	2009–10
Scheduled tribes	−20.4	−23.7	−17.2	−28.8	−18.5	−9.5
Scheduled castes	−13.9	−15.0	−11.9	−19.2	−27.9	−27.2
Other backward classes	−2.5	−0.4	−1.6	−14.0	−17.2	−15.4
Others	18.8	22.6	21.6	17.6	24.1	24.3

Source: National Sample Survey Organization 2011.

Note: Figures are deviations in percentages of levels for various categories, with the level for overall population taken as 100.

the bottom being just half of that in the state at the top, both in urban and in rural areas.

There are also inequalities among social groups, both in rural and in urban areas. The average monthly per capita expenditure for households in rural areas is lowest for scheduled tribes and gradually higher for scheduled castes, other backward classes, and "others," in that order (table 2.1).[3] In urban areas, scheduled tribes fare somewhat better. Generally, the average monthly per capita expenditure of scheduled tribe households is about 20 percent lower than the overall level, while that of "others" is about 20 percent higher. There is little evidence that these differences are declining. On the contrary, the category "others," whose position is generally considered to be socially or economically high, improved during the last decade, with per capita consumption expenditure almost one-fifth to one-quarter higher than the level overall (table 2.2).

Are Evaluations the Answer to Every Problem?

Can evaluations help to accelerate the attainment of equitable development goals? The answer seems to be that they can. However, evaluations of development policies, programs, or projects by themselves do not directly enhance equity, just as they do not directly bring about development results.

Evaluations only help policy makers, program implementors, and project managers to make informed decisions on how to shape development interventions to attain their objectives in an optimum manner and with the greatest beneficial impact. Equity-focused evaluations inform policy makers and others about the equity aspects and impacts of development interventions.

The process of achieving equitable development is not a one-step activity but a process of successive approximations through a string of evaluations and reviews of policies or programs. Evaluations can stimulate and guide action to contain inequalities in the following ways:

- Highlighting inequalities through periodic reviews of information
- Evaluating the impact of general economic or social policies on different segments of society (for example, the impact of energy pricing policy on the poor)
- Evaluating the impact of development programs or projects (for example, laying roads) to assess the likely impact on society by asking whether the program reduces or enhances inequality
- Evaluating completed development projects by assessing the flow of benefits to different segments of society
- Evaluating development projects aimed specifically at reducing inequalities and identifying whether benefits are indeed flowing to the intended beneficiaries

Policies and programs are not conceived in a vacuum. They are created to respond to an observed problem. If the situation suggests the existence of developmental inequalities, policies and programs should seek to reduce them. Thus reviews of the current situation, which may be baseline studies or ex ante evaluations, prompt action to contain inequalities and promote equitable development. For example, the household sample surveys regularly carried out by the National Sample Survey Organization collect data on employment and household consumption expenditure in rural and urban areas, among males and females, in different regions, and among different social categories. At the same time, policies and programs that seek to achieve development in general but not to reduce inequality in particular could have fallout effects that exacerbate inequalities.

Evaluation culture is gradually evolving in India. It is becoming mandatory to evaluate all major development interventions. Management information systems have been established for 14 major flagship programs. Evaluations create an enabling environment and help to address the issues of equity and equality. The success varies, as evaluations are not the sole agents of change. Figure 2.5 details how evaluations and other variables have an impact on change.

Figure 2.5   Role of Evaluations in Promoting Equity and Equality

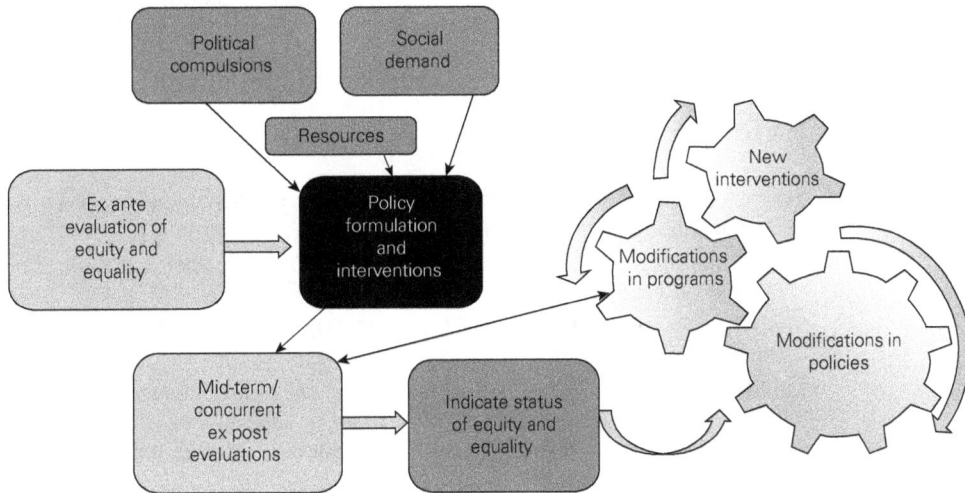

Conclusion

The theoretical formulations and examples from Indian experience indicate the manner in which equity-focused evaluations could help to promote an environment of equal opportunity for all segments of society and eventually to minimize inequalities. Evaluations could highlight the existence of inequalities, assess the impact of specific development policies, programs, and projects relating to equity and inequalities, and suggest ways to accelerate the movement toward an egalitarian society. Whether they achieve these goals depends on the commitment of policy makers and program managers to them and their willingness to use evaluation information.

At the same time, it is also important to have high-quality evaluations. The quality of evaluations is a global concern, which calls for reexamining the demand for evaluations, on the one hand, and for building the capacity for evaluation, on the other. An explicit evaluation policy is needed to address all of these issues.

Notes

1. Community development blocks are subdivisions of a district with a focus on development in the area. Districts are subdivisions of a state.
2. The literacy rate is the percentage of people who can read and write with understanding in any language out of all people seven years of age or more.

3. According to the National Sample Survey, the proportion of scheduled tribes, scheduled castes, other backward classes, and others in the population is 8.7, 19.9, 41.7, and 29.7 percent, respectively.

References

Bamberger, M., and M. Segone. 2011. "How to Design and Manage Equity-Focused Evaluations." Evaluation Working Paper, UNICEF, New York.

Kirk, C. 2012. "Preface." In *Evaluation for Equitable Development Results*, edited by M. Segone, vii. New York: UNICEF.

Ministry of Finance. 2013. *Economic Survey 2012–13*. New Delhi: Ministry of Finance.

Ministry of Human Resource Development. 1998. *The National Educational Policy, 1986 (as Modified in 1992) with National Policy on Education, 1968*. New Delhi: Ministry of Human Resource Development. mhrd.gov.in/sites/upload_files /mhrd/files/NPE86-mod92.pdf.

———. 2011. *Education for All: Annual Report 2010–11*. New Delhi: Ministry of Human Resource Development.

Ministry of Labour and Employment. 2009. *National Policy on Skill Development Policy*. New Delhi: Ministry of Labour and Employment. http://labour.gov.in /policy/NationalSkillDevelopmentPolicyMar09.pdf.

Ministry of Law and Justice. 2007. *The Constitution of India. As Modified up to 1 December 2007, Chapter III Fundamental Rights, Articles 15(3) and 15(4)*. New Delhi: Ministry of Law and Justice.

Ministry of Statistics and Programme Implementation. 2012. *Millennium Development Goals. India Country Report 2011*. New Delhi: Ministry of Statistics and Programme Implementation.

National Sample Survey Organization. 2011. *Level and Pattern of Consumer Expenditure: National Sample Survey 66th Round (July 2009–June 2010)*. New Delhi: National Sample Survey Organization.

Pickett, K., and R. Wilkinson. 2009. *The Spirit Level: Why Equality Is Better for Everyone*. New York: Penguin Books.

Planning Commission. 2007. *The Eleventh Five-Year Plan (2007–12) and Approach to Twelfth Five-Year Plan (2012–17)*. New Delhi: Planning Commission.

———. 2011. *Faster, Sustainable, and More Inclusive Growth: An Approach to the Twelfth Five-Year Plan (2012–17)*. New Delhi: Planning Commission.

Registrar General of India. 2011. "Provisional Population Totals." Census of India Paper 1, Registrar General of India, New Delhi.

University Grants Commission. 2012. *Higher Education in India at a Glance*. New Delhi: University Grants Commission.

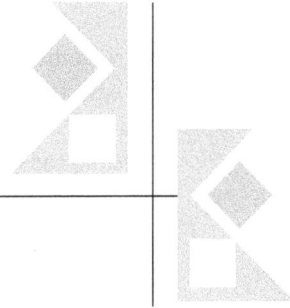

CHAPTER 3

Evaluating Value Chain Development Programs: Assessing Effectiveness, Efficiency, and Equity Effects of Contract Choice

Ruerd Ruben

Introduction

An increasing part of international cooperation is oriented toward programs for private sector development, including public-private partnerships (PPPs) for strengthening value chains. The development rationale of such multiagency programs is usually that their activities reinforce either the size or the value of production and trading activities or reduce transaction costs through closer integration of activities undertaken. Typical examples are programs for certification of fair and sustainable value chains (coffee, tea, chocolate) and co-investment activities for infrastructure or services delivery (water and sanitation, health care, roads, energy).

Ruerd Ruben is at Wageningen University.

Only a few empirical assessments apply rigorous methods for impact evaluation to value chain programs. These studies tend to indicate that registered net welfare effects are rather modest, since substitution effects dominate growth effects, while externalities for neighboring nonparticipants can be substantial. Far less attention is usually given to the impact of value chain programs on the distribution of added value throughout the chain, based on, for example, spatial reallocation of activities, achievement of economies of scale and scope, or upgrading of the quality of production systems. Moreover, issues of additionality deserve more attention.

This chapter provides insights regarding the possible procedures for assessing welfare, efficiency, and equity effects of value chain development programs, taking advantage of available analytical tools derived from impact analysis, transaction cost theory, and contract choice approaches. It briefly outlines the strengths and weaknesses of different measurement approaches for value chain appraisal based on empirical counterfactual analysis, dynamic value chain modeling, and systematic contract choice analysis of public-private partnerships, arguing that an integrated sequential framework is required to assess the impacts on effectiveness and efficiency and the implications for equity of value chain programs for poverty alleviation.

Setting the Stage

Development aid policies are currently subject to an important reorientation. Shifts in international patterns of poverty and a broader understanding of the dynamics of poverty reduction have led to a fundamental reappraisal of the role of private agents in the strategies for linking international trade and cooperation.

Involving the private sector in development programs is considered a major—albeit complementary—strategy for creating employment opportunities and fostering economic growth, which are key goals of poverty alleviation programs. Such programs typically include two dimensions: (a) support for improvement of the national business and investment climate (reducing constraints) and (b) support for business development activities at the enterprise or sector level (creating opportunities).

Whereas evaluations of private sector activities are still rather scarce and generally limited to the appraisal of specific public policy instruments (like microfinance support, business development services, or investment guarantees), the range of developmental programs with private sector involvement is rapidly expanding and new instruments are appearing that cannot be assessed in a straightforward manner using conventional evaluation techniques. Most attention in evaluations concerning private sector development (PSD) is usually given to the effectiveness of programs that involve private enterprises in the provision of public goods and services and the strategic coherence between public and private aid activities (EuropAid 2005). Far less sound evaluation material is available to assess public co-financing programs for upgrading private sector production, processing, and marketing processes.

In addition to common evaluation questions related to the effectiveness, efficiency, and relevance of PSD interventions, general issues that emerged from these and other ongoing PSD evaluations refer to the conditions that guarantee (ex post) "additionality" and the safeguards against creating new market distortions. Moreover, specific questions are raised with respect to the distributional implications of PSD programs and the likelihood of reaching sustainability.[1]

This chapter focuses on the possibilities and pitfalls that are likely to appear in the evaluation of value chain development (VCD) programs. These programs usually focus on the inclusion of smallholder producers in cross-border commodity chains, providing producers with support in the areas of (micro) finance, technical assistance, and information exchange that permits them to increase traded volume, improve the quality of produce, and increase the reliability and frequency of delivery. VCD programs seek to reduce transaction costs and share risks for the private partners involved in international trade. These efforts are expected to lead to improved outputs, higher-quality and better yields, higher prices, lower price volatility, and, ultimately, higher income and improved rural welfare (IFC 2013).

Different analytical approaches are available for evaluating VCD programs, both from a theoretical perspective and from an empirical viewpoint. Specific issues that deserve attention are related to the involvement of multiple stakeholders (producers, traders, processors, retailers, and consumers) and the interactive nature of an exchange process that takes place over long distances (that is, producers in developing countries need to respond to quality requirements defined by retailers and consumers in Western countries). Moreover, part of the information in the middle of the value chain is confidential company information that is not readily available for evaluation purposes. Finally, the outcomes of VCD programs are the result not just of the delivery of project inputs, but also of bargaining among stakeholders. Therefore, VCD evaluations also need to be addressed from an agency perspective.

The remainder of this chapter is structured as follows. First, it discusses the increasing role of PSD programs in development cooperation and the implications of this shifting aid paradigm for the meso-level locus of evaluation research. Second, it outlines three major analytical approaches for assessing VCD effectiveness, based on a combination of business management and development analysis. The discussion then distinguishes between (a) robust methods of impact measurement at the micro level, (b) value added distribution and transaction cost models at the supply chain level, and (c) contract choice simulation approaches at the behavioral agency level. Third, it presents some empirical examples of each of these approaches, drawing on a variety of research methods from the field of development evaluation studies and arguing that an integrated and sequential combination of approaches could generate better insights into the welfare and distributional effects of VCD programs.

The Rise of Private Sector Development Programs

International cooperation has long been considered the exclusive domain of public and civic aid agencies, focusing on the supply and delivery of key services that are important for poverty alleviation (education, health care, drinking water, and sanitary services). In addition, a major part of aid has been used to create global political and institutional conditions for development in areas of good governance, public finance management, democracy, safety, and security.

The growing attention paid to the role of the private sector in development came in two waves. The first wave started in the 1980s and aimed to privatize publicly provided services and turn them into private market-based entities within the framework of ongoing structural adjustment programs. Former marketing boards for export promotion were largely abolished, and many public utilities were transferred to private companies. The second wave became more prominent after 2000. It sought to support private sector enterprises through improved input delivery, training programs, and finance and marketing services and, ultimately, to create local employment, increase value added, and enhance economic growth (IFC 2013).

Initially, much attention was devoted to programs focusing on reducing trade barriers. Public support for enhancing international trade activities (aid for trade) has been subject to several, usually rather positive, evaluations that focus on the effectiveness of reducing trade constraints and improving market access for increasing the volume and value of international trade transactions. It is expected that growing trade also benefits producers, workers, and traders involved in market exchange (Bird 2009). These programs essentially enable developing countries to reap the fruits of their comparative advantage.

Many current PSD programs distinguish two dimensions: (a) supporting the improvement of the national business environment and investment climate and (b) supporting concrete private business activities at the enterprise or sector level. While the former focuses on reforms of the state and the adoption of enabling macroeconomic policies to enhance business and investment opportunities, the latter are oriented more toward specific enterprises, clusters, or sectors that can develop or exploit specific competitive advantages in international trade.

Whereas most concrete PSD activities were either launched at the macro (country) or micro (enterprise or firm) level, the recent focus on value chain development introduces a meso-level perspective (Korfker 2013). At this level, VCD programs intend to bridge the gap between macro policies and local action and rely on notions of linking up, networking, building connections, and strengthening interactions between participating firms within a particular commodity supply chain. Primary attention is given to the objectives of (a) reducing information constraints (and thus diminishing risks and transaction costs), (b) upgrading production and exchange processes (generating efficiency, quality, and value added), and (c) enhancing willingness to invest and thus promoting better entrepreneurship.

Expectations regarding the effectiveness and efficiency of PSD programs are generally high, but the availability of sound evaluations is still far too limited to be able confirm this. The scarce delivery of PSD evaluations is the result of different conceptual and strategic challenges. First, PSD programs are unlikely to rely on randomized evaluations since participating clients are typically selected by private lead firms. Second, counterfactual analysis is notably difficult, and self-selection is likely to take place in many PSD programs. Third, information on commercial transactions and financial performance is not widely available and tends to be protected for competitive motives. Fourth, mixed funding and blending arrangements for co-financing of activities are frequently used, making attribution analysis more complex. Fifth and finally, the sample size of participating producers and processors tends to be rather small, limiting the prospects for thorough statistical analysis.

Value Chain Development: An Analytical Perspective

The outcomes and impacts of VCD programs need to be analyzed empirically based on a thorough theoretical understanding of the agency structure and dynamics of the interactions between agents involved in the supply chain. Most value chain theories originate from the field of business management and enterprise administration and tend to devote ample attention to the timely exchange of transactions (lean supply chains), logistics organization (lower transaction costs), and information exchange (risk management).

Analysis of supply chain management addresses the network of interconnected businesses involved in the provision of products and services required by end customers in a supply chain. It spans all movement from the storage of raw materials, work-in-process inventory, and finished goods from the point of origin to the point of consumption as well as the reversed streams of information to guarantee adequate agency coordination (figure 3.1). Linking upstream and downstream interaction and tailoring the components of the supply chain require deliberate planning and

Figure 3.1   Supply Chain Structures

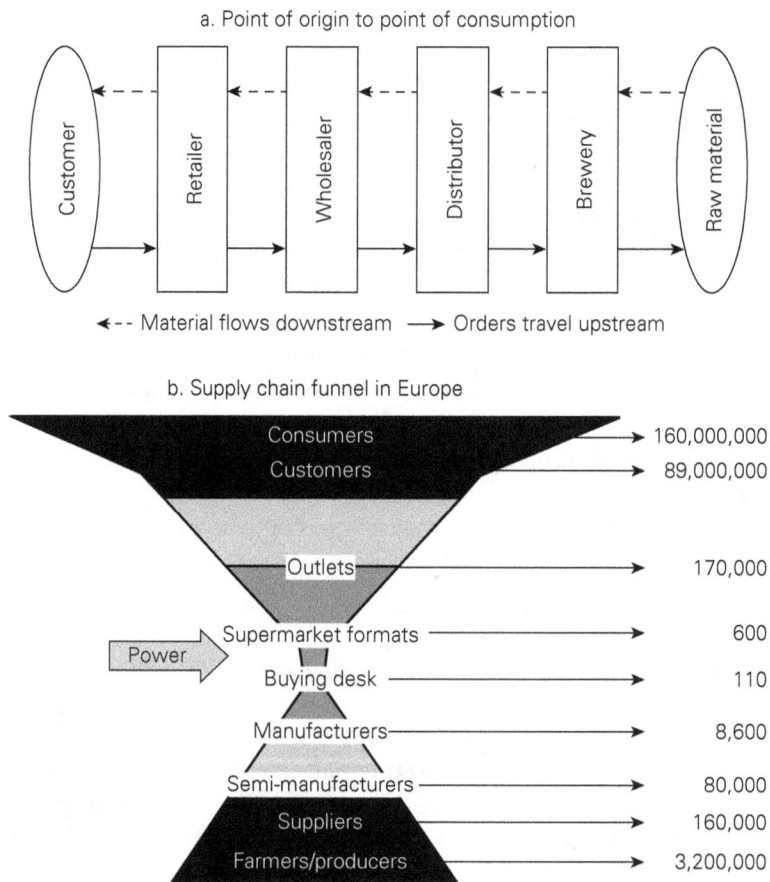

a. Point of origin to point of consumption

◄-- Material flows downstream   ──► Orders travel upstream

b. Supply chain funnel in Europe

Consumers	160,000,000
Customers	89,000,000
Outlets	170,000
Supermarket formats	600
Buying desk	110
Manufacturers	8,600
Semi-manufacturers	80,000
Suppliers	160,000
Farmers/producers	3,200,000

management of all activities involved in sourcing, procurement, conversion, and logistics through careful coordination and purposeful collaboration with all relevant partners (Kouvelis, Chambers, and Wang 2006).

The empirical analysis of the interactions between supply chain partners faces some practical challenges. Most important, representative data sampling is only possible at both extremes of the supply chain (among smallholder producers and final consumers). In the middle only a few observation points are available, and many data are kept confidential. This funnel-shaped data structure makes statistical analyses rather complicated, requiring multilevel approaches that link input data from one stage in the chain to outcomes at other stages.

Another major challenge refers to the contractual nature of exchange transactions. Relations between supply chain partners are guided by multiple objectives, and trade-offs are likely to occur (between revenue generation and risk reduction). In addition to efficiency motives (short-run profit), equity considerations (distribution of revenue shares) and long-term continuity criteria (loyalty between chain partners) are also of crucial importance for maintaining fruitful supply chain cooperation.

In analytical terms, three different—albeit related—approaches are available for evaluating the impact of supply chain performance on development:

- *Robust impact measurement* studies focus on the generation of (net) income and (net) employment at the upstream (suppliers) level, using microdata that inform about revenues, costs, labor intensity, prices, and product quality.[2] Such analyses can rely on counterfactuals outside the targeted supply chain (noncertified producers). Much of the empirical literature in this field focuses on the effectiveness of certification and labeling practices.
- *Transaction cost modeling* at the value chain level relies on empirical studies that analyze the value added distribution among supply chain partners, relying on transaction cost approaches that identify the cost-effectiveness of different configurations of the supply chain. Primary attention is given to information and enforcement costs to guarantee loyalty and trust.
- *Contract choice analysis* is based on simulation studies that analyze the interactions between different partners in the value chain at the systemic level, while addressing the structure of alternative contractual arrangements and the implicit behavioral incentives that result from mutually agreed procedures for sharing distribution costs, revenues, risks, and responsibilities.

The following section provides some empirical examples of these three approaches and outlines their analytical relevance for understanding the implications of particular value chain approaches for effectiveness, equity, and sustainability.

Value Chain Impact Analysis: Focus on Development Effectiveness

Analytical procedures and empirical approaches for robust impact measurement have been generally established in the field of development cooperation, particularly for assessing the net effects of project interventions in key areas of education, health care, water and sanitation, and microfinance. The application of impact measurement in VCD programs is, however, still rather scarce and meets specific methodological challenges.

Major difficulties for using robust impact measurement in VCD programs include the occurrence of simultaneous input contributions by various (public and private) agents, the interactions between farm-household and village-level effects, and selection effects that are likely to occur due to explicit targeting of trade propositions to specific segments of producers. The latter aspect makes randomized control trial methods inappropriate for evaluating VCD programs; most value chain impact measurements thus rely on pseudo experimental approaches.

Internal evaluations of VCD programs focus largely on the efficiency of operations between chain partners. Therefore, a wide variety of measures and metrics are available to assess timely delivery (lead time, order path), capacity utilization, and consumer satisfaction (see Gunasekaran, Patel, and McGaughey 2004 for a concise overview). These intercompany frameworks usually provide adequate insight into the operational performance of VCD activities and are critical for assessing the competitiveness of the organizational arrangements in place.

External evaluations that also consider the effects of VCD on development outcomes need to go a step further. Primary attention is given to the net income and employment effects at the upstream level of the supply chain (primary producers) or the welfare effects at the downstream level (final consumers). It is therefore important to pay due attention to impact at the household level (including possible substitution effects) and to consider likely spillover effects on nonparticipating households (externalities for third parties due to pricing effects).

Figure 3.2 provides some empirical examples of such impact measurement based on the case of fair trade (FT) certified products. Panel a shows

Figure 3.2 Impact of Fair Trade Certification

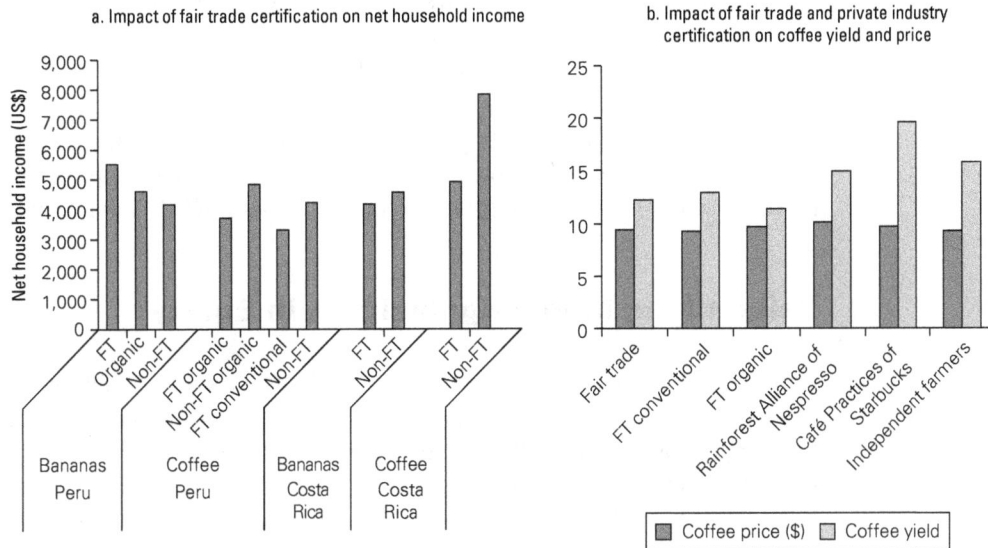

a. Impact of fair trade certification on net household income

b. Impact of fair trade and private industry certification on coffee yield and price

Sources: Ruben, Fort, and Zúñiga-Arias 2009; Ruben and Zúñiga-Arias 2011.

Note: FT = fair trade.

net income effects of FT certification for primary producers of coffee and bananas in Costa Rica and Peru. In many cases, non-FT producers—particularly in coffee—have higher net income than FT producers due to (a) substitution effects (higher prices lead to more specialization in coffee production and the neglect of other income-generating activities like food production and off-farm employment) and (b) general price effects (FT pushes up local market prices and thus non-FT producers also reap major benefits). Insights into these net effects can only be generated with a sound counterfactual analysis and adequate matching procedures that rule out individual effects and include village-specific effects.

Panel b of figure 3.2 reveals the effects of voluntary labels (FT), with private industry labels (Rainforest Alliance of Nespresso, Café Practices of Starbucks) used as a counterfactual. The disaggregation of price and yield effects reveals that private labels focus more on technical assistance for productivity and quality improvements that lead to higher market prices. The net effect of private labels tends to outcompete the prospects provided by fair trade through a guaranteed minimum price. This illustrates the importance of analyzing VCD interactions beyond the simple perspective of "output pricing" and of paying attention to other exchange relationships (input provision, technical assistance, knowledge exchange) that may lead to productivity or quality improvements.

Evaluating the development effectiveness of VCD programs requires an analytical framework that considers a relevant counterfactual, controls for self-selection, and is based on a sound theoretical understanding of the likely effects at the plot, farm, and household levels. This type of analysis provides, however, limited insight into the distribution of value added and the procedures used for distributing costs, revenues, and risks among value chain partners. The next section discusses some complementary approaches that are useful for constructing a more complete image of VCD operations.

Value Chain Modeling: Insights in Equity

Impact measurement with counterfactual methods is hardly possible at the downstream level of the value chain, since data are rarely available for the full comparison of several alternative cost-benefit structures. Figure 3.3 provides some insight into the added value distribution within four typical international supply chains for fresh fruits and vegetables. It illustrates the percentile share of the price paid by the consumer that accrues to farmers, processors, exporters, traders, importers, and retailers (and the state).

The input-output structure for these typical fruits and vegetables value chains is useful for understanding the structure of value added distribution among partners in the chain. Although many tasks are undertaken at upstream stages in the supply chain, only a relatively small percentage of the retail price is captured by developing-country agents. On average, the stages located within developing countries capture between 9 and 32 percent of the

Figure 3.3 Distribution of Value in International Horticultural Value Chains

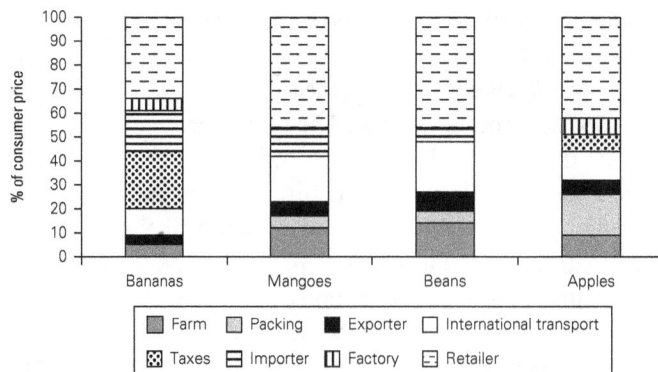

Source: Ruben and van Eyk 2007.

free-on-board value. The value captured by primary producers (growers) ranges from 4 to 14 percent of the total retail price. International transport accounts for 11 to 21 percent of the retail price and thus captures a significant part of the value in the chain. This share is even higher than the value captured by local growers. In most cases, about half of the cost-insurance-freight value is assumed by international transport. The tax share in the supply chain is highly variable and sometimes not fully reported. Retailers clearly capture most value in the fruits and vegetables chain, ranging from 34 to 46 percent of the consumer price. This implies that, from every dollar of banana or mango imports, about 40 cents accrues to the retailer. Since retailers also face significant costs in terms of shelf space, wastage, loss, and no-sale, their net profit margin is about 20 percent.

Such an empirical analysis is important for understanding the structure of the power relations within the value chain, but it gives insufficient insights into the alternatives for evaluative purposes. Simulation approaches provide deeper insight into the alternative value added options under different types of market procurement (Ruben and Kruijssen 2007). Based on common transaction cost theory, differences in governance costs, changes in trust relationships, economies of scale, and degrees of opportunism can be simulated for direct deliveries to local wholesale markets and for contractually arranged deliveries through preferred supplier arrangements.

A linear programming approach is used here to assess the net value added share received by primary producers. In the baseline run (with the same capital costs for each channel), local spot market deliveries offer a positive net margin due to generally low production costs (figure 3.4). The net margin for farmers engaged in value chain integration under preferred supplier arrangements (runs 1, 2, and 4) can rise due to lower governance costs or the sharing of production costs (credit for input purchase provided by the processor). On some occasions, the increase in variable production costs (run 3) or the high fixed investments required to participate in integrated value chains (run 5) might outweigh the advantages of lower governance costs.

These simulation models can be useful for exploring alternative options under different types of cooperation scenarios and for assessing the effects of reduced governance costs (run 1), higher fixed investments (run 2), higher production costs (run 3), economies of scale (run 4), and improved trust or reduced opportunism (run 5). For each case, the outlet permitting the highest net margin for the producer can be detected.

The reliance on value chain simulation models enables us to appreciate the net effects of the interactions between value chain partners on the transaction costs for market exchange. These savings are occasionally even larger than the direct net profits realized in production and thus represent a major

Figure 3.4 **Simulation of Transaction Costs under Different Procurement Regimes**

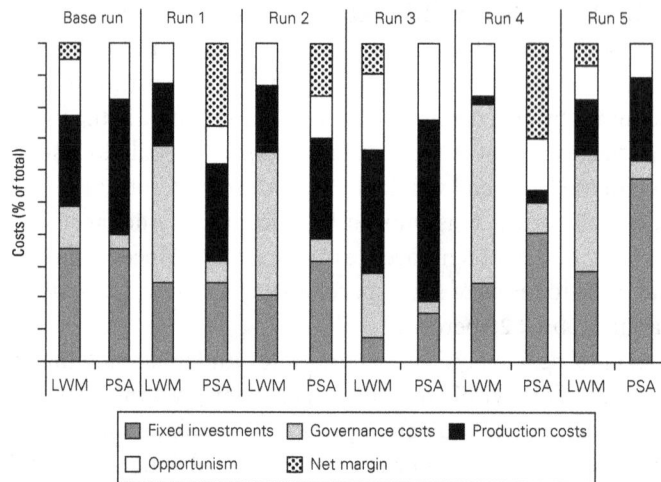

Source: Ruben and Kruijssen 2007.

Note: LWM = local wholesale market; PSA = preferred supplier arrangements.

outcome of value chain programs. Transaction cost approaches also permit an appreciation of the outcomes in terms of enhanced *trust* among chain partners, reduced costs of information search, and cost savings from greater *loyalty* between producers, traders, and processors. Making these "unobservables" more transparent remains a major challenge for evaluation studies.

Contract Choice in Value Chains: Understanding Uncertainty

Many VCD programs take place within the framework of a public-private partnership relationship. These PPPs are defined as a form of cooperation between government and business agents—sometimes also involving voluntary organizations (nongovernmental organizations, trade unions) or knowledge institutes—that agree to work together to reach a common goal or carry out a specific task, while jointly assuming the risks and responsibilities and sharing their resources and competences. While many conceptual studies provide insights into the core principles and the potential of PPPs in international development cooperation, empirical evidence that highlights the (developmental) rationale and the actual outcomes for VCD stakeholders is still extremely scarce. Analyzing the contractual structure that governs the relationships between supply chain agents is critical for understanding the behavioral incentives of such cooperative arrangements.

In theory, PPPs can be considered a suitable contractual option if market or institutional failures prevent the delivery of goods and services with a net development impact. In practice, however, many PPPs are motivated by financial reasons to mobilize additional resources that enable them to execute large investment programs. Few evaluation reports mention overcoming financial market failures and product or market risks as motives for public engagement. Market failures are a reason to pursue PPPs in medical research and agricultural product development, where high sunk costs inhibit private start-ups. Government failures can also be a reason to pursue PPPs if the adequate provision of public goods is at stake.

Many PPP evaluations focus on resource sharing and pay little attention to the risk-sharing and revenue distribution dimensions of partnerships. More than half of the PPP evaluative case studies pay no attention to the distribution of risks between public and private partners. The partnership is usually conceived as a cooperative agreement focusing on common goals and sharing of inputs and resources. Clear arrangements for distributing revenues and rules for assigning responsibilities for potential losses are commonly absent. Moreover, rules for distributing public and private shares are defined rather mechanically or on an ad hoc basis; bidding schemes are hardly used to identify appropriate private partners.

A systematic review of the available evidence regarding the development impact of PPPs was conducted based on a careful search and selection process following the guidelines and procedures of the Campbell protocol (IOB 2013). From an initial collection of 1,433 studies derived from several sources (articles from scientific portals and development evaluation studies), 81 studies qualified as valid evaluative reports. After a further screening regarding the reporting on PPP results, 47 studies offered empirical evidence on PPP effectiveness, including 18 case studies and 29 reviews. Many of these PPPs refer to value chain cooperation programs.

Figure 3.5 provides an overview of the contract choice arrangements that are included in PPPs. Five contractual dimensions are distinguished: rules for cooperation, decision-making arrangements, joint funding, revenue sharing, and risk distribution between PPP partners. These dimensions are related to whether positive or negative outcomes of the PPP are registered.

The contractual terms for PPP arrangements require an explicit definition of the mutual contributions (inputs), the generated output, and the distribution of risks and rights for the residual value of the program. Whereas most contracts offer clear mechanisms for cooperation and mutual

Figure 3.5 Contract Choice Characteristics of PPP Arrangements

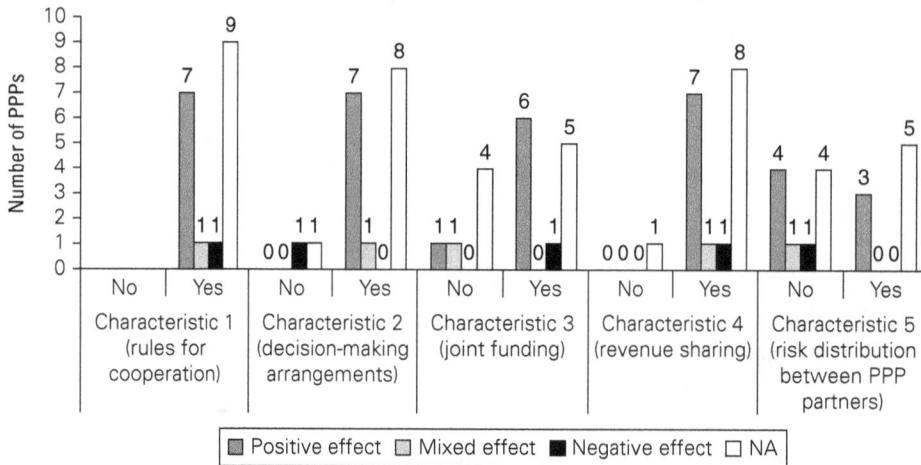

Source: Ruben and Kruijssen 2007.

Note: NA = not applicable; PPP = public-private partnership.

agreements, co-funding mechanisms are usually defined rather loosely. More important, clear arrangements for revenue sharing and risk distribution are notably absent in many PPPs. Less positive outcomes are registered if the latter arrangements are not in place.

The absence of conscious and systematic attempts to manage and arrange negotiation processes at the start of PPPs may result in contractual arrangements that are largely *incomplete* with respect to the allocation of risks, distribution of lifetime costs, and allocation of rights to residual value (Nisar 2007). The completeness of the contractual dimensions of VCD programs represents a key criterion for assessing the prospects for achieving developmental outcomes. Since contracts provide behavioral incentives for agency coordination, the overall performance of supply chains requires a set of procedures that (a) encourages trust between chain partners and (b) guarantees loyalty in delivery relationships. The better the PPP arrangements can guarantee mutual trust and loyalty, the more savings can be realized in control and surveillance. The reduced uncertainty for VCD agents can be expected to create incentives for intensification and investments that finally lead to product or process upgrading.

Given the large heterogeneity in product quality that is common to supply chains originating in developing countries, guaranteeing trust and improving loyalty are of crucial importance for VCD performance (Zúñiga-Arias, Ruben, and van Boekel 2009). Heterogeneity is caused by diversity in human behavior and variability in product management procedures. Producers that

Poverty, Inequality, and Evaluation

want to deliver to export market outlets have to satisfy international quality and safety regulations, forcing them to maintain strict production and management standards.

Controlling the heterogeneity in product quality usually requires strict monitoring and control, occasioning high costs associated with supervision that can also undermine trust relationships (Ruben, Saenz, and Zúñiga-Arias 2005). Otherwise, uncertainty is mainly due to asymmetric information regarding prices and market requirements. Long-term contracts can be extremely helpful for reducing such uncertainties and mitigating adverse and opportunistic behavior among supply chain agents. In a similar vein, contracts are crucial for enforcing loyalty between producers and traders or processors, thus removing the temptation of farmers to engage in side-sales with other agents. Reducing uncertainty through input-sharing arrangements that are matched with output deliveries at agreed prices is critical for effective, efficient, and sustainable VCD programs.

Conclusions and Outlook

With the growing emphasis on private sector development in international cooperation, the availability of sound evaluation procedures for assessing the effectiveness, efficiency, and equity effects of cross-border VCD programs is becoming increasingly important. VCD programs share some typical characteristics that make their evaluation rather complicated, such as (a) the simultaneous engagement of multiple stakeholders, (b) the upstream and downstream linkages between various agents, and (c) the implicit contractual arrangements for guiding transactions and exchange between supply chain partners.

This chapter has distinguished three different—albeit complementary—approaches for evaluating VCD programs, focusing on (a) effectiveness in terms of net welfare effects, (b) efficiency through reduction of transaction costs, and (c) equity in contractual terms and distribution of risks for enforcing loyalty and trust. Each aspect requires a specific approach to guarantee the availability of relevant counterfactuals. Whereas effectiveness analysis can rely on empirical field data and common diff-in-diff procedures, efficiency analysis of transaction costs asks for a simulation modeling framework. Finally, contract choice analysis offers opportunities for gaining insights into the incentives for guaranteeing long-term cooperation.

The integrated analysis of VCD performance can thus rely on a careful combination of analytical tools derived from the academic traditions of robust impact analysis, transaction costs theory, and agency approaches.

The precise way of interlinking these analytical frameworks asks for an explicit sequential approach that enables the evaluator to identify potential synergies or trade-offs between effectiveness, efficiency, and equity considerations. Many VCD programs start from efficiency considerations (that is, reduction of losses in supply chain deliveries) but subsequently develop options for improving quality or reducing risks that can be translated into revenue gains for several chain partners. The final welfare distribution effects throughout the value chain depend mostly on the bargaining framework between the PSD partners and the contractual terms of engagement agreed among them.

In the medium and long run, it is likely that the dynamic development of VCD interactions will evolve according to globalization tendencies in the competitive market environment. Whereas short-run welfare and efficiency gains are still preserved for direct VCD partners, externalities for other agents are likely to emerge if sectorwide propositions are reached. This will eventually drive VCD partners toward the development of new competitive advantages. Such a life cycle of subsequent VCD propositions reflects the dynamics of PSD programs that continuously adapt to changes in the public policy environment and the private sector competitive space.

Notes

1. Issues related to improving public procurement procedures and practices are also receiving increasing attention within the framework of guaranteeing private sector engagement in development programs.
2. Impact analysis at the downstream level (focusing on consumer benefits) is usually based on shopping and expenditure surveys, asking whether "bottom of the pyramid" consumers benefit from supply chain management arrangements.

References

Bird, K. 2009. *Second Global Aid for Trade Review: Assessing Impact and Effectiveness.* London: ODI.

EuropAid. 2005. *Evaluation of European Community Support to Private Sector Development in Third Countries.* Brussels: EuropAid.

Gunasekaran, A., C. Patel, and R. E. McGaughey. 2004. "A Framework for Supply Chain Performance Measurement." *International Journal of Production Economics* 87 (3): 333–47.

IFC (International Finance Corporation). 2013. "Building a Roadmap to Sustainability in Agro-Commodity Production." IFC (with the Sustainable

Trade Initiative, Dutch Ministry of Foreign Affairs, and the Swiss State Secretariat of Economic Affairs), Washington, DC, October.

IOB (Policy and Operations Evaluation Department). 2013. "Systematic Review of Public-Private Partnerships." IOB Study, Ministry of Foreign Affairs, The Hague.

Korfker, F. 2013. "Reflections on Private-Sector Evaluation in the European Bank for Reconstruction and Development 1991–2010." *Evaluation* 19 (1): 85–96.

Kouvelis, P., C. Chambers, and H. Wang. 2006. "Supply Chain Management Research and Production and Operations Management: Review, Trends, and Opportunities." *Production and Operations Management* 15 (3): 449–69.

Nisar, M.T. 2007. "Risk Management in Public-Private Partnership Contracts." *Public Organization Review* (7) 1–19.

Ruben, R., R. Fort, and G. Zúñiga-Arias. 2009. "Measuring the Impact of Fair Trade on Development." *Development in Practice* 19 (6): 777–88.

Ruben, R., and F. Kruijssen. 2007. "Smallholder Procurement in Supply Chain Development: A Transaction Costs Framework." In *Development Economics between Markets and Institutions: Incentives for Growth, Food Security, and Sustainable Use of the Environment*, edited by E. Bulte and R. Ruben, 291–304. Wageningen: Academic Publishers.

Ruben, R., F. Saenz, and G. Zúñiga-Arias. 2005. "Contracts or Rules: Quality Surveillance in Costa Rican Mango Export." In *Hide or Confide? The Dilemma of Transparency*, edited by G. J. Hofstede, 51–58. The Hague: Emerging World of Chains and Networks, Reed Business Information.

Ruben, R., and K. van Eyk. 2007. "The Dynamics of the Global Fruit and Vegetable Chains: Export-Oriented Agriculture as a Pro-Poor Strategy?" *Faith and Economics* 50 (Fall): 42–63.

Ruben, R., and G. Zúñiga-Arias. 2011. "How Standards Compete: Comparative Impact of Coffee Certification in Northern Nicaragua." *Supply Chain Management: An International Journal* 16 (2): 98–109.

Zúñiga-Arias, G., R. Ruben, and T. van Boekel. 2009. "Managing Quality Heterogeneity in the Mango Supply Chain: Evidence from Costa Rica." *Trends in Food Science and Technology* 20 (3–4): 168–79.

CHAPTER 4

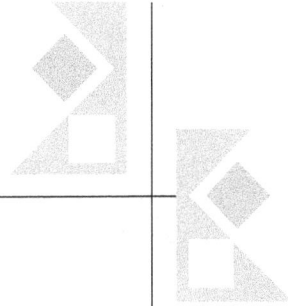

Assessing Growth and Its Distribution in IFC Strategies and Projects

Ade Freeman and Izlem Yenice

Introduction

Growth is good for the poor, but the impact of growth on poverty reduction depends on both the pace and the pattern of growth. A pattern that enhances the ability of poor women and men to participate in, contribute to, and benefit from growth should not come at the expense of the pace of growth. Including the poor in the growth process is also good for the pace of growth. This relationship underscores the critical importance of the pattern of growth for poverty reduction.

Support for private sector development is crucial for driving broad-based growth, reducing poverty, and achieving the Millennium Development Goals. The International Finance Corporation (IFC) is the world's largest

Ade Freeman and Izlem Yenice are with the Independent Evaluation Group at the World Bank.

multilateral development bank providing financial support and technical advice to private firms in developing countries. Its mission is to create opportunities for people to escape poverty and improve their lives through support for private sector development.[1] Paying attention to the type of growth that the institution supports is therefore critical to fulfilling its mission.

The IFC's approach to poverty has evolved from supporting private sector–led growth in general to promoting environmentally and socially sustainable growth and—more recently—to paying explicit attention to inclusive growth. A substantial increase in the IFC's activities in poor and middle-income countries has drawn attention to the corporation's development effectiveness in these countries. Attention has been paid to how IFC's support for private sector development is helping to tackle poverty. Yet there is limited evidence of what poverty means within the IFC's development context or how its interventions reach and affect the poor.

This chapter is based on an evaluation by the World Bank's Independent Evaluation Group (IEG) of IFC strategies and investment projects designed over a 10-year period from 2000 to 2010.[2] It aims to assess the relevance and effectiveness of the corporation's poverty focus and results, giving explicit attention to its strategies, policies, and investment operations. In the context of the IFC's business model, poverty focus is defined as support for private sector development that contributes to growth as well as patterns of growth that enhance opportunities for the poor. This type of growth is often referred to as inclusive, pro-poor, or broad-based growth.

This assessment uses the conceptual framework shown in figure 4.1 to evaluate how IFC support for growth through private sector development contributes to poverty reduction. It assesses the relevance and effectiveness of the IFC's poverty focus, specifically (a) the IFC's strategic directions on poverty, (b) the extent of poverty focus at the project level, and (c) the contribution of IFC projects to growth and distributional patterns of growth that create opportunities for the poor.

Poverty Focus at the Strategic Level

The private sector, comprising small and large firms, individuals, and businesses, is an engine of growth. It is responsible for investments and economic activity that make a major contribution to gross domestic product and employment. Because the private sector has been the dominant engine of growth, its role has been associated with increasing the pace of growth. Private sector activities can have considerable effects on the pace of growth as well as on the distribution of rising average incomes (see box 4.1).

Poverty, Inequality, and Evaluation

Figure 4.1   Conceptual Framework Guiding Assessment of IFC's Contribution to Poverty Reduction

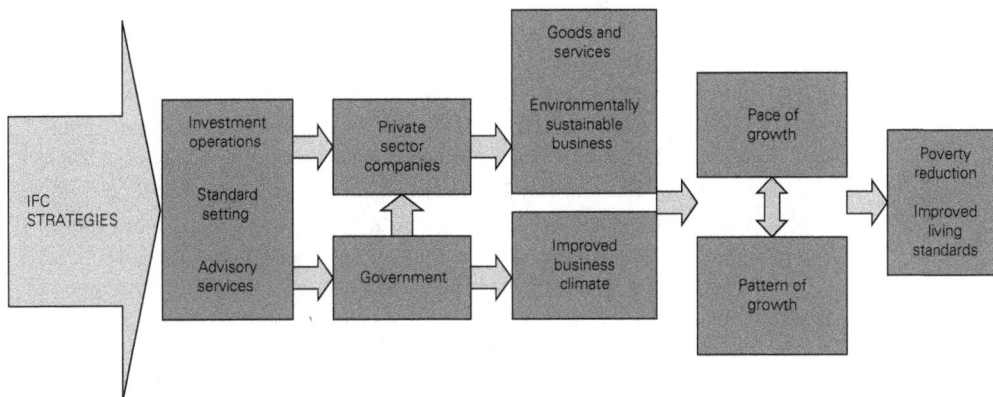

Source: IEG 2011.

Note: IFC = International Finance Corporation.

Box 4.1   The Private Sector, Growth, and Poverty Reduction

The private sector can be involved in growth and poverty reduction in various ways:

- *Jobs and opportunities.* Jobs created by private investment provide opportunities and upward mobility that improve living standards for poor families. The World Bank's Voices of the Poor Initiative at the turn of the new century showed that poor people identify a paid job and self-employment as key to moving out of poverty (World Bank 2001).
- *Role of micro, small, and medium enterprises.* Privately run micro, small, and medium enterprises (MSMEs) span a wide range of sectors and provide important sources of livelihood for the poor in low- and middle-income countries. MSMEs, characterized mainly by informality, account for about 72 percent of nonfarm employment in Sub-Saharan Africa, 65 percent in Asia, 51 percent in Latin America, and 48 percent in North Africa.
- *Contribution to human development.* Governments remain the largest source of financing for health and education, but private companies are extensively involved in delivering these services in many developing countries. For instance, in many countries in Africa and Asia, private companies are the main providers of health and education services to the urban and rural poor. In addition, private companies lead the development of innovative approaches to expand access to health and education services to the poor, including through partnerships with governments and nongovernmental organizations.

(continued next page)

Assessing Growth and Its Distribution in IFC Strategies and Projects

Box 4.1 *continued*

- *Investment in infrastructure.* Infrastructure investments are essential for economic growth and poverty reduction. Private financing of infrastructure is growing in importance, particularly in International Development Association (IDA) countries. Between 1995 and 2008, total per capita private investment in IDA countries was 64 percent of the levels in IDA-blend countries and only 23 percent of that in non-IDA countries, pointing to a major investment gap. The private sector is also significantly more efficient in the delivery of infrastructure services than the public sector.
- *Source of innovation.* Private enterprises play key roles in developing and bringing innovative products, services, and processes to the marketplace. Many innovations expand access to affordable goods and services for the poor and more affluent consumers. They also provide income and livelihood opportunities for the poor and investment opportunities for private businesses.

The IFC's approach to addressing poverty has evolved over the years. Since its inception, the IFC has grappled with the basic challenge of combining successful business operations with development impact. From its early days, the assumption was that any project that met the IFC's criteria and generated an economic rate of return of 10 percent or more contributes to reducing poverty. Recent strategic direction papers, however, demonstrate a stronger commitment to a focus on the poor.

At the strategic level, the IFC's priorities in frontier areas and sectors such as infrastructure, agribusiness, health and education, and financial markets are largely consistent with a poverty focus in that they reflect geographic, sectoral, and equity aspects that are correlated with enhanced opportunities for the poor. The IFC's five strategic pillars are important parts of its poverty agenda. Three of these—frontier markets, targeted sectors with potential engagement of the poor, and certain types of financial services—explicitly aim to support the kind of growth that provides opportunities for the poor to participate in, contribute to, or benefit from growth. But strategic sectors are defined in such broad terms that, although they are consistent with a pro-poor orientation, they need to be designed and implemented in ways that enhance the opportunities for and impact on poor people.

Over the evaluation period, from 2001 to 2010, the IFC increased the volume and share of investments in poor countries, represented by commitments in IDA countries. The share of its total commitments in IDA countries rose from 19 to 31 percent. The number of IDA countries with IFC investments nearly doubled, from 32 to 58. Investments and country coverage in Sub-Saharan Africa also increased significantly. Involvement in IDA countries accelerated in fiscal 2005, due mainly to the Global Trade Finance Program (GTFP). The IFC's relative investment share in IDA countries is higher than that of foreign direct investment (FDI). However, IFC investments in IDA countries have been heavily concentrated in just a few countries. Four countries have accounted for more than half of total IFC investments in IDA countries since fiscal 2001, reaching a peak of 78 percent in 2005 (figure 4.2). In fiscal 2010, the top four countries—India, Nigeria, Pakistan, and Vietnam—accounted for 59 percent of IFC investments in IDA countries. From 2000 to 2007, the IFC's level of concentration in the top four IDA countries was higher than that of FDI flows as well as IDA's own lending.

The IFC's relevance and additionality in middle-income countries depends on how well it defines its poverty agenda there. Frontier regions in middle-income countries are defined on the basis of a per capita income differential between country and regional averages. This criterion tends to focus the IFC on regions with the highest poverty rates. However, poverty maps developed for Brazil (map 4.1) show that the largest concentrations of

Figure 4.2 Concentration of IFC and World Bank Investment and FDI in Top-Four IDA Countries, 2000–10

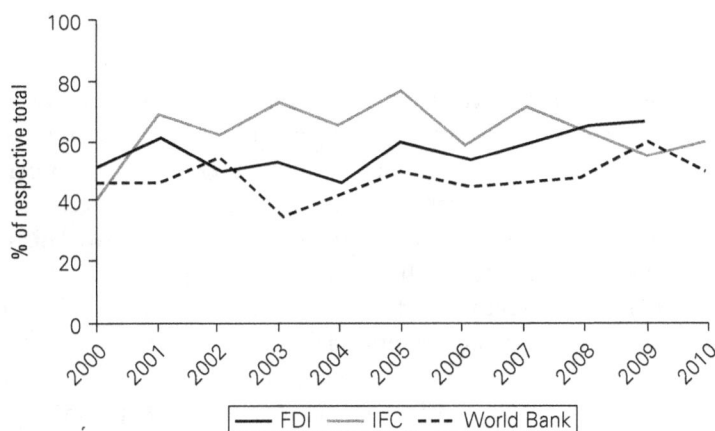

Source: IFC Management Information database, June 2010.

Note: FDI = foreign direct investment; IDA = International Development Association; IFC = International Finance Corporation.

Map 4.1 Poverty Map of Brazil

a. Poverty rate

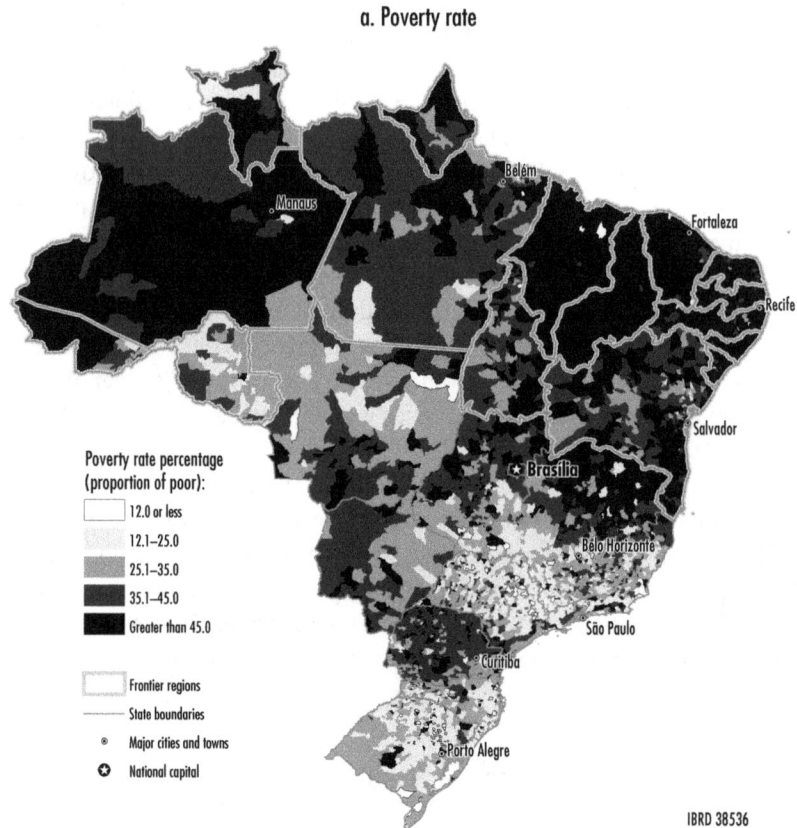

Poverty rate percentage (proportion of poor):

- ☐ 12.0 or less
- 12.1–25.0
- 25.1–35.0
- 35.1–45.0
- Greater than 45.0

- ☐ Frontier regions
- —— State boundaries
- ⊙ Major cities and towns
- ✪ National capital

IBRD 38536

(continued next page)

poor people are not in the locations with the highest poverty rates. This, together with the diversity of poverty in middle-income countries and the importance of nonincome dimensions of poverty, such as providing access to opportunities, suggests the need for a broader set of criteria that includes income and nonincome dimensions of poverty and spatial distribution of the poor (Department for International Development 2008).

The IFC is also targeting sectors with the potential for widespread engagement of the poor, such as financial markets, infrastructure, health and education, and agribusiness. Investments have also been highly concentrated within these sectors. In fiscal 2010, IFC commitments in financial markets accounted for 75 percent of total investments in targeted sectors. In IDA countries, the concentration was even higher. Within financial markets, investments are highly concentrated in the GTFP, which grew rapidly

Map 4.1 (continued)

b. Poverty density

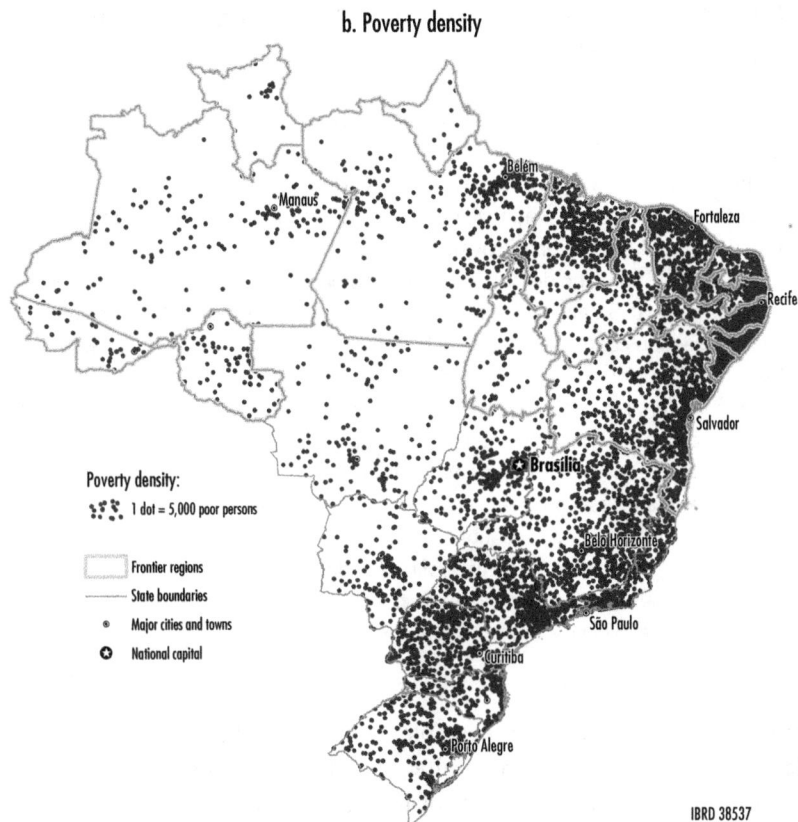

Poverty density:

⋮ 1 dot = 5,000 poor persons

▢ Frontier regions

— State boundaries

∘ Major cities and towns

⊙ National capital

IBRD 38537

after 2005. Through the GTFP, the IFC increased its presence in the poorest countries, helped to fill finance gaps for essential goods, and increased activity in sectors such as agribusiness. Yet the development and poverty impacts of these interventions have not been assessed at the project level (IEG 2013).

In relative terms, IFC investments in infrastructure, agribusiness, and health and education have changed little over time. The extent to which projects in these sectors actually benefit the poor depends on strategic choices relating to (a) the type of projects selected, (b) the incorporation of design features that benefit the poor, and (c) the robustness of monitoring and evaluation systems to track progress, take corrective actions, and assess impacts on the poor. Box 4.2 highlights a project that has incorporated such features into its design.

MSMEs account for the largest part of the private sector in many developing countries. The IFC provides the bulk of MSME financing through

Box 4.2   Evidence from Case Studies: Affordable Services and Expanded Access to Services

An IFC-supported microfinance bank provides a good example of how innovations that reduce costs can enhance the poor's access to services (Hammond et al. 2007).

Innovations in savings deposits, such as not requiring minimum deposits or personal references when clients open an account, were important factors driving the expansion of savings deposits by the poor. For example, the number of account holders in the bank increased from 3,679 in 2005 to 111,935 in 2010. Small depositors were specifically attracted by the relatively low transaction costs. As a result, 64 percent of customers had balances of less than US$100.

Respondents from field surveys confirmed the massive growth in savings deposits among low-income households, stating that the affordability of these services made savings accounts very attractive. In two urban areas where new bank branches had been opened, about 75 percent of respondents reported having a savings account. In contrast, in two areas that did not have bank branches, less than 20 percent of respondents reported having a savings account. In these areas, 73 percent of the people interviewed reported that they would like to have a branch of the microfinance bank in their area.

financial intermediaries (for example, commercial banks and specialist microfinance institutions). In parallel, the IFC's strategic directions consider MSMEs as a major element of its growth and poverty agenda. The IFC's total investment commitments in MSMEs grew from US$400 million in fiscal 2000 to US$3.1 billion in 2010, accounting for 17 and 24 percent of investments, respectively. The IFC's strategy of supporting MSMEs through financial intermediaries has reached a large number of MSMEs. The share of MSMEs being supported this way rose from 66 percent of total MSME support in fiscal 2000 to 83 percent in 2010 (figure 4.3). Empirical evidence on the poverty impacts of microfinance institutions is mixed: some studies show a positive impact on borrowers' welfare; others point to significant risks and downsides. Small and medium enterprises (SMEs) tend to face greater constraints to growth than large firms. Thus there is a strong development rationale for IFC support.

However, research and a recent IEG evaluation shows that there are many questions about the efficacy and welfare impacts of interventions seeking to support SMEs (IEG 2014). These questions need to be addressed to enhance the impact of SMEs on growth and poverty reduction. The magnitude of the challenges implies that carefully targeting investments in these

Figure 4.3   IFC and IDA Support to MSMEs through Financial Intermediaries, 2000–10

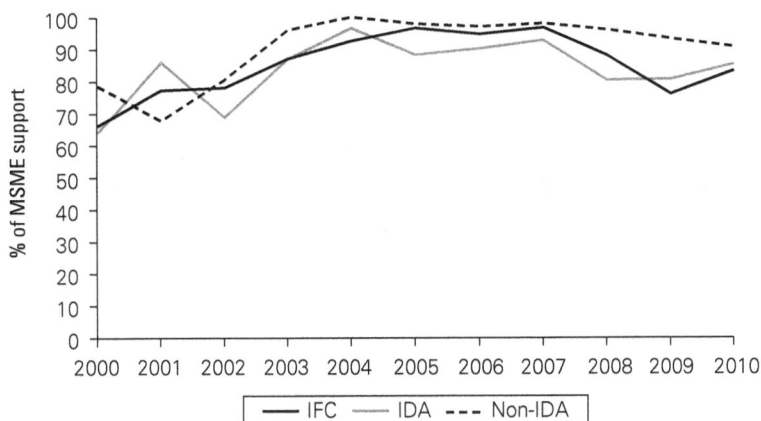

Source: IFC Management Information database, June 2010.

Note: IDA = International Development Association; IFC = International Finance Corporation; MSME = micro, small, and medium enterprise.

diverse situations will be critical for leveraging growth and poverty impacts in both IDA and non-IDA countries.

Poverty Focus in IFC Projects

At the project level, 481 IFC investment projects approved between fiscal 2000 and fiscal 2010, including 158 projects evaluated between 2005 and 2009, were randomly selected to examine how they addressed growth and distributional issues. A project's contribution to growth is measured by its expected economic rate of return (ERR), insofar as it is well estimated. The incorporation of distributional aspects of growth in projects was assessed based on features of their design and implementation using one or more of the following criteria:

- Project objective focused explicitly on the poor or underserved.
- Project identified mechanisms, such as geographic and household criteria, for targeting the poor and underserved.
- Project design paid attention to distributional issues, measured by explicit consideration of poverty characteristics (geographic, community, individual) of intended beneficiaries.
- Mechanisms were incorporated to track poverty and social outcomes during project implementation.

Most IFC projects are designed to contribute to growth. Of 211 nonfinancial sector projects, 86 percent reported estimated ERR of more than 15 percent. Given a benchmark ERR of 10 percent, this shows that the majority of projects are expected to generate net positive returns in the economies in which they are being implemented.

The link from growth to poverty reduction is, however, not automatic, particularly in situations where market failures and other inefficiencies limit participation of the poor. Thus deliberate action is often required to incorporate distributional aspects of growth into project design and implementation. Box 4.3 describes a project where deliberative action was taken to incorporate such aspects into a project.

With respect to distributional issues, based on the IEG's definition, 13 percent of projects across the sample had objectives with an explicit focus on poor people. Of projects with an explicit focus on the poor, 87 percent had interventions that engaged poor people directly through employment or the provision of goods and services.

Box 4.3   Innovations Making Services Affordable

An IFC-supported water concession used several innovations to make water services affordable to the poor. The number of customers in the concession area doubled, from 3.1 million in 1997 to 6.1 million in 2009.

In 1998 the water concession company launched a program that used local and community-based mechanisms for planning and implementation. This program emphasized the role of the poor as active decision makers with clear responsibilities for choosing the connection scheme and collection arrangements for their communities.

An output-based aid financing facility provided a subsidy for connection costs that helped to reduce the initial cost of connections for poor households. Connection fees for an individual residential connection ranged from about US$170 for an unsubsidized connection to US$64 for a subsidized one. Cross-subsidy-based innovative pricing schemes that considered variations in minimum consumption rates across different categories of consumers also kept rates affordable for the poor (Haughton and Khandker 2009).

These rates significantly reduced the cost of obtaining water. Households in the survey reported that, on average, they spent about US$17 a month for irregular supplies of water before the project and about US$4 a month for 24-hour water supply with the project. Households in a comparison area not covered by the water concession reported spending about US$25 a month for irregular water supply. Households also reported significant time savings—up to four hours a day—after the project.

Few projects incorporated a clear mechanism for targeting the poor. In cases where projects did target the poor, geographic targeting—such as focusing project activities in frontier and rural areas or urban slums—was the most frequently used mechanism. The identification of distributional effects on the intended beneficiaries was the most frequently used design feature to address poverty issues at this level.

Incorporating distributional issues into projects has been challenging for the IFC. Despite the increase in poverty focus at the broader strategic level, less than half (43 percent) of projects (a) had an expected ERR greater than the benchmark and (b) included at least one type of mechanism that addressed distributional issues during design or implementation. Box 4.4 provides several perspectives on how IFC-supported companies addressed business and social development objectives.

Box 4.4   Evidence from Case Studies: Integrating Business and Social Motivations

Companies in the IEG case studies invested in goods and services that benefit poor and underserved communities, using a mix of business and social motivations. The companies used a range of approaches to integrate business and social focus at the project level. These examples reflect how the IFC and its clients engage the poor.

One IFC client company involved in a village phone project did not have a clear development objective. It adopted mainly a business approach, although it did target its services to underserved rural areas, engaging SMEs as distributors of village phone services.

A microfinance bank considered itself a full-service bank, with a development mission and a socially responsible approach. It used geographic targeting and an appropriate mix of financial services to provide financial services to an underserved banking population.

A company involved in a farm forestry program had social objectives (a corporate social responsibility program), but these were not integrated into the farm forestry program. The company engaged low-income farmers as suppliers of pulp for the company's plant. The program also integrated farmers into markets for seedlings, credit, and the company's supply chain.

In a water concession project, the social objective was fully integrated into the company's business focus. Its corporate social responsibility initiative identified providing water to the urban poor as one of three focus areas. This initiative contributed to the company's business goals and its poverty alleviation objectives.

Poverty Outcomes in IFC Projects

The IFC's evaluation framework does not quantify benefits to poor and vulnerable groups and thus has no specific indicator for measuring a project's effect on poverty. Therefore, the majority of investment projects generated satisfactory economic returns but did not provide evidence of identifiable opportunities for the poor to participate in, contribute to, or benefit from the economic activities that the projects supported. The fact that projects did not provide evidence of identifiable opportunities for the poor does not necessarily mean that they did not contribute to poverty reduction. The findings reflect a failure to articulate the poverty effects of projects that focus primarily on economic growth.

Projects that supported a more inclusive pattern of growth performed as well as, if not better than, other IFC projects with regard to development and investment outcomes. This suggests that a poverty focus need not come at the expense of financial success. Projects were more likely to provide evidence of poverty outcomes when expected development outcomes focused on the poor, when project activities targeted the poor, when distributional issues were made explicit, or when poverty outcomes were tracked during project implementation.

Given the limited attention paid to distributional issues in the monitoring and evaluation framework, a poverty index was used to characterize project benefits on the basis of their contribution to growth and inclusion of the poor (figure 4.4). A project's Inclusiveness Index characterizes the project's contribution to economic growth and delivery of benefits to the poor. The Inclusiveness Index is based on a project's ex post ERR, a quantitative measure of net benefits to society, and qualitative descriptions of project benefits to the poor. Project evaluation findings that describe a project's nonquantified benefits are used to identify cases where there is evidence of direct benefits for the poor through (a) creation of employment and entrepreneurial opportunities, (b) access to goods and services, (c) access to finance, and (d) improved capacity to engage in productive or market activities. The analysis is based on 58 real sector projects from the random sample of 158 investment projects with evaluative findings.

Projects that incorporated distributive mechanisms were more likely to be associated with satisfactory poverty outcomes. In the sample, 53 percent of projects with at least one distributive mechanism achieved an identifiable direct impact on the poor. In contrast, only 6 percent of projects that did not have evidence of such a mechanism actually delivered benefits that could be traced to the poor. Inclusion of distributive mechanisms in project design and implementation enhanced the likelihood of creating opportunities for

Figure 4.4 Inclusiveness Index and ERR

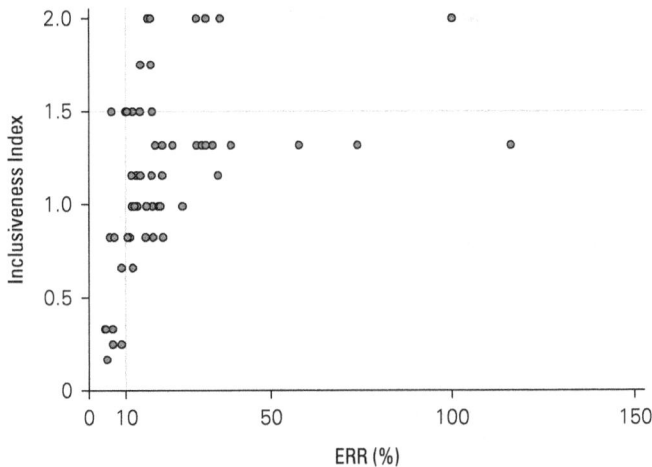

Source: IEG 2011.

Note: A project's Inclusiveness Index characterizes the project's contribution to economic growth and delivery of benefits to the poor. ERR = economic rate of return.

the poor. Box 4.5 provides examples of projects that showed less than successful results because they did not adequately consider the priority needs of beneficiaries.

Very few projects fall in the quadrant with low growth and evidence of low inclusiveness outcome, confirming that most IFC projects make important contributions to growth in the countries where they are implemented. The majority of IFC projects—59 percent of the sample—are positioned in the quadrant where they make a positive contribution to growth, but without evidence of discernible benefits to the poor. The fact that the majority of projects show strong contributions to growth but limited evidence of benefits to the poor does not mean that projects did not have an impact on the poor. Rather, there is no conclusive evidence of how the benefits from growth created employment for poor people or delivered goods and services that reached the poor. These findings reflect a failure to articulate the poverty effects of projects that focus primarily on economic growth.

Only a few of the sample projects delivered high levels of growth and demonstrated evidence of inclusion of the poor. Such projects provide learning opportunities that are useful for enhancing the IFC's poverty focus. They are also useful for understanding the poverty implications of projects in the high-growth, low-poverty-outcome quadrant and for articulating and better understanding how the IFC's overall poverty focus can be enhanced.

Box 4.5 Understanding Beneficiaries' Needs

Projects that focus on expected outcomes, target the poor, make distributional issues explicit, and track poverty outcomes tend to be more successful than projects with limited focus on these issues, such as the two described here.

In an agribusiness project, a major explanation for the low adoption of tree cultivation for pulpwood in a farm forestry project was the limited understanding on the part of project planners of the resource endowments and livelihoods of farmers. Only 10 percent of targeted farmers were cultivating pulpwood, much lower than expected.

This low adoption rate was partly due to the fact that the project design did not adequately take farmers' livelihood situations into account. The bulk of targeted farmers were small, marginal farmers whose priority was to generate cash flow to meet household expenditures throughout the year. Such households need immediate cash and were not willing to undertake long-term investments in pulpwood, with high initial costs and income streams that accrue four to five years in the future.

All of the small farmers in the survey reported that they would choose paddy cultivation, with a four-month growing cycle and investment return of US$333 per acre, over pulpwood cultivation, with a growing cycle of four to five years and an investment return of US$1,333 per acre.

In a microfinance project, microentrepreneurs in villages with a village phone operator program did not use these phones for commercial purposes because they owned cell phones. Villagers also did not want to discuss their business operations in public places. Thus even though pricing innovations made the cost of information services affordable, use was much lower than expected. In the case studies, 20 of the 29 entrepreneurs (69 percent) owned cell phones and stated that they would not use the village phone operator for conducting business.

A lack of understanding of the demand for information was also a key factor explaining the limited use of information disseminated through village phones. Respondents reported that they were not using the village phone operator to get access to information on agriculture and on services such as health care. In the case of agriculture, most participants in focus group discussions suggested that they would be willing to pay for information if it helped them to get better prices or farm more productively (OECD 2004).

Conclusion

The review finds that the IFC's strategic focus on economic growth and the needs of the poor is highly relevant for addressing the pressing development challenges in poor and middle-income countries. Projects by IFC-supported companies engaged poor people directly or through community activities. Some projects have limited or unknown engagement with the poor, but activities may have important impacts on the poor through indirect pathways.

The IFC's ability to reduce poverty by supporting the private sector needs to be based on a clear understanding of who the poor are and where they are located. To know what helps to reduce poverty, what works and what does not, and what changes over time, poverty has to be defined and measured. Such insights are important in developing an effective poverty-focused agenda, because the definition of poverty within the IFC context will drive the strategies and approaches for tackling it.

At the strategic level, the IFC's poverty focus can be enhanced by adopting a more strategic approach to addressing poverty, including sharpening the definition and shared understanding of poverty and poverty impact within the IFC context. In particular, in middle-income countries the organization needs to adopt more nuanced concepts of poverty when defining frontier regions, taking into consideration the incidence of poverty, spatial distribution of the poor, and nonincome dimensions of poverty (Word Bank 2001).

At the project level, there is a need to reexamine the stakeholder framework to address distributional and poverty issues in project design. Development institutions, such as the IFC, that support the private sector as a vehicle for boosting growth and sustainably reducing poverty can sharpen their poverty focus by making explicit the causal pathways, transmission channels, and underlying assumptions about how their strategies and projects can contribute to growth and about patterns of growth that provide meaningful opportunities for the poor.

With regard to measuring results, most IFC investment projects generate satisfactory economic returns but do not provide evidence of identifiable opportunities for the poor. The relatively high proportion of projects that do not generate such identifiable opportunities suggests that operations focus primarily on the pace of growth for poverty reduction at a time when the institution's strategies support focusing on the pattern of growth. For projects with poverty reduction objectives, poverty outcomes ought to be defined ex ante and then monitored and reported. For projects that focus primarily on growth but anticipate poverty reduction outcomes, the assumption underlying the expected relationship should be stated at approval with a rationale based on prior results or lessons from similar projects. These assumptions need to be tested periodically using field data and selected in-depth evaluations to learn about what works, what does not work, why, and in what contexts.

Notes

1. As of 2013, the mission of the World Bank Group, including the IFC, is to end extreme poverty and boost shared prosperity.
2. IEG (2011) covers both IFC investments and IFC advisory services.

References

Department for International Development. 2008. *Private Sector Development Strategy: Prosperity for All; Making Markets Work*. London: DFID.

Hammond, A. L., W. J. Kramer, R. S. Katz, J. T. Tran, and C. Walker. 2007. *The Next 4 Billion: Market Size and Business Strategy at the Base of the Pyramid*. Washington, DC: World Resources Institute and International Monetary Fund.

Haughton, J., and S. R. Khandker. 2009. *Handbook on Poverty and Inequality*. Washington, DC: World Bank.

IEG (Independent Evaluation Group). 2011. "Assessing IFC's Poverty Focus and Results." World Bank, Washington, DC.

———. 2013. "Evaluation of the International Finance Corporation's Global Trade Finance Program, 2006–12." World Bank, Washington, DC.

———. 2014. "Big Business of Small Enterprises." World Bank, Washington, DC.

OECD (Organisation for Economic Co-operation and Development). 2004. *Accelerating Pro-Poor Growth through Support for Private Sector Development: An Analytical Framework*. Paris: OECD.

World Bank. 2001. *World Development Report 2000–01: Attacking Poverty*. New York: Oxford University Press.

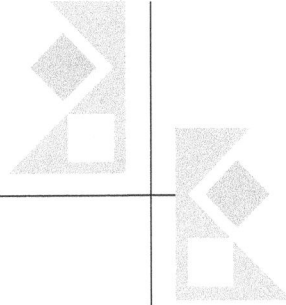

CHAPTER 5

Addressing Inequality and Poverty: An Evaluation of Community Empowerment in Jordan

Ann M. Doucette

Introduction

Depravation of basic resources and lack of sufficient "well-being" are often used as markers for poverty. The absence of consensus as to what level of depravation constitutes poverty has led many evaluators to take a monetary approach, in which income inequality serves as a primary indicator of relative poverty. While poverty can be assessed as the income disparity between rich and poor, this disparity says little about the importance of social indicators and how they exacerbate or ameliorate income inequality or how the individual experiences this inequality. Poverty in terms of income distribution is a myopic approach, as poverty can be conceived in terms of opportunities (choice and access to education, health, security and safety, and self-fulfillment) as well as outcomes (income level). The presumption is

---

Ann M. Doucette is with the Evaluators' Institute at George Washington University.

that higher levels of income inequality lead to increased social adversity for segments of the population, resulting in limited access to resources, which further contributes to poverty.

In contrast, a focus on inequality emphasizes the distribution of wealth and opportunity, from the highest strata to the most impoverished. The focus on the range of disparity between the "haves" and the "have-nots" may be a distraction. What may be of more consequence is social mobility, the opportunity to move within the social and economic hierarchy.

This chapter questions the sufficiency of inequality as a primary marker of poverty. It describes a comprehensive approach using a community empowerment framework that is implemented by the Jordan River Foundation (JRF) to address the socioeconomic challenges experienced in poverty pocket areas of Jordan. It addresses the distinction between poverty and inequality, highlighting findings from an external evaluation of the JRF community empowerment approach in the following areas: (a) facilitating the growth of community or village self-agency, solution-focused decision making, and civic engagement; (b) building social networks within tribal village communities and promoting gender and tribal equality; (c) developing successful community-selected entrepreneurial income-generating activities and businesses; and (d) involving youth in meaningful civic, employment, and volunteer activities to target poverty reduction and enhance social mobility.

Jordan River Foundation

The Jordan River Foundation, established in 1995, is a nongovernmental, nonprofit organization chaired by Her Majesty Queen Rania Al Abdullah. Its mission is "to engage Jordanians to realize their full economic potential and overcome social challenges." The JRF focuses primarily on Jordan's most vulnerable populations with initiatives to empower citizens by enabling them to identify concerns that challenge and compromise their ability to protect child and family well-being, to achieve community-level economic potential, and to develop strategies to address and ameliorate such challenges.

The identification of concerns and issues as well as the strategies used to address them are *home grown* and idiosyncratic to each participating community and village. Jordan is a highly diverse country, as exemplified by its tribal history, and this diversity calls for diverse interpretations of community and village needs and the development of unique strategies for addressing them. The JRF recognizes the uniqueness of the communities in which it works and does not implement a *one-size-fits-all* approach.

To empower communities, the JRF targets vulnerable communities (poverty pockets) and engages community members by supporting training, coalition building, and the development of local and regional capacity through community-based organizations (CBOs). JRF activities help communities to explore and develop entrepreneurial options and opportunities, to strengthen their management of community resources, and to strengthen community engagement in cooperative and productive civic governance.

While the quality of JRF programs is publicly acknowledged, there is a lack of systematic evaluation of the impact of JRF efforts across time and diverse programs. For example, the JRF's annual and sustainability reports emphasize program goals and outputs, but provide little detail on how these efforts or events changed perceptions or attitudes, improved the well-being of individuals, or strengthened community or village organizations and governance.

To address these concerns, the JRF engaged an external impact evaluation of its Community Empowerment Program (CEP). The evaluation sought to answer the following question: How did the JRF improve the quality of life of the communities served and achieve good governance at local levels? Specifically, how did the JRF accomplish the following?

1. Improve the employment opportunities through revolving loans and income-generating projects for the communities served
2. Alleviate poverty in the communities served
3. Empower women and youth in the communities served
4. Promote good governance through building the capacities of local CBOs

The Context

Jordan is located in a global region characterized by political turbulence and regional conflict. It is a constitutional monarchy under the reign of King Abdullah II, with a parliamentary system consisting of a lower house (Chamber of Deputies) that is elected and an upper house (House of Notables) that is appointed by the king. Jordan's population is approximately 6.5 million people (2012), with about 70 percent under 30 years of age and roughly 36 percent of the population 14 years and younger.[1] The ratio of males to females is consistent across the population age span. About 70 percent of the population lives in urban areas.

While Jordan is considered a middle-income country, with gross domestic product (GDP) per capita of US$6,000, GDP growth of 2.6 percent in 2012, and an expected ratio of debt to GDP of 65 percent (IMF 2012), the kingdom is challenged by a scarcity of natural resources and water supplies, pressures exerted by a large refugee population (from the West Bank and Gaza, Iraq, and the Syrian Arab Republic), declining tourism in the wake of the Arab Spring, and a growing need to import energy sources (IMF 2012). The debt burden and budget constraints have resulted in the change or elimination of several subsidies, intensifying the effects of poverty for many.

Although the national poverty rate, reported by the Ministry of Planning and International Cooperation, has hovered around 14 percent (13.3 percent in 2008, 14.4 percent in 2010), both urban and rural areas have substantial pockets of concentrated poverty. Also contributing to the slow economic growth is a rising unemployment rate. Large segments of the Jordanian population are available for work, but lack employment opportunities. Of specific concern is the unemployment rate for youth between the ages of 15 and 24, which is estimated at 27 percent (22.5 percent for males; 45.9 percent for females). Despite some incremental growth in GDP, economic, employment, and development efforts, especially those pertaining to Jordanian youth, are a central focus for reform.

Community Empowerment Program

The CEP is committed to beneficiary-targeted *sustainable human development*. Its primary goal is to enable communities and villages to identify existing community resources, to craft economic opportunities, and to develop effective strategies to take advantage of these opportunities and improve the quality of life of direct beneficiaries and the communities in which they live.

The CEP is based on a community capacity-building training model. It begins with community outreach and the establishment of local community committees. Building community identification and awareness about shared concerns and the importance of community participation is the foundation that leads to the development of a community profile, the identification of potential development projects, the formation or mobilization of existing CBOs, and the implementation of proposed projects. Community leadership, CBO members, and villagers learn and acquire the skills and expertise needed to design, implement, and manage their projects, to monitor progress, to modify and adapt strategies as necessary, and to sustain and expand the scope of their activities. In addition, participants gain proficiency in advocacy and governance as a result of training that uses information gained through successful community projects to campaign for policy changes that positively affect and improve life in the community.

Despite their diversity, CEP projects take a systematic approach that includes

1. A participatory methodology that ensures meaningful community involvement,
2. Commitment to the long-term sustainability of projects and activities, and
3. Economic endeavors that lead to community-level job creation, employment, human capital returns, and revenues for CBOs (cooperatives) and their members.

Evaluation Approach

This chapter defines impact as the positive and negative lessons learned and the primary, secondary, and tertiary long-term effects on the intended beneficiaries that result from the intervention or program. It therefore examines the direct and indirect effects of the program and explains how it contributed to sustained outcomes for direct and indirect beneficiaries.

A contentious debate continues within the evaluation community regarding the design and methodological approach needed to determine the level of *causal* impact associated with a program or intervention. Many evaluators consider randomization to be essential to determining program impact. In theory, randomization is the optimal safeguard against potential bias in estimating impact; in practice, it presents several challenges, especially for developing communities. Random control designs answer the important question of what would have occurred if the program or intervention had not taken place—the *counterfactual*—using a well-defined comparison considered to be equal in every way except exposure to the program or intervention.

It is not always feasible to implement a randomized design, nor does this design always yield accurate and actionable data for policy decision making. For example, with regard to the CEP, it is difficult to identify equivalent comparisons. The Bedouin tribal communities are not homogeneous; neither are the refugees seeking safety and asylum in Jordan. The definition of target constructs such as quality of life, well-being, and community capacity building are ambiguous. Moreover, given the expectation that participating communities and villages will generate their own definitions as well as develop and implement village-specific programs, it is impossible to maintain the control and stability needed to implement a randomized design that assumes the equivalence of program and comparison groups. Interventions implemented in remote areas of Jordan present even more challenges, as villages often are too small to provide sufficient samples for randomized participation in controlled comparison groups. In many, if not most, instances equivalent cross-village comparisons simply do not exist.

The lack of adequate comparisons is especially pertinent given that this impact evaluation was conducted after the programs had been implemented. While some program communities and villages may be similar to those not experiencing the program, they may not have been similar when the programs were implemented, in some cases more than a decade before the evaluation. In addition, JRF programs have grown via *word of mouth* from village to village (diffusion of innovation; Rogers 1962), making the identification of suitable villages not exposed to or engaged in any part of the program even more challenging.

Because JRF initiatives are grounded in a community participatory model, whereby the community shapes and defines the program and the manner in which it is implemented, this evaluation takes a largely *developmental* approach. Developmental evaluation recently emerged in the evaluation literature in response to programs and interventions that do not have a clear progression in which the identification of a problem and implementation of a program lead to a set of hypothesized outcomes (Patton 2011). While JRF programs share the same goals, their conceptualization varies from community to community or village to village. Nonetheless, they share similarities. The developmental evaluation framework allows us to identify and integrate the shared patterns and guiding principles promulgated by the JRF, the unique contextual characteristics of the initiatives, the social structure of the participating communities or villages, and the dynamic relationships of stakeholders that continuously shape and influence them.

This impact evaluation takes three approaches: (1) a theory-based approach that examines the causal mechanisms from input to outcome, essentially examining the *theory of change* used by the Jordan River Foundation; (2) a participatory evaluation approach that examines the role of diverse stakeholders, heavily emphasizing the experiences of direct and indirect beneficiaries and observing expressions of knowledge and shifts in attitude and demonstrated behavior; and (3) within and across case studies of communities participating in the JRF community empowerment initiatives.

Theory-Based Approach

The impact evaluation uses a theory of change to understand the mechanisms that contribute to change and support the data interpretation. The CEP projects are community based. The JRF provides support to the community for building capacity through education, awareness building, and managerial and technical training. Meaningful engagement of the community is the crucial component for achieving a positive impact and sustainability. The JRF continues to consult with the community, but the community is expected to conceptualize, implement, adapt, and sustain the project. While the initial involvement of the JRF's capacity-building efforts triggers the potential for community change, the mechanisms associated with the changes that occur are contextual and unique from community to community.

Participatory-Focused Approach

Community participation is an integral component of the JRF's theory of change. Essentially, participation in the development of community-based CEP projects promotes a sense of ownership and optimizes the potential for success. As David Ellerman (2005) suggests, participatory approaches see beneficiaries as having *agency* and the actions of beneficiaries as contributing to favorable outcomes. This chapter examines the *participatory role* of beneficiaries and other appropriate community stakeholders in shaping the program. Using data collected from multiple stakeholders provides an opportunity to examine the correspondence and discord across diverse groups of stakeholders, such as cooperative managers, direct beneficiaries, and community members not participating directly in CEP activities.

Case-Based Approach

Emerging patterns across JRF program sites were examined using a case-centered approach. Data collected from observations, documents, interviews, focus groups, and most significant change stories were examined within a site to determine the consistency of beneficiary experiences and the extent to which outcomes were positive or negative. Process tracing (Collier 2011), linked to the theory of change, was used to assess and identify causal mechanisms, stakeholder and beneficiary actions and beliefs, community events, and phenomena that provide evidence that the program was associated with the change that occurred.

Case data were examined for empirical regularities—patterns that reoccur within and across cases (villages). Given the lack of a comparison group, the counterfactual was examined using descriptive evidence asserting what would have occurred if the CEP initiatives had not occurred (plausible alternatives). The congruence of presumed causal mechanisms was examined using a within-case and across-case approach. The limited time spent in each site and limited familiarity with the site challenge the rigor of this approach. Nonetheless, process tracing provides a conceptual framework for examining the theory of change associated with the CEP and a context for exploring community-centered data.

Most Significant Change

The most significant change (MSC) technique was used to collect primary data (Davies and Dart 2005; Serrat 2010). MSC is a qualitative and participatory method that systematically collects stories about the changes and outcomes that beneficiaries have experienced as a result of participating in a project or intervention. Developed by Davies (1996), the method addresses the specific challenges associated with evaluating complex programs characterized by diverse implementation and, sometimes, unexpected outcomes. Ideally, the process uses a nomination process whereby community stakeholders select the most meaningful of the stories collected.

In this study, the MSC approach was adapted to address time constraints. Stories were collected from beneficiaries about the most significant change(s) they experienced as a result of the CEP. Although the stories were shared with community and village beneficiaries and CEP program staff, there was no systematic selection of the most significant of the stories collected or identification of specific domains of change to investigate. Instead, program beneficiaries were free to tell us about the changes that were most meaningful to them. Beneficiaries were also asked to describe challenges they experienced and to reflect on how things might have been different. MSC is an ideal method for this study, as it intentionally and purposefully focuses on program impact.

An advantage of MSC is its inductive approach. It is not prescriptive, does not define the data collection strategy a priori, and does not constrain stakeholder participation to a structured or semistructured question protocol. Rather it enables broad participation at diverse program levels. It captures unexpected as well as anticipated events and outcomes and incorporates diverse perspectives. In addition, MSC is adaptive, allowing a change of focus when appropriate, and is amenable to favorable organizational learning. The MSC technique has been successfully used internationally to examine community empowerment, maternal and child health, educational reform, and local governance by organizations such as the U.S. Agency for International Development, the U.K.

Department for International Development, the Aga Khan Foundation, Oxfam International, and CARE.

MSC has been criticized as subjective. However, the use of a systematic process, the review and analysis of stories in terms of patterns and repetition of stories by other beneficiaries and stakeholders, and the correspondence of MSC stories with other data sources (documents, reports, observations, interviews) strengthen this approach. Furthermore, the analytic process is transparent. MSC is quite different from other qualitative approaches (traditional case studies, interviews, focus groups), where the evaluation team decides what information will be included and what will be discarded. All stories are accompanied by sufficient descriptive details allowing for verification of the story's accuracy. The MSC approach is flexible, providing the ability to gather additional information about events pertinent to the story or events that occurred after the story that support or dispute the project's impact and sustainability. Because MSC supports a diversity of perspectives, as opposed to seeking a consensus of stories, it provides a safeguard against bias. As noted, the process can verify the story details.

Figure 5.1 illustrates the basic theory of change for the JRF's CEP. It represents the basic *causal* chain that characterizes the CEP projects independent of their focus. It builds on community outreach, awareness, and training (inputs) to support community participation, strengthen leadership,

Figure 5.1 Basic Theory of Change for the Jordan River Foundation's Community Empowerment Program

INPUT	OUTPUT	OUTCOME	IMPACT

• Outreach
• Awareness
• Training
• Support
• Existing community structures (CBOs)
• Funding
• Collaborative opportunities
	• Improved CBO and community
	  – Engagement
	  – Participation
	• Increased community and CBO skills and expertise
	• Strengthened leadership
	• Strategies for improvement
		• Increased
		  – Personal agency
		  – Community responsibility
		  – Skills and expertise
		  – Community well-being
		  – Entrepreneurial opportunities
		  – Employment
		  – Income
			• Increased
			  – Economic independence
			  – Family income
			  – Educational opportunities
			  – Job creation
			  – Resource efficiency
			  – Participation in governance
			• Poverty reduction

Note: CBO = community-based organization.

and generate strategies for improving community well-being (outputs). The CEP model asserts that this will lead to a sense of personal agency, community action, increased skills and expertise, as well as opportunities, employment, and income (outcomes). Impact is defined as longer-term outcomes such as economic independence, job creation, poverty reduction, and long-term benefits and social mobility for children, youth, families, and the community.

Data Collection

Data were collected during site visits to JRF programs from Ajloun in the north to Aqaba in the south (map 5.1). Many of the CEP projects are intentionally located in what Jordan has identified as *poverty pockets*, subgovernorate areas where more than 25 percent of the population is below the

Map 5.1 Jordan River Foundation Locations Visited

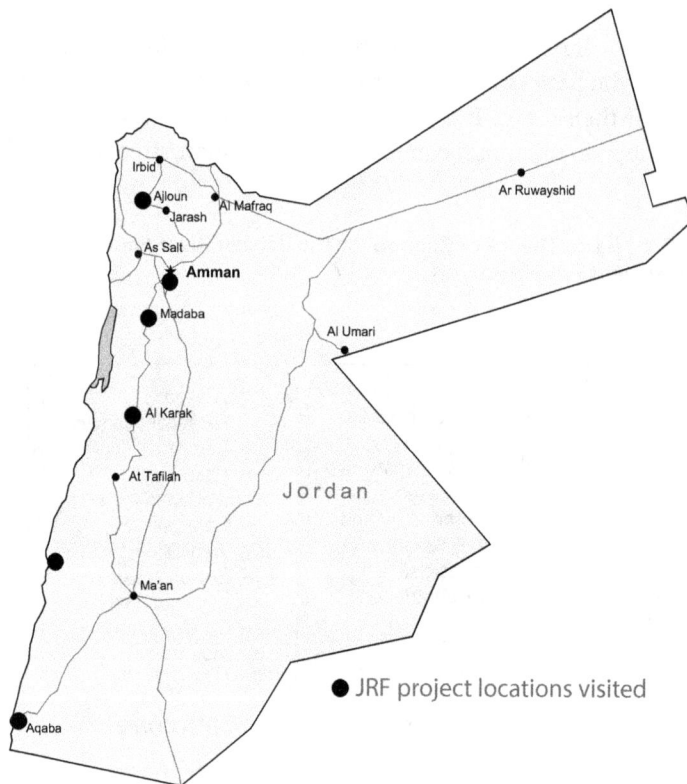

Source: www.mapresources.com.

Poverty, Inequality, and Evaluation

Jordanian poverty level.[2] JRF staff selected the sites to illustrate the diversity of CEP projects across a variety of geographic contexts, but the evaluator was free to request additional information and to speak with any member of the community or program staff. It was not unusual for community members not directly affected by or associated with JRF projects to volunteer their perspectives and opinions.

Data sources also included reviews of existing statistical data and JRF reports and project documents; direct observations of community program activities; conversations with programs staff, which included JRF staff as well as community members leading CBO initiatives; direct program beneficiaries (and their families); randomly selected community members not directly affected by the program; and individuals volunteering their perspectives on JRF programs and life in the community. The conversations took place in one-on-one interviews and in community focus groups, as well as in CBO buildings, in community and village meeting places and shops, and in the streets, walking from shop to shop, meeting to meeting.

Conversations were audiotaped with permission from the individuals involved. Individuals were informed that reports would not identify them by name. Conversations were conducted in Arabic, with near simultaneous translation into English provided by a professional interpreter, who was not part of JRF staff. During the few instances when professional interpretation services were not available, JRF staff provided translation. Various JRF staff provided translation on these occasions to ensure the accuracy of what was spoken in Arabic. On occasions when a translation was questioned, the audiotape was marked and later reviewed by Arab-speaking colleagues of the evaluator. Many individuals from the project sites had an understanding of English. Both Arabic and English conversations were recorded, enabling further verification of translations as necessary.

The evaluators collected 156 audiotapes ranging in duration from brief five-minute conversations to more than hour-long group conversations, for a total of approximately 42 hours of taped conversations. Audiotapes were compared to the notes taken during the interview and focus group conversations. Selected audiotapes, representing each site visited, were coded using NVivo, a text-based software program,[3] to produce an initial report of findings. In the near future, all tapes will be coded using NVivo, which will enable the quantification of perceptions and the examination of associations among codes.

Coding was developed using an etic-emic approach, in which a randomly selected portion of randomly selected audio files were used to develop codes, and the remaining tapes selected were used to test the adequacy of the coding structure. This process led to an inductive discovery of the characteristics of the JRF community empowerment initiatives and the similarities and differences among these initiatives.

Evaluation Findings

The CEP projects sought to achieve the following objectives:

- Improve well-being and socioeconomic status, especially among persons in poverty pockets
- Increase managerial and entrepreneurial skills and expertise of local community members and community-based organizations, especially for marginalized groups (women and youth)
- Examine and reorganize local resources to increase efficiency and productivity (CBOs, cooperatives)
- Engage local communities, individuals, and institutions in advocacy, municipal decision making, and governance activities targeting issues that affect their well-being and livelihoods

Box 5.1 summarizes the CEP projects evaluated. The evaluation looks at how these initiatives addressed poverty and inequality.

Box 5.1   Summary of CEP Projects Evaluated

Ajloun Governorate: Rasoun Village. JRF has been working in Ajloun Governorate since 2002. In 2007, it piloted a holistic approach to community building that includes education, health, infrastructure, youth, and economic empowerment. In 2008, it signed an agreement with Orange Jordan and Orange Foundation to create and support sustainable social, economic, and cultural programs derived from local needs and priorities. In 2007, it established the Rasoun Cooperative as the umbrella and steering arm of the project's activities. Of 191 members, 120 are female.

The following projects were evaluated: small revolving loans for small and micro business projects (of 87 beneficiaries, 47 are female); a nursery and child care; Rasoun Secondary School for Girls (structural project); revolving loans for a bakery, sheep breeding, and a supermarket; and a health center.

Ajloun Governorate: Ras Munif. An income-generating project owned and managed by the Qura Shamal Ajloun Cooperative is under the Rural Community Cluster Development Program (RCCDP), which is funded by the

(continued next page)

Box 5.1 *continued*

Ministry of Planning and International Cooperation and implemented by the Jordan River Foundation and Mercy Corp. The project promotes citizen participation in economic and social revitalization efforts by empowering local communities with similar needs to develop income-generating projects.

The following projects were evaluated: an agricultural complex for storing and freezing fruits and vegetables; an agricultural nursery for growing high-quality fruit seedlings; a business for manufacturing vinegar and molasses; a multipurpose hall for holding meetings, workshops, and trainings; an olive press for serving local farmers; AI and a fodder block for generating organic heat that was manufactured using olive pressing by-products.

Madaba Governorate: Al Areed area and Bani Hamadi Village. The JRF has been working in Al Areed since 2002 and in Bani Hamadi Village since 1998. This JRF-supported effort includes development of a transportation-bus complex that houses several local markets. Implemented in 2002 through the RCCDP, the project provides 15 full-time jobs.

The Bani Hamida Women's Weaving Project was originated by Save the Children in 1985 and merged into the Jordan River Foundation in 1998. This project revived traditional Bedouin rug weaving, helping to maintain the social fabric of the Makawir area. Since its inception, the project has employed 24 full-time employees and provided part-time work for more than 1,650 women, including spinners, weavers, and dyers. Approximately 450 women work part time in the project.

The following projects were evaluated: a bus complex, including a bakery, grocery store, and variety store, and the Bani Hamadi Women's Weaving Project.

Al Karak Governorate: Al Ghor Mazra'a. Recognizing the need to empower youth and make youth centers youth-friendly places, the JRF has worked with community-village stakeholders at the district level to identify needs and priorities with a focus on youth and their surrounding environment. Funded by the Ministry of Planning and International Cooperation, the initiative has enhanced the socioeconomic status of youth by creating volunteer positions in municipal government, some of which have led to paid jobs.

Another project supports the local committee for the mentally and physically disabled in Ghor Al Mazra'a. Implemented in partnership with the Embassy of Japan, the project supports a rehabilitation center that provides physiotherapy and other services for the mentally and physically disabled.

Revolving loans have been given to community members including youth to implement small and micro business projects. Of 132 people who have received revolving loans, 49 are female.

(continued next page)

An integrated agriculture project was implemented in 2007 to offer agricultural services to local farmers. It provides four jobs. The Wadi Salam Cooperative was established to oversee project activities. Of 153 members, 23 are female.

The following projects were evaluated: a park and recreation center with a youth club and knowledge center; a center for the physically and mentally disabled; and revolving loans for projects such as radio and television repair, a supermarket, and bird breeding.

Aqaba Governorate: Rahma Village (Wadi Araba). The JRF has been working in Rahma Village since 2002. A project was implemented in 2007 through the Local Development Program for Less Privileged Areas, offering agricultural services to local farmers. The initiative provided four jobs. The project is run by Rahma Cooperative and has 288 members, of which 46 are female. Although the cooperative was visited, no projects were observed.

Aqaba Governorate: Wadi Araba Risha Village and city of Aqaba. The JRF has been working in Wadi Araba since 2002, supporting several interventions through the RCCDP and the Local Development Program for Less-Privileged Areas.

An integrated project with local farmers provides 25 jobs. The Ga'a Seedyeen Cooperative was established in 2002 as the umbrella and steering arm of the project's activities. It has 873 members (no females). Other projects include the Al-Risha Folklore Group, with 14 youth members who provide traditional music, and the Old Town (Aqaba) Neighborhood Development Activity.

The following projects were included in the evaluation: agricultural projects, such as well and irrigation systems, organic farm fields, greenhouse, and a dam project (water collection and use of sediment); glass-bottom boats (city of Aqaba); and revolving loans (city of Aqaba) for a play station and video game station, dress shop, and computer electronic repair.

In all, 21 unique CEP projects were visited. Some projects had several sites. Sites within these integrated projects were considered as one project and are not listed separately.

Capacity Building in Agriculture Projects

In the Ras Munif area, Ajloun, CBO and cooperative members manage and operate an olive press, with community input. After deliberation, it was determined that purchasing the olive press and providing it as a service to olive growers in the region was more beneficial than using the press to make and sell olive oil. The pressing service was offered to growers for a fee sufficient to maintain the press and operating staff. Growers would then sell their own products. This decision yielded funds for the cooperative to expand its efforts and enabled growers to become independent entrepreneurs. As agricultural knowledge increased, community and individual economic growth also increased. For example, growers learned that olives stored in inexpensive plastic bags decay quickly. Burlap bags, though more expensive than plastic bags, have a higher return because they do not retain ethylene gas and thus prevent decay.

The cooperative's business plan demonstrates sufficient demand for a second olive press. The purchase was expected to double productivity and income and be cost neutral in terms of operation. No expansion of staff or increase in overhead was needed. The cost-benefit analysis was impressive, as was the hardcopy record keeping of farmers' use of the press (see photo 5.1).

An integrated agricultural project in Wadi Araba provides another example. Members of the Ga'a Seedyeen Cooperative presented plans for expansion of the agricultural project, identifying irrigation needs, concerns about the quality of the soil, and a strategic process for expansion. Their planning was impressive. A tour of a "plantation" (farm) where the soil was unfit to grow most crops due to high concentrations of salt and sediment revealed a high level of agricultural knowledge and a long-term commitment to the project. Cooperative members explained that they need to plant and harvest at least three rotations of crops (corn) before the soil would be

Photo 5.1   Record Page: Olive Press

Credit: © Ann Doucette. Used with permission. Further permission required for reuse.

Photo 5.2   Tractor Transportation, Wadi Araba

Credit: © Ann Doucette. Used with permission. Further permission required for reuse.

suitable for growing food products. Crops grown to leach the soil of salt and sediment were used for fodder.

"Change takes time," they said many times. The planning and attention to both the growing and the marketing potential of their produce were impressive, as was their investment in growing crops that need less water. Cooperative members proposed using plastic greenhouses to conserve water and producing unique varieties that would yield higher returns. This project collaborates with the Regional Center for Agriculture, which conducts research, providing an opportunity for mutual learning.

The agricultural projects have direct and indirect benefits. For example, in Rahma Village, Wadi Araba, four permanent jobs were created to assist in offering agricultural services to local farmers. A man holding one of the four jobs said that, while his salary was small, the fact that he could use the tractor for transportation was a great advantage (see photo 5.2).

Empowerment of Women

The tribal customs in Wadi Araba are not open to women working or participating in most cooperatives. This attitude is changing slowly. For example, in Rahma Village, the cooperative now includes women: out of 288 members, 46 are women. Women are also beginning to work in agricultural projects. For example, six women work part time in the plastic greenhouses harvesting cucumbers and collecting the bottom leaves that are beginning to wither. These leaves are used for livestock fodder (see photo 5.3). When asked how working has changed their lives, one woman volunteered that she can now send her daughter to university. Her daughter receives tuition, but there is no money for books or bus transportation. A follow-up question was asked about the seasonality of this work and how it affected her ability to send her daughter to university. She explained that she borrows money from women whose children are not old enough to attend university yet. "When they send their children to university, they can borrow from me," she said. These women had set up their own revolving loan system, an indirect effect of a small loan program from the cooperative and the training they

Photo 5.3   Harvesting Cucumbers, Wadi Araba

Credit: © Ann Doucette. Used with permission. Further permission required for reuse.

received, not to mention the sense of empowerment that is evident when they describe their accomplishments and hopes for their children.

Perhaps the best illustration of the impact of the CEP on social mobility and how it reduces poverty and enhances equality is the Bani Hamadi Women's Weaving Project, which produced the most significant empowerment change stories (Al Areed, Madaba Governorate). Hand weaving on floor looms is a tradition of the women of the Bedouin tribe of the Bani Hamadi. The area is a poverty pocket, with minimal transportation, a lack of roads, insufficient health care services, scarcity of potable water, and low social status for women. In 1985, under Save the Children, the Bani Hamadi Women's Weaving Project began to mobilize. In 1998 it merged with the JRF. During this time, women became organized. The JRF offered training in leadership, marketing, and computers. Prior to this initiative, rugs were woven at home in a haphazard manner, with no systematic patterns or sizes. Women simply worked in isolation, using the yarn they had on hand, using toxic dyeing processes, and having little or no knowledge of what other women were weaving.

Halima Al-Qa'aydeh, from the Bani Hamadi Village, now manages this project. She introduced quality control, using a marked stick to size the weaving of the rugs (see photo 5.4). With the other women, she implemented some regulation of traditional Bedouin designs and instituted

Photo 5.4   Halima Al-Qa'aydeh Introduced Quality Control to the Bani Hamadi Women's Weaving Project

Credit: © Ann Doucette. Used with permission. Further permission required for reuse.

health-conscious processes for dyeing the wool used in the rugs. She went house to house, working with the women, and over time some women began to work collectively outside their homes.

Halima's success exemplifies the JRF's efforts to empower women in Jordan. She became the first woman to obtain a driver's license in her village and the first woman to run for municipal office, which she won. She announced in our meeting that she recently became the first woman in her village to go to the beauty salon to get her hair done. When asked about how men in the villages responded to all of this, she laughed, offering that her father worried about other people on the road when she decided to get her driver's license. On a more serious note, she stated that the income the women earned enhanced the well-being of families and that the men grew to appreciate that. At the height of its productivity, the weaving project employed 24 full-time workers, but the numbers have diminished as the market for rugs has become saturated. To date, the project has provided wages to more than 1,650 women.

Halima's story has been widely written about, and other women are following in her footsteps. As of 2013, six other women in the weaving project had licenses to drive and were taking advantage of opportunities to gain more education and skills. While the women expressed concerns about the future of the weaving project, their sense of accomplishment and empowerment continues to grow, as they collectively strategize the next steps for bringing new products to market.

Collective Ownership: Success and Disappointment

No one in any of the 21 projects visited complained about the training, support, or capacity-building workshops and activities. All provided positive stories linking the activities to significant changes (economic and educational opportunities, increased status in the community, increased social mobility) that occurred as a result.

This is not to say that the CEP initiatives and projects were without shortcomings or disappointment. Among those mentioned was the difficulty of obtaining funding for cooperative initiatives and drawbacks with some of the projects chosen—choices that they acknowledged were theirs.

The bus complex in Al Areed in Madaba Governorate is an example. The area is remote, and transportation linking the villages was nonexistent. People took buses back and forth to Madaba, a distance away, to shop and secure health and other services. A decision was made to purchase two buses that would link the villages. A complex was built around the bus station, with shops (income-generating opportunities for the community),

Photo 5.5   Grocery Store at Bus Complex

Credit: © Ann Doucette. Used with permission. Further permission required for reuse.

storage (for products to sell and ship), and meeting places (photo 5.5 illustrates one such popular shop). A bus runs more frequently to and from the complex and Madaba.

The community is divided as to whether this was a good decision. The bus does not stop at each house, making it inconvenient for some. Some people use cars and think that a gas station would have been a better choice, as they must drive to Madaba to get fuel, which means that they use almost twice the fuel they would if there were a local gas station. The bus does not generate sufficient revenue to support other projects. As one cooperative member said, "To please 100 percent is impossible."

Talking with people around the bus complex yielded mixed opinions. Several people thought that the shops were too expensive. However, when asked what they did before the complex, they quickly responded, "We'd go to Madaba," and followed up by saying, "This is better." When the cost of the bus trip to Madaba and the time to get there were factored in, people recognized the benefits of the complex. The effort to get a local gas station continues.

Youth-Focused Initiatives

Some CEP projects focused on the needs and opportunities for community engagement of youth. The recreation complex in Wadi Araba is an example.

The center houses a knowledge and cultural center offering computer classes and skills training for the community, a playground for children, a soccer field for youth, and two youth clubs (photo 5.6 shows part of the playground).

This is a remote area of Jordan, with limited resources. Groups of youth roam the streets. When asked why, several said, "There is nothing to do but be in the street." The JRF has begun to change this, offering training opportunities for youth in Amman. Participating youth receive JRF training in basic skills and entrepreneurship. In summarizing youth experience with JRF activities, one youth shared, "We didn't have goals, didn't have ideas, skills. Through training and collaboration, we have goals, vision, and success."

What the youth had learned became obvious during the site visit. A sequence of individual meetings was scheduled with municipal, cooperative, and youth leaders in the park. However, all groups came at the same time. Youth led much of the discussion and felt confident to offer opinions, positions, and recommendations that differed from those of adults representing the municipality and cooperative. They took a leadership role in much of the discussion. They openly discussed the lack of employment opportunities and the need for meaningful activities. They told us about the surrounding villages and how they formed competitive soccer teams. About 300 players compete, using the recreation center

Photo 5.6   Community Recreation Center

Credit: © Ann Doucette. Used with permission. Further permission required for reuse.

fields morning and evening. Demand to use the fields is growing and exceeds capacity.

Particularly inspiring was the youth discussion about volunteering. They said, "Volunteering is not new, but the methodology is." Further explanation revealed that helping out is the norm, but with nothing to do, a sense of "laziness develops." Now, youth accept meaningful unpaid positions to learn skills and gain experience. Volunteer positions can lead to employment and, in this case, an interest in governance. Two youth mentioned their interest in running for elected office in the municipality.

Without being asked, youth said that the JRF influenced change in the community and provided important opportunities for them and others. Many said that, without the JRF, they "would be walking the street, like them" (pointing to a group who had been walking back and forth for much of the four-hour site visit). This example clearly illustrates the potential to mobilize youth and enhance their *social capital* (the perception that youth are a vital part of the community network), *human capital* (expertise, skills, volunteerism), and *status capital* (value as contributing members of community and cooperative decision making).

Summary and Conclusions

There is little question that the CEP has had an impact through its participatory methodology, its commitment to sustainable projects and activities, and its focus on capacity and skills building, income generation, community volunteerism, and civic engagement.

Impact was determined in reference to the counterfactual—what would have happened if the program or intervention had not occurred. Among its successes are productive plantations (farms) in Wadi Araba with lemon trees growing in the sandy soil; six women harvesting cucumbers in an integrated agriculture project overseen by a cooperative whose membership is restricted to men; a woman in Rasoun Village with a household well to collect rainwater so she no longer has to travel to the far-away water tank and pay for potable water; the Bani Hamadi Women's Weaving Project, where more than 1,650 women have received income support, six women are now driving, and one is a municipal official; and a video game and play station shop that provides both family income for private schooling and university training and a safe place for children living in the community. These project outcomes and many others not described in this chapter are evidence of the impact of the JRF's CEP initiative.

The CEP initiative, through its participatory community-centered efforts, demonstrates how awareness raising and training can lead to community agency in identifying, strategizing, and solving community problems and concerns; how a sense of ownership enables communities to work through disappointment and discouragement; and how income-generating projects lead to educational opportunities and social mobility, mobility that will have potential impact for generations to come. Approximately 90 percent of the *change stories* focused on being better able to educate children. Many of these stories resulted from participation in cooperative-sponsored small revolving loan programs to start businesses.[4] Education, coupled with skills training, entrepreneurship, empowerment for women and youth, and cultural change, albeit slow, provide a foundation for social mobility that goes beyond focusing solely on reducing poverty and inequality. Labor markets influence poverty and inequality. Although subsidies have helped to address poverty, especially in the area of inadequate nutritional resources, Jordan's relatively high unemployment, especially among youth, continues to exacerbate the effects of both poverty and inequality.

CEP projects reduced the relative poverty experienced by many participants and their families. The entrepreneurship and job-focused volunteerism supported through cooperatives (community projects, small loan programs) changed the structure of the communities and villages. The opportunity for growth (mobility) through entrepreneurship (Naudé 2010) and educational opportunities may well be a channel through which to ameliorate poverty and inequality, changing the perceived status and sense of self-agency of Jordan's most vulnerable.

Notes

1. According to the U.S. Central Intelligence Agency.
2. National poverty levels were set at JD 57 per month in 2008, equivalent to approximately US$81.
3. NVivo (www.qsrinternational.com).
4. Participants receive training and apply to cooperatives that manage the loans. Data on the number of loans provided by cooperatives were variable. Some could report on the number of loans and the proportion given to women, but the details of the time interval for these numbers were uncertain. Cooperatives estimated that between 95 and 98 percent of loans were paid back on time, an estimate that represents a far better return than that of most lenders in industrial countries.

References

Collier, D. 2011. "Understanding Process Tracing." *Political Science and Politics* 44 (4): 823–30.

Davies, R. 1996. "An Evolutionary Approach to Facilitating Organisational Learning: An Experiment by the Christian Commission for Development in Bangladesh." *Monitoring and Evaluation News.* http://www.mande.co.uk/docs/ccdb.htm.

Davies, R., and J. Dart. 2005. "The 'Most Significant Change' (MSC) Technique: A Guide to Its Use." *Monitoring and Evaluation News.* www.mande.co.uk/docs/mscguide.pdf.

Ellerman, D. 2005. *Helping People Help Themselves: From the World Bank to an Alternative Philosophy of Development Assistance.* Ann Arbor: University of Michigan Press.

IMF (International Monetary Fund). 2012. "Jordan: 2012 Article IV Consultation." IMF Country Report 12/119, IMF, Washington, DC.

Naudé, W. 2010. "Entrepreneurship, Developing Countries, and Development Economics: New Approaches and Insights." *Small Business Economics* 34 (1): 1–12.

Patton, M. Q. 2011. *Developmental Evaluation: Applying Complexity Concepts to Enhance Innovation and Use.* New York: Guilford Press.

Rogers, E. M. 1962. *Diffusion of Innovations.* New York: Free Press.

Serrat, O. 2010. *The Most Significant Change Technique.* Manila: Asian Development Bank.

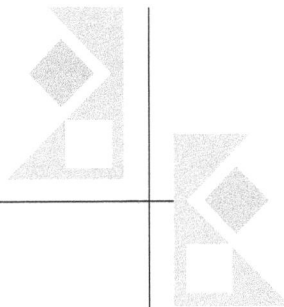

CHAPTER 6

Determining the Results of a Social Safety Net Program in St. Lucia

Paulette Nichols, Bobb Darnell, and Frederic Unterreiner

Introduction

The evaluation research presented in this chapter reflects the experiences of the Koudmen Sent Lisi, a two-year pilot program managed by the St. Lucia Social Development Fund (SSDF). It is based on an evaluation conducted in St. Lucia from October to December 2012. The full evaluation report was commissioned by the SSDF, with financial and technical support from the United Nations Children's Fund (UNICEF), Office for the Eastern Caribbean Area.

As part of its global mandate, UNICEF promotes a culture of results and performance management and builds national capacity for monitoring and evaluation. It is in this context that UNICEF responded positively to a

Paulette Nichols is a consultant; Bobb Darnell is with the Saint Lucia Social Development Fund; and Frederic Unterreiner is with the UNICEF Office for the Eastern Caribbean Area.

request of the Ministry of Social Transformation (MOST) and the SSDF to support implementation of Koudmen Sent Lisi.

From UNICEF's perspective, evaluation of the Koudmen Sent Lisi pilot was critical to (a) support the country's ongoing discussion on social protection reform, (b) build national capacity for monitoring and evaluation of social assistance programs, and (c) promote learning through the conduct of a multistakeholder, participatory evaluation. From the beginning, key stakeholders and SSDF staff members were included in the evaluation process with the objective of having a structured and informed learning process and informing a broader policy dialogue about social protection reform.

The evaluation was also critical to UNICEF as a vehicle for (a) promoting and institutionalizing a multidimensional, equity-focused response to poverty,[1] as inspired by Puente Chile (a comprehensive poverty eradication effort) but "creolized" by St Lucia; (b) demonstrating how social assistance programs targeting households can be made more gender sensitive and child focused by refining the content of assistance delivered and increasing coordination for effective and adaptable service delivery among line ministries and agencies; and (c) serving as an example for other countries in the region.

This chapter, based on the full evaluation report, is composed of five sections. After reviewing the Koudmen Sent Lisi's initial design and objectives and examining the beneficiary households, the chapter presents the evaluation's methodology, describes the findings, and offers recommendations.

Initial Design and Objectives

Koudmen Sent Lisi was adapted from the Puente Chile experience, which served as a model offering a timely paradigm shift for national policy to move away from a silo approach to poverty reduction and toward multidimensional social protection interventions accompanied by integrated psychosocial support. The intent of the two-year pilot (2009–11) was to reduce poverty of 46 indigent families by facilitating access to income, employment, housing, health, education, family counseling, and networks that fortify family assets.

The island of St. Lucia, with a population of 177,800, is ranked 82 among the 187 countries and territories in the *Human Development Report 2011* (UNDP 2011). Life expectancy at birth in 2000–05 was 73.1 years, under-five mortality (per 1,000 live births) was 14, and other social development indicators such as infant mortality and school enrollment rates were showing signs of improvement (Renard 2008). However, unemployment rates were rising (17.5 percent in 2000 and 18.7 percent in 2005), particularly among youth (39 percent), as were gender-based violence and sexual offenses (with reported sexual offenses of 164 in 2000 and 174 in 2005). In addition, as early as 2002, inequality and deprivation of income, wealth, and access to social services were challenging development initiatives in the subregion by causing labor market imperfections, persistent stratification, and a "culture of poverty."[2]

Before the onset of the global recession and Caribbean financial crisis in 2001, the St. Lucian economy was struggling through a transitional period brought on largely by the shrinking agriculture sector. The country had placed great hope and investment in expansion of the tourism industry. In 2009 St. Lucia struggled to find new sources of growth and to resist economic vulnerability in a context of increasing competition at global and regional levels, shifting trends in trade preference, and shrinking donor funding.

St. Lucia was becoming a lower-middle-income country with a strong commitment and political will to pursue all eight of the Millennium Development Goals and principles reflected in the Paris Declaration. Considerable public policy reform was undertaken, and the Interim Poverty Reduction Strategy and Action Plan (IPRSAP) was approved by the Ministry of Social Transformation in 2003 (MOST 2003). During that same period, MOST drafted a Social Policy for Human Development with the intention of creating greater political space for mechanisms and instruments that support social protection. The poverty assessment conducted by the Caribbean Development Bank in 1998 helped to establish the IPRSAP, and the country poverty assessment, completed in 2007, further positioned the country to increase investments in the social protection sector.

Learning from the Puente Chile experience, a multidimensional poverty framework was designed to take full advantage of the government's commitment and political dedication to eradicating extreme poverty. The design team took full advantage of findings from six major, high-quality poverty studies carried out during the previous 12 years (CDB 1996, 2006; DFID, CDB, and European Union 2004; European Union 1998; MOST 2003; World Bank 2000).

The adoption of this approach was very timely for the Koudmen Sent Lisi pilot. It placed at the core of the program the theory that if a household's portfolio of capabilities (that is, basic education) is not sufficient or the family does not have the opportunity to acquire them, its ability to escape poverty will remain limited. The Puente model offered a paradigm shift for St. Lucia to move from the classic provision of basic services and toward social protection interventions accompanied by integrated psychosocial support that addresses the social disadvantages, risks, and vulnerabilities of the poor. The model was adjusted to the St. Lucia context, retaining the "rights-based approach," which affords families the right to human dignity. The principles of equity and community participation are central to the design and methodology adopted by the Koudmen Sent Lisi, which, as Puente Chile, embraces a contextual or qualitative approach. This is essential in efforts to end extreme poverty, as the application of human rights principles exposes the underlying cultural causes and manifestations of poverty while reinforcing the psychological and emotional development of the family, the cornerstone of St. Lucia society. In adapting selected aspects of Puente Chile to St. Lucia realities, Koudmen Sent Lisi targeted the reduction of poverty and vulnerability with an emphasis on overcoming extreme poverty (indigence).

The objectives of the Koudmen Sent Lisi include the following:

- Improve the socioeconomic living conditions of indigent, poor, and vulnerable households
- End extreme poverty in St. Lucia (1.6 percent of the population and 1.2 percent of households)
- Reduce poverty by building sustainable livelihoods, devising coping strategies, and improving the quality of human relationships and interactions
- Develop opportunities in poor communities and vulnerable populations by establishing a targeted program of support designed to transform household units

To do so, the program's intervention theory focused on providing opportunities to access basic services and achieve the minimum conditions needed to improve the quality of life. It focused on the delivery of goods and services in seven areas or pillars: personal identification, health, education, family dynamics, housing, employment, and income.

Pillar 1: Personal Identification

The personal identification pillar is designed to assist households to obtain certain formal documentation and certification. Possession of key documents is often a barrier for poor families or individuals to accessing social grants and entitlements (child welfare and disability grants, pensions). Other documents are needed to participate fully in civic life, such as voting, driving, and obtaining education and skills training. This pillar helps family members to access and understand the knowledge of the grants and entitlements policies and to access and complete the application forms. Common difficulties include having all national documents in place, knowing someone who can assist the application process, and traveling to complete an application. With the guidance of family caregivers (FCGs), families examine the factors that facilitate access to personal identification, establish what needs to be done, or set minimum conditions to address the difficulty.

Pillar 2: Health

Health care services, the second pillar of Koudmen Sent Lisi, is extended to every member of the household in an effort to safeguard the complete well-being of families. It includes standard health promotion, prevention, and care services. Access to the national health care network is largely fee based. While there are no documented functional barriers to accessing health care in St. Lucia, access to certain health care services is determined by an individual's financial resources; poorer persons have less access than richer persons and rural persons have less access than urban persons (Renard 2008). Most of the Koudmen Sent Lisi communities are close to community nursing services and a bus ride from regional health center services. The FCG helps families to envision health standards that they would like to achieve and to identify the necessary steps to achieving them (access to health facility, early detection services), giving special attention to women, children, elderly, and disabled.

Pillar 3: Education

The education dimension of the program is central to the intervention strategy, as it helps to define the families' capability to build and expand social and human capital. Education is the pillar for improving the opportunities for social inclusion of all members of the household and community. The program connects households to services and benefits that assist each family member in accordance with his or her stage of development. For example, fees, uniforms, and transport for primary and secondary school are of concern in St. Lucia. The FCG guides the family through the process of analyzing and setting goals and examining the challenges and opportunities to access, continue, and complete education.

Pillar 4: Family Dynamics

A functional family is defined by the quality of the relations within the family and the interaction and ability of family members to meet the demands of living together and fully asserting themselves socially. The stronger the household dynamic, the tighter the bond necessary to meet the challenges of family development and social integration. Activities under this pillar are at the core of the work carried out by the FCG, who provides guidance and counseling on how best to address the issues and priorities with limited resources and how best to involve family members in solving problems.

Pillar 5: Housing

This pillar addresses the physical conditions of the dwelling as well as the surrounding site and the care and upkeep of the home. Many structures are no larger than 14 feet by 14 feet and are constructed of plywood and cardboard. For poor families, outdoor access to water, toilet, and standpipe is often shared with several neighbors, making it especially difficult for children to use these facilities on "cold" mornings.

Pillar 6: Employment

Targeting adults and young adults in the household, pillar 6 is strategically separated from pillar 7, the income pillar, in order to emphasize work issues associated with finding and maintaining a stable source of income.

Pillar 7: Income

The income dimension is designed to move indigent families away from short-term survival strategies that inadequately use scarce resources to meet day-to-day activities and toward building the ability to mobilize a combination of resources (state benefits, including cash transfers) that will result in income above the poverty line. This pillar targets all family efforts to generate resources. In working with family members, the FCG first focuses on the resources, capacities, and energies that family members themselves have developed and then helps to activate whatever benefits St. Lucia offers for poor families. Although Koudmen Sent Lisi was designed as a cash transfer program, this pillar does not emphasize gaining access to cash. FCGs counsel family members on budget planning and organization and use of family resources.

Summary of the Pillars

In all, the seven pillars represent an interesting mix of strategies and assistance that constitute an appropriate response to the poverty typology and patterns observed. Together, they aim to achieve a more equitable uptake by households of opportunities through minimal cash transfers, increased access to basic social services, and effective psychosocial support.

Each pillar is addressed through minimal conditions established by Puente Chile and designed to address the common situations that are imperative for poor families to overcome in order to graduate from extreme poverty.

These seven dimensions are considered "pillars" of the program and are closely accompanied by a group of FCGs or counselors specifically trained to provide psychosocial support and guidance to the families. Each household agrees to a family-specific set of minimal conditions during the phase of intensive work guided by the FCGs.[3] The FCG works with the families to renew and reinforce the household's capabilities and basic functions.

Beneficiary Households

The 46 beneficiary households were identified using a national test or proxy means test, a targeting mechanism, and a formula using multidimensional characteristics to measure well-being and eligibility. After the process of eligibility and targeting of households, steps were taken to engage and assess each family's situation and to secure agreements from families on the elements of expected success at the end of the program.

The following presents a snapshot of the beneficiaries:

- There are 216 beneficiaries in 46 households: 116 adults and 100 children.
- Women head 31 of the households.
- Less than 15 percent of the children are under 5 years of age.
- Nearly half of the heads of household are over 50 years of age.

Domestic violence (mentioned 13 times), rape (mentioned 8 times), and drug addiction (mentioned 17 times) are noted in the family histories of the households, particularly among participants in the Bruceville District.

Of the participants, 11 families are squatting on Crown land occupying ancestral homeland. This figure is assumed to be much higher, as several clusters of family dwellings are known to be situated on Crown land zoned for commercial development. Conditions of the houses are generally unacceptable. Dwellings, in most cases, consist of one- or two-room shanties without running water, toilet facilities, or electricity.

Of the participants, 37 indicated that they frequently had to go without cash income, enough food, or rent monies. Many said that they experienced shortfalls in medicines and were unable to procure basic and specialized medical treatment during the previous year. Nearly 87 percent the households initially screened stated that they had been unemployed for more than six months over the previous year.

A review of a randomly selected number of the eligibility tests found a cycle of poverty suggesting that successive generations inherit inadequate basic requirements, financial and material resources, and intangible assets, notably with regard to access, investments, and clear entitlements.

Evaluation Methodology

In addition to using the evaluation standards and criteria of the Organisation for Economic Co-operation and Development's Development Assistance Committee, specific effort was made to (a) emphasize the intervention theory; (b) use an equity-focused approach and gender- and child-sensitive perspectives in designing the data collection instruments, conducting the interviews, and treating and analyzing the data; and (c) collect evidence from all 41 surveyed households and key stakeholders through the use of mixed methodologies.

After considering the available program planning and design documents and minutes from national consultations, three key people involved in the early development and application of the pilot were interviewed in order to recreate a results framework for the program. In the absence of key program plans and documentation, it was important to look at factors that would support a theory of change process, including:

- Mapping and causal analysis of the context and problems: Was analysis of the problem based on credible and reliable data?
- Availability of studies and assessments: Was a wide range of studies and assessments available for review?
- Interaction with others: Did the program design process consider a range of perspectives?
- Open mind: Was there a willingness and opportunities to challenge and change the design?
- Consensus: Was there consensus on program strategies and assumptions?
- Facilitation: Was there outside facilitation?
- Creativity: Was there ample time for creative thinking?

The design process documented a minimum of three active discussions at the national level with a diverse group, including government, nongovernmental organizations (NGOs), faith-based organizations, and the private sector. Presentations and discussions took place at an Organization of American States (OAS) forum. Briefing sessions were held with political leadership.

Although implementation of the Koudmen Sent Lisi pilot was from March 2009 to February 2011, the preparation process was lengthy and feasibility reviews took place. This helped to build an a posteriori logical model, wherein the core of the change theory is "if the household's portfolio of capabilities (that is, basic education, confidence in household management) is not sufficient or the family does not have the opportunity to acquire them, its ability to escape poverty will remain limited," as presented in figure 6.1.

Specific efforts were made to focus on equity in the evaluation. In the absence of records, it was decided to address equity issues by looking at equity in terms of added value, reduced disparity, and expected long-term societal gains. Using this equity-focused framework, the initial analysis of Koudmen Sent Lisi led to the findings presented in table 6.1.

An evaluation plan and appropriate tools (questionnaires, focus group discussion questions) were then designed to match the field research questions and collect credible data. This process was valuable on two levels: (a) it guided the probing necessary to answer essential questions put forth under each of the five evaluation criteria (effectiveness, efficiency, relevance, sustainability, and impact) and (b) it focused on the most critical questions and identified the most informative stakeholders. The mapping also made it easier to develop protocols and data collection tools that made the triangulation and analysis of data more coherent.

Given the multidimensional nature of Koudmen Sent Lisi and the complexity of the information needed to evaluate the pilot, the use of a mixed methodology was the most appropriate approach. The evaluation methodology included (1) a review of accessible research and documentation relevant to the design and implementation of the pilot in St. Lucia; (b) household interviews with 41 of the 46 families who participated in the pilot, targeting communities in four areas: Malgretoute, Bruceville, Anse la Verdue, and Roseau Valley; (c) focus group discussions with children and adolescents from each of the target communities as well as all the FCGs; (d) interviews with 17 relevant political, government, and program stakeholders; and (e) debriefing and exit meetings with all stakeholders. These are discussed in turn.

The *review of accessible research and documentation* included early poverty studies, workshop reports, material available from the OAS website, and several reports, but the documents directly associated with the design phase were limited to a few conceptual papers. The original program document, including the log frame, was lost during the transition of key staff shortly after the launch of the pilot. Consequently, the evaluation was

Figure 6.1   A Posteriori Logical Model of the Koudmen Sent Lisi Pilot Program

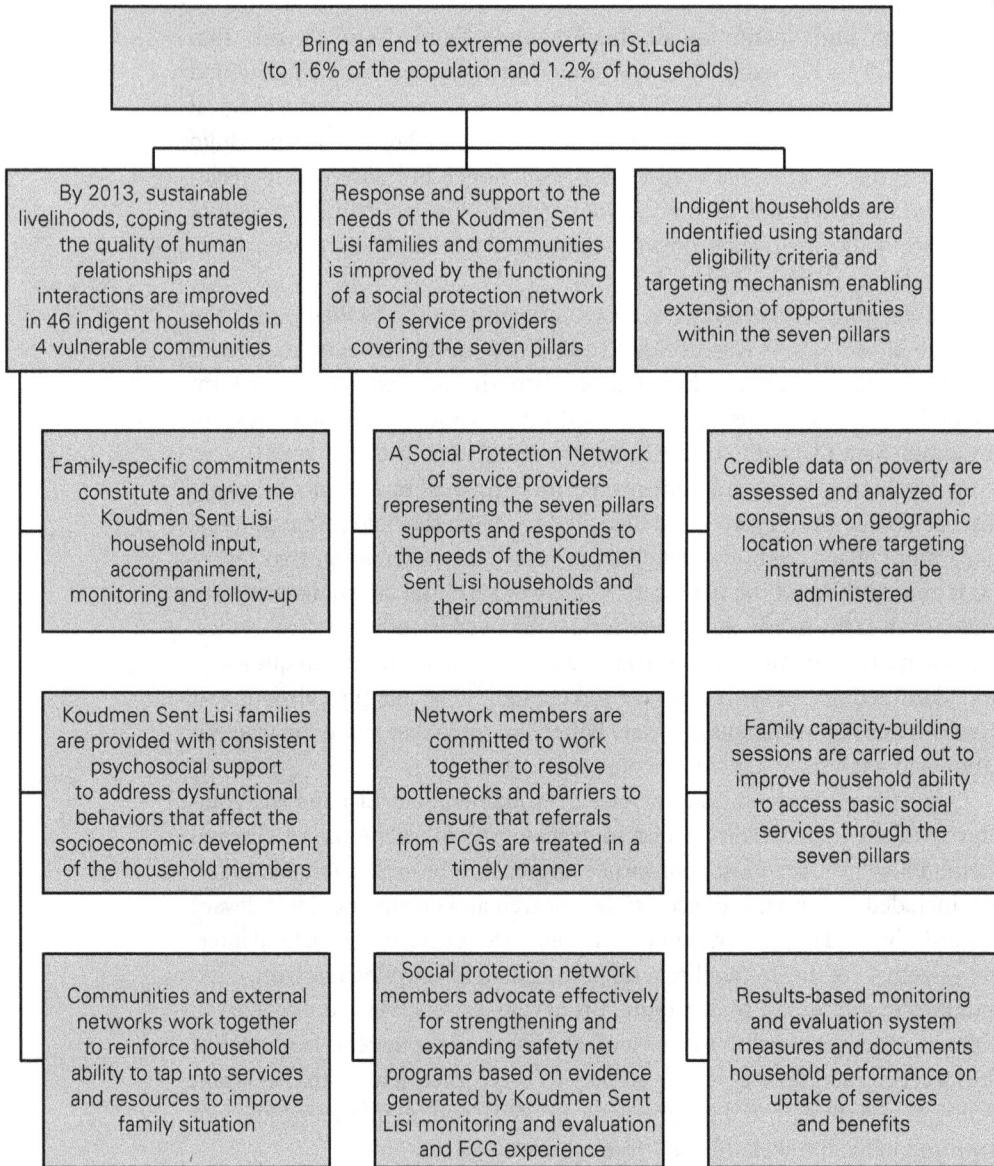

	Bring an end to extreme poverty in St.Lucia (to 1.6% of the population and 1.2% of households)	
By 2013, sustainable livelihoods, coping strategies, the quality of human relationships and interactions are improved in 46 indigent households in 4 vulnerable communities	Response and support to the needs of the Koudmen Sent Lisi families and communities is improved by the functioning of a social protection network of service providers covering the seven pillars	Indigent households are indentified using standard eligibility criteria and targeting mechanism enabling extension of opportunities within the seven pillars
Family-specific commitments constitute and drive the Koudmen Sent Lisi household input, accompaniment, monitoring and follow-up	A Social Protection Network of service providers representing the seven pillars supports and responds to the needs of the Koudmen Sent Lisi households and their communities	Credible data on poverty are assessed and analyzed for consensus on geographic location where targeting instruments can be administered
Koudmen Sent Lisi families are provided with consistent psychosocial support to address dysfunctional behaviors that affect the socioeconomic development of the household members	Network members are committed to work together to resolve bottlenecks and barriers to ensure that referrals from FCGs are treated in a timely manner	Family capacity-building sessions are carried out to improve household ability to access basic social services through the seven pillars
Communities and external networks work together to reinforce household ability to tap into services and resources to improve family situation	Social protection network members advocate effectively for strengthening and expanding safety net programs based on evidence generated by Koudmen Sent Lisi monitoring and evaluation and FCG experience	Results-based monitoring and evaluation system measures and documents household performance on uptake of services and benefits

Note: Seven pillars are personal identification, health, education, family dynamics, housing, employment, and income. FCG = family caregiver.

Table 6.1 Design Features of the Koudmen Sent Lisi Pilot Program in St. Lucia

Objective	Action
Promote equity as a value	• Shift away from the classic provision of services and toward addressing social and economic disadvantages, risks, and vulnerabilities of the poorest households
	• Focus on community support and build household capacity for resilience (capacity to know where to go to claim rights and entitlements) and strengthen interactions with the community and networks
	• Operationalize the theory of change that promotes solutions through psychosocial support for families and offers bridges or opportunities for extremely poor households to help themselves
Promote equity as a way to measure reduction of disparities	• Identify seven pillars under a multidimensional approach to poverty that reduces disparities in access to and use of services and benefits for the poor
	• Use objective evidence to identify and select Koudmen Sent Lisi beneficiaries and program dimensions in which issues of deprivation should be addressed and corrected
Promote equity as a way to build long-term benefits for society	• Emphasize family dynamics to address (a) household issues such as violence and lack of capacity to prioritize needs and (b) household connectedness to the community and society to support action to correct destructive behaviors (drug abuse, violence, crime) and build social capital over time
	• Build or strengthen a portfolio of capabilities within the family and at the household level

Note: Seven pillars are personal identification, health, education, family dynamics, housing, employment, and income.

conducted without a baseline. Remarkably, the individual family files were available and mostly intact, providing important details on the FCGs' routine household visits.

Household interviews were conducted with 41 of the 46 participating families using a face-to-face questionnaire, with 36 questions covering all seven pillars and the relationships between the household members, their psychosocial capacities, and basic family function. The interview began with five general questions and a final question asking for general comments on how to improve the program.

Originally intended to be administered to the head of the household, at the house, after the pretest, it was decided to conduct the interviews in a neutral setting for convenience and to protect the participant's dignity.

It was determined that while the family caregivers were welcome in the homes, admitting other personnel from the program and the SSDF created some tension.

All but 6 of the original 47 households were surveyed. One participant voluntarily dropped out of the program in the first quarter, another was considered an error of inclusion, and four were not available due to work, travel, or illness. The questionnaire was administered by seven SSDF project officers and supervised by the consultant. The 41 interviews were conducted by geographic location and completed in two weeks.

Focus group discussions were held with 32 children and adolescents. Three discussions were conducted, one in each of the geographic study areas. The group meetings were organized by the family caregivers for each of the locations. One had to be rescheduled due to poor turnout. The others took place in spite of very heavy rain. There was relatively good gender balance as well as a fairly good distribution of ages (10 to 18 years).

A focus group discussion was also organized with the FCGs, permitting them to discuss the program, openly review the reporting process, and describe the main steps and forms used for the intake and psychosocial assessments of adults and children. The four family caregivers were all women. A final focus group discussion took place with the seven SSDF project officers and staff (only one male) who had conducted the household interviews. The discussion was intended to capture their perceptions of the process and the general views of the participants.

Interviews with 17 national stakeholders were carried out over a period of two weeks, which allowed the collection of often high-spirited comments from SSDF management, the board of directors, the Social Protection Network, NGOs, government stakeholders, and former staff members.

Two debriefing and exit meetings with all stakeholders were organized toward the end of the fieldwork. The first was intended to provide feedback to key informants. It was attended by the Social Protection Network members, the deputy representative for the UNICEF Office for the Eastern Caribbean Area, and the UNICEF monitoring and evaluation specialist who supervised the work of the consultant. The second was organized to present and discuss the emerging recommendations with high-level decision makers. The minister of social transformation participated along with current SSDF board members.

The data collection instruments were pretested in the third week of the fieldwork, resulting in minor changes to the questionnaires and process. The changes were related mainly to language. Household interviews were conducted in English and, during the initial interviews, sometimes by two interviewers per household, permitting more experienced staff to guide

Figure 6.2   Koudmen Sent Lisi Program Timeline

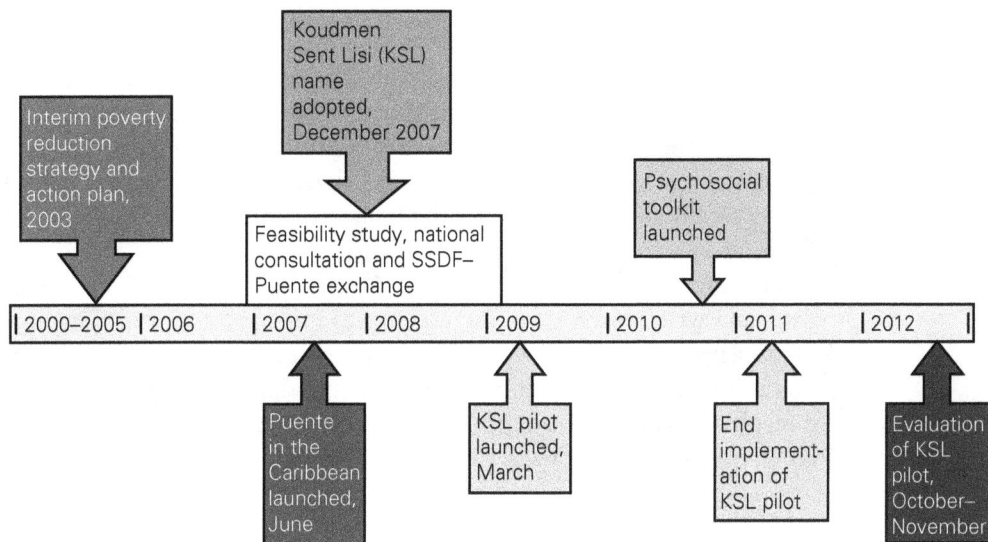

Interim poverty reduction strategy and action plan, 2003	Koudmen Sent Lisi (KSL) name adopted, December 2007	Psychosocial toolkit launched

Feasibility study, national consultation and SSDF–Puente exchange

| 2000–2005 | 2006 | 2007 | 2008 | 2009 | 2010 | 2011 | 2012 |

Puente in the Caribbean launched, June

KSL pilot launched, March

End implementation of KSL pilot

Evaluation of KSL pilot, October–November

Note: SSDF = St. Lucia Social Development Fund.

junior staff in interview techniques. All interviews and focus group discussions were recorded for reference and accuracy.

As per the terms of reference, the evaluator had enough time to cover the seven pillars of the Koudmen Sent Lisi and to consult with all 46 of the program families (figure 6.2). This was thought necessary due to the program's design and structure (central role of psychosocial support pillar, multidimensional approach) and made possible because of the relatively small number of households targeted in the pilot phase. Covering all of the program participants delivered the additional advantages of (1) hearing from all of the families and many of their members, (2) capturing diverse perceptions about the program and what changes occurred, if any, within the family and individual family members, and (3) learning how Koudmen Sent Lisi made that change possible.

Despite all of these efforts, the methodology had some limitations. The paucity of original program documents was a major limitation. This was complicated by the absence of a relevant institutional memory among SSDF staff. Reports and meeting minutes were difficult to collect, as the program coordinator had just moved offices and files were still boxed up during the evaluation. Like many small island states, St. Lucia is still very much a "paper culture." Hence, computerized file systems remain a distant prospect. SSDF staff and other stakeholders (MOST and NGOs, among others) were very cooperative, easily accessible, and highly motivated to contribute to the evaluation and learn from it.

As discussed during the review of the evaluation's terms of reference, questions regarding costing and cost evaluation could not be pursued due to time constraints and concerns regarding the gathering and preparation of necessary documents on program expenditures. These concerns were indeed relevant, as evidenced by the challenges faced in obtaining budget and expenditure documents and the limited number and weak quality of financial data accessed during the fieldwork.

The time required to collect data, build staff capacity, treat and analyze data, and write and finalize the report was underestimated in the terms of reference. Despite adding an additional week to the fieldwork, an evaluation of this complexity (multidimensional, multiple geographic sites) and difficulties (paucity of program documents, weak institutional memory) required more time than was allocated.

Evaluation Findings

Although Koudmen Sent Lisi was planned as a multifaceted cash transfer program, a serious delay in government financing resulted in cancellation of the cash dimension of the program. The SSDF decided to divert cash (US$300,000 over the two-year period) from the HOPE Program (the Holistic Opportunities for Personal Empowerment Program is designed to generate employment opportunities) to Koudmen Sent Lisi and to use in-kind contributions such as housing materials contributed by the European Union, valued at nearly US$150,000.

Relevance

Koudmen Sent Lisi was piloted to test the extent to which the basic principles and approaches of Puente Chile were relevant and consistent with the national and local culture, policies and priorities, and needs of program families. Modified for the context in St. Lucia, Puente Chile offers a vehicle for enabling poor communities and families to reduce their economic and social vulnerability.[4] The model and the Koudmen Sent Lisi's intended outputs and outcomes continue to be consistent with national and local policies and priorities and the needs of the intended beneficiaries. This is evidenced by government's funding and support for a second phase that is slightly scaled up.[5]

With regard to the cultural relevancy of the program, 40 of the 41 households interviewed suggested that the program should be continued.

Interview comments support this: "[The program] helped in as many ways as it could with the limited resources available"; "Although it was better in the beginning, skills training was A+"; or "[My] situation improved even though the program did not deliver all the benefits promised." The strategic use of family caregivers was culturally acceptable, as 23 households continued to use the FCG counseling services even after the pilot had closed. The data examined suggest that Koudmen Sent Lisi had a high level of cultural acceptance of the activities and method of delivery and was feasible within the local context.

With moderate levels of success in the nonincome pillars, program staff may find it helpful to examine the timing and level of cash transfers before considering this dimension in the next phase. Household interviews indicated that appropriate and timely discussions with FCGs clearly helped to reinforce the family's attributes and to change the family head's ability to manage the household situation.

The integrated design of the program requires significant and dedicated fiscal and human capacity for effective delivery. Putting in place the proper institutional arrangements proved to be a formidable challenge, beginning with a system to track family progress toward their established minimum conditions. The evaluation found fragmented effort to establish and monitor these minimum conditions. Therefore, it is difficult to ascertain whether (a) the important logical connection was established and respected between achieving the minimum conditions and "graduation" and (b) the relations between poverty levels and life events were followed, understood, or addressed. In the absence of this vital overview, the question of equity comes into view. FCG responses to household requests appear to have been somewhat subjective and ad hoc.

The weaknesses and strengths of the program's Social Protection Network, the technical steering committee for the pilot, were discussed in detail. The Social Protection Network met with difficulties in facilitating cross-sector, multiple-sector responses. With the constraints faced by the Social Protection Network, the FCGs spent a great deal of time coordinating both within and between pillars. They often used personal contacts to achieve this coordination, robbing time needed to establish and track family goals or minimum conditions.

To maximize success, the program needs to focus not just on poverty levels, but also on persons struggling in a cycle of poverty (cumulative effects of discrimination, risk, vulnerability, exclusion) and on persons on the margin of poverty. In doing so, a well-designed program will consider a continuum of age and life stages, where the needs of an individual change throughout his or her life, from conception to death.[6] An examination of economic and social vulnerability at different stages of the life cycle will help to analyze how risk and vulnerability are influenced by factors linked to the life cycle, relations between generations, and social exclusion. While this type of analysis was undertaken in the design phase, there is little indication that the roles, relationships, and links between different age groups were considered in great detail.

Given the proper resources and their efficient use, the program could have a marked impact on the reduction of poverty in St. Lucia. With the advent of the new Labour government, elected in November 2011 after five years in opposition, efforts to address the levels and patterns of poverty in St. Lucia have accelerated. Reform of the policy framework that guides social safety net programs has taken a front seat among the priorities established by the incoming administration. For example, there is support for establishing a central beneficiary system to track and monitor families receiving assistance and avoid duplication and waste of limited funds. The reform has also taken on the need to standardize eligibility criteria and use of a multidimensional proxy means test for scoring vulnerability. Of the 30 social assistance programs listed in Blank (2009), Koudmen Sent Lisi is the only one that employs a multidimensional approach. Its experience could be useful to informing the dialogue on reform in general and to establishing good practices in social safety net programs in particular, including the issue of conditionality in cash transfer programs, which is a subject of debate.

Effectiveness

A two-part questionnaire (part 1: household filter; part 2: individual) was administered, scoring households in multiple categories, including housing conditions, education, employment, and income. In exploring whether this targeting mechanism was effective in selecting the intended beneficiaries, the research findings indicate that low errors of inclusion were made, with the selection of only four single-person households who were likely eligible for other state-run programs (for the elderly or disabled, for example).

Data analysis suggests some inefficiency in the use of family caregivers' time. For example, they could spend more time counseling larger families, particularly those with children, and less time counseling single male-headed households. A well-targeted program will achieve maximum coverage, but, which is more important, the program should examine the use of a standardized proxy means test, with costs offset by a reliable local poverty impact analysis.

Opportunities for social integration, a major goal of the program, are determined largely by changes in the attitudes of family members. These changes were most notable in the pillars of family dynamic and the effort to create and restore family psychosocial capacities and basic functions. Applying the gains made in this area, household interviews noted that, after the end of the pilot, family members continued to remain "extremely confident" in their ability "to manage their family situation" and maintain the "improved environment for the family to work together."

Although the FCGs lived relatively close to the program sites, their knowledge and ability to connect to the local networks was not maximized. If they had mapped out all of the potential resources in the community and made courtesy calls to the NGOs and churches, for example, they could have better understood these networks and facilitated strategic connections between the household and the community. Instead, they were too dependent on the "connections" provided through the Social Protection Network or, in the best-case scenario, on personal contacts. Conducting a mapping exercise and nurturing priority contacts would have strengthened the role of family caregivers in creating linkages.

The changes in how members of the household relate to one another were important in enabling the family to take advantage of social inclusion opportunities. However, the quality and quantity of those opportunities was limited because family caregivers took insufficient action to make and protect linkages to local networks and benefits.

While stakeholder and household interviews linked positive results in several of the seven pillars to the pilot's ability to deliver some inputs in a timely manner (Christmas vouchers, skills training, identification documents), the achievements in operationalizing psychosocial support and strategies were the most effective, despite the delays in funding. More than half of the 41 households interviewed indicated that participation in the program resulted in a better understanding and use of the family's assets, including cash or materials, friendships and acquaintances, and general knowledge and parental skills.

The Social Protection Network was properly formed and, for a brief period, functioned with full awareness of the processes and methodologies employed by the program. According to stakeholder interviews, the Social Protection Network also had a good understanding of the indispensable contribution and role of each of its agency members. However, the network ceased to function during the pilot, and its absence left Koudmen Sent Lisi struggling to survive and to maintain the synergies with major stakeholders. Although the network members came to the table with much enthusiasm, they had weak capacity for program development, and their enthusiasm was not able to drive the momentum. In essence, their experience and skills did not strengthen the coordination and leadership, as anticipated and required.

Efficiency

Koudmen Sent Lisi was never intended to provide direct services and benefits under each of the seven pillars. It was intended to facilitate the delivery of services from existing government departments and NGOs to program participants. Its attempt to access existing state and nonstate benefits and services for poor families met with limited success due to weak coordination between the different service providers.

The pilot initially validated a communication strategy that used culturally sensitive local radio programs broadcasting routine public messages in Creole about the program's objectives, strategies, and basic operating procedures. This strategy, designed to generate a feeling of ownership toward the program, was discontinued due to funding constraints.

The original budget requested for the pilot totaled well over EC$3 million per year and included a substantial line item for cash transfers. The HOPE budget diverted resources to keep the pilot afloat, totaling little more than EC$300,000 for the two years of the pilot. These funds were used largely to employ the FCGs, pay for annual food vouchers distributed to the 46 households at Christmas, buy materials and technical assistance for the housing pillar, and pay for a very small amount of training, including tuition and exams. As a result, there was more of an "ad hoc" use of very limited resources. This undermined the ability to achieve expected results. Based on the pilot experience, the program could benefit from some reflection on what it will *cost* the program to deliver cash to more than 46 households, as the scaled-up phase of the program intends to do.

From an equity perspective, the fact that more than 20 percent of the available funds went to provide new or improved housing for 24 percent of the 41 households interviewed leads one to question how equitably and efficiently the scarce program resources were allocated. Household interviews indicated that the donated windows, doors, and inside building materials were largely not appropriate for warm-weather structures and that much of this in-kind donation remains stored. It is uncertain whether the donor was informed of this fact or whether attempts were made to sell, return, or donate these materials and apply the profit to the purchase of local materials or technical assistance to fulfill the many expectations for housing assistance among participating families. A more efficient handling of this in-kind donation and the housing pillar in general might have avoided much of the disappointment expressed by well over half of the pilot families and key informants.

The key role of family caregivers was critical to program effectiveness and efficiency. The FCG intervention included two phases, over a period of 24 months, that aimed to build trust and establish a bond of support with the family: intensive work with the family (first 6–8 months), including monitoring and follow-up (16–18 months). The key was for the family caregiver to help the family without making them dependent. The end goal was to strengthen or empower self-management capabilities in order for the family to take full advantage of the opportunities offered by community-based social capital and networks.

Another critical element affecting the efficiency of the program was the role of the Social Protection Network. Building a technical network that is responsive to and supportive of the need to create multidimensional opportunities to accelerate the reduction of poverty and economic and social vulnerability is an important outcome of the pilot.

Impacts

On the one hand, Koudmen Sent Lisi accumulated knowledge about and experience with transmitting capacities that enable households to address their problems and take advantage of development processes and opportunities.[7] On the other hand, the pilot demonstrated the importance of the family's connection to social networks for exercising these capacities or for spending the social capital required to escape poverty. To a certain degree, the program was able to broker this connection. These two achievements contributed to the short- and long-term effort to reduce poverty in St. Lucia and provided a strong basis for scaling up the Koudmen Sent Lisi. They also promote equity as a means to build long-term benefits for society by strengthening the portfolio of capabilities within the family and reinforcing the linkages of the household to the community and networks and eventually changing behaviors. This success was confirmed by 36 of the 41 households surveyed, which declared that they were the same, a little better, or much better off after participating in the Koudmen Sent Lisi pilot. In terms of continued benefits, a third of households said that they had more confidence and capability to access assistance in their community (14 of 41) and more than half said that they had more confidence and capability to manage vulnerabilities, difficulties, and responsibilities better as parents and heads of household (24 of 41).

Sustainability

Program benefits have been only partially achieved with regard to coverage and effectiveness. For example, the household interviews acknowledged that families had an improved awareness about how to access preventative health care services for children and that direct beneficiaries had changed their attitudes. However, lack of disposable income continues to make accessing these services problematic.

While most of the evaluation research shows an understanding of the program's assets and efforts, there is also recognition of the challenging environment and factors influencing sustained efforts. A few common themes are elaborated below and should be examined when considering how to take the Koudmen Sent Lisi pilot to scale.

The multidimensional approach can be effective and sustainable if the program makes a marked improvement in the efficient use of resources and is successful in linking services among the pillars. Despite the success in achieving several outputs, the inability to provide sufficient assistance in complementary pillars prevented the program from achieving the overall outcome. The buy-in, commitment, and follow-through from other services are essential for the program to achieve and sustain success.

The human-rights-based approach, adapted from Puente Chile and at the core of the Koudmen Sent Lisi pilot, is visible, for example, in the targeting of households and efforts to strengthen family dynamics. The ability of family caregivers to establish direct links and trust with the household is an effective force and could be focused more sharply on addressing children's vulnerabilities. Recognizing the importance of breaking the intergenerational transmission of poverty is the basis for Puente Chile's strategy to focus on ensuring services and benefits for children, particularly in the area of early childhood development. The Koudmen Sent Lisi pilot covered few of these needs. Only 5 of the 41 households interviewed said they had received services and benefits for child care for children under the age of six, for example.

The pilot made real progress in engaging targeted households in the struggle to bring about positive change for family members. However, progress in terms of a successful exit or graduation from the program will require considerable effort. The pilot had no procedure for closing the program, and the families were not aware that it had been discontinued.

Recommendations

The recommendations of the evaluation support opportunities for Koudmen Sent Lisi to become more equity focused and child sensitive in a scaled-up phase of the program:

1. Formulate an evaluation policy to support the establishment of a monitoring and evaluation framework and system
2. Establish an effective coordination function

3. Use Koudmen Sent Lisi to deliver services and benefits for children and to promote equal opportunities for children to grow, develop, and reach their full potential
4. Institute quality standards and distribution principles to ensure equitable access to the program's goods, services, and benefits
5. Strengthen and streamline connections among SSDF programs and other social safety net initiatives, particularly, but not limited to, the decentralized levels
6. Strengthen the national institutional structure or framework to provide strategic guidance and improve the coordination of social assistance initiatives
7. Provide technical support to help the SSDF to implement the evaluation recommendations and set up a monitoring and evaluation framework for the SSDF as a whole
8. Convene with stakeholders at all levels to share the evaluation findings and support the national discussion on a comprehensive, integrated social protection system and share the findings with partners at the regional level (Puente in the Caribbean, among others)

Because of the nature of the pilot (multidimensional approach to poverty reduction) and its content (strong emphasis on psychological support coupled with household-specific delivery services), the recommendations pertain to the overall architecture of the pilot and how it was implemented (family caregivers, social network) as well as to the mix of seven pillars and their content and potential to address the poverty of targeted households.

Specific recommendations were also made to increase the focus on children, the sensitivity to gender, and the capacity to address equity issues:

- *Promote equity as value.* (1) Focus the Koudmen Sent Lisi brand (the meaning of "Koudmen" in Creole) on the potential for the community to contribute to reversing the trends that keep the extremely poor in poverty and remove social and cultural barriers (hindering interaction with the community) and (2) question the effect(s) of introducing a cash transfer in phase 2 of the program.
- *Promote equity as a way to measure reduction of disparities.* (1) Focus resources on age- and gender-specific poverty issues facing each family member and adopt a more child-sensitive approach, (2) revive and reinforce the Social Protection Network to achieve optimal coordination of service and benefit delivery, including the convergence of sector-specific services on family members, and (3) introduce a monitoring and

evaluation framework with adequate metrics that define graduation of household members in each of the program pillars.

• *Promote equity as a way to build long-term benefits for society.* (1) Strengthen the horizontal and vertical linkages among St. Lucia social assistance programs to improve the effectiveness in building bridges and networks and offering opportunities for all household members and (2) emphasize the role of family resilience and capacity to interact with the community in an effort to remove barriers and bottlenecks.

Conclusion

This chapter has presented the findings of the evaluation of the Koudmen Sent Lisi pilot. The evaluation was conducted (a) to promote learning by national counterparts from the pilot (phase 1) and support the implementation of phase 2 and (b) to inform the current national dialogue about social protection reform.

The evaluation gained from the inclusion of national stakeholders at all levels of the process. The participative process allowed beneficiaries to provide direct feedback on the relevance and effectiveness of the program and the visible effects on their lives. Meetings were held with key decision makers, who have been or still are key to the success of Koudmen Sent Lisi and who can influence the coordination of service delivery among ministries.

In addition, equity issues were analyzed through three aspects (promotion of equity values, reduction of disparities, and achievement of longer-term gains for the community and society). The focus on equity looked at (a) the effect of the intervention theory, not just on the targeted households but also on individual family members, including girls and boys, and (b) the capacity of households, as a sum of individuals, to reconnect with the community and society as a way to remove barriers that prevent them from acquiring capabilities and accessing opportunities that will help them to stop being poor. The program can address gender- and child-specific poverty issues by having family caregivers and the Social Protection Network deliver specific assistance. Such assistance can produce some long-term positive effects for children, as evidence regarding early childhood development and good parenting show.

The evaluation also found that the existing social protection framework in St. Lucia needs to be reformed, while the adoption of a multidimensional approach to accelerate the reduction of extreme poverty and vulnerability needs to be encouraged. Poverty reduction programs in the past have focused solely on income poverty, seeking to create jobs and generate income. The Koudmen Sent Lisi approach of providing a cross-cutting package of social services in seven areas has the potential to address the various dimensions of poverty faced by households in St Lucia.

Although this chapter does not present final results, it does identify trends with regard to the degree of success in meeting coverage targets and effectiveness in complying with the minimum conditions set by families, which, once met, would track the family's move out of extreme poverty. This improvement would indicate the exit strategies and compliance percentages in each of the seven dimensions of family life.

Finally, this chapter reaffirms the importance of:

- Linking social protection mechanisms with sector-specific services to enhance outcomes at different life stages of household members, especially children;
- Basing the social protection framework on a coherent policy that sets forth interministerial regulations, coordinates national priorities and a multisectoral network, and establishes norms and standards while promoting child-sensitive social protection with equity; and
- Recognizing that household members can solve their problems once they have the capabilities and opportunities to do so at the family, community, and society levels.

Notes

1. UNICEF defines an equity-focused approach as one that promotes the realization of children's rights and ensures equal outcomes for all groups of children through increased redistribution and assistance to those who need it the most and removal of barriers and bottlenecks to equity (bias, favoritism and discrimination, social norms and values, and inequitable policies and institutions, among others).
2. Koudmen Sent Lisi program proposal.
3. "The minimal condition is a specific measurable indicator which is used to assess the progress of the family from the start to the end of the intervention" (OAS 2010, 44).
4. For excellent and recent reviews, see Barrientos and Villa 2013 and Robles Farias 2012.
5. A second phase was initiated in April 2011, with initial funding from government of EC$3 million.
6. See the work of psychologist Albert Bandura, for example.
7. Given the nature of the intervention, the type of evaluation, and the information available, this evaluation has tried to determine outcomes rather than impact.

References

Barrientos, A., and J. M. Villa. 2013. "Evaluation of Anti-Poverty Transfer Programmes in Latin America and Sub-Saharan Africa." UNU-WIDER, New York.

Blank, L. 2009. "Saint Lucia Social Safety Net Assessment." UNICEF, World Bank, and UN Fund for Women, Castries, August.

CDB (Caribbean Development Bank). 1996. "Poverty Assessment Report, St. Lucia." CDB, St. Michael.

——. 2006. "Poverty Assessment Report, St. Lucia." CDB, St. Michael.

DFID (Department for International Development), CDB (Caribbean Development Bank), and European Union. 2004. "Review of Social Protection in St. Lucia." DFID, London.

European Union. 1998. "A Socio-Economic Impact of Banana Restructuring in St. Lucia." European Union, Brussels.

MOST (Ministry of Social Transformation). 2003. "Interim Poverty Reduction Strategy and Action Plan." MOST, Castries.

OAS (Organization of American States). 2010. "Puente in the Caribbean Operations Manual." Executive Secretariat for Integral Development, OAS, Washington, DC.

Renard, Yves. 2008. "Saint Lucia MDGs: A Plan of Action for Localising and Achieving the Millennium Development Goals (MDGs)." MDG Series 4. Report prepared for the United Nations Development Programme and the Organization for the Eastern Caribbean States. OECS Secretariat, Castries.

Robles Farias, C. 2012. "Social Protection Systems in Latin America and the Caribbean: Chile." ECLAC, Santiago.

UNDP (United Nations Development Programme). 2011. *Human Development Report 2011: Sustainability and Equity; a Better Future for All*. New York: UNDP.

World Bank. 2000. "Social Assessment Study." World Bank, Washington, DC.

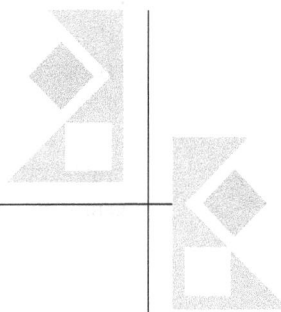

CHAPTER 7

HIV/AIDS Services Delivery, Overall Quality of Care, and Satisfaction in Burkina Faso: Are Some Patients Privileged?

Harounan Kazianga, Seni Kouanda, Laetitia N. Ouedraogo, Elisa Rothenbuhler, Mead Over, and Damien de Walque

Introduction

The human immunodeficiency virus (HIV)/acquired immune deficiency syndrome (AIDS) remains a major public health problem in Sub-Saharan Africa. The latest estimates of the United Nations HIV/AIDS Program

Harounan Kazianga is at Oklahoma State University; Seni Kouanda and Laetitia N. Ouedraogo are with the Institut de Recherche en Sciences de la Santé, Ouagadougou; Elisa Rothenbuhler and Damien de Walque are with the World Bank; and Mead Over is with the Center for Global Development. This work was supported by the Bank Netherlands Partnership Program, the Research Committee of the World Bank, and the William and Flora Hewlett Foundation. The authors thank the patients and medical staff who participated in the survey for their time.

(UNAIDS) reported that 35 million people worldwide were living with HIV by the end of 2010 (UNAIDS 2013a). More than two-thirds (71 percent) of them were living in Sub-Saharan Africa (WHO 2015). Initially, antiretroviral treatment (ART) was only available for a small number of patients in a few health facilities located mainly in urban areas. With the support of governments, associations of persons living with HIV/AIDS (PLWHA), and multilateral, bilateral, and private donors, the number of PLWHA who have access to ART has increased dramatically since 2003 (UNAIDS 2013b). As of June 2014, an estimated 13.6 million people worldwide were receiving antiretroviral drugs (UNAIDS 2014), representing 38 percent of those needing them. In 2003 the estimated coverage in the region was only 2 percent (UNAIDS 2008, 2014). In Burkina Faso, the number of PLWHA was 110,000 persons (99,000–130,000) at the end of 2012 (UNAIDS 2013b), 54,000 of whom were estimated to need antiretroviral treatment. The number of PLWHA under treatment increased from 3,000 in 2004 to 39,047 (72 percent) in 2012, concomitant with a rise in the number of facilities delivering ART, from 44 in 2005 to 76 at the end of 2007 (UNAIDS 2013b).

In Africa HIV infection occurs in a general context of health system crisis and underuse of health services. Health services were not prepared to confront the HIV/AIDS epidemic. The 1987 Bamako Initiative for primary health care aimed to strengthen the geographic, financial, and cultural accessibility of care for the population. However, most of the studies conducted in the continent show that access to care and the performance of health facilities remain low (Baltussen and Ye 2006; Das, Hammer, and Leonard 2008; Fowler, Adhikari, and Bhagwanjee 2008; Mapunjo and Urassa 2007; O'Donnell 2007; Zere et al. 2007).

There are many challenges in successfully scaling up ART, ensuring access to care, and reorienting the delivery of health care services for people with chronic diseases. In many studies, insufficient human resources in health care are often cited as the most important obstacle to providing adequate access to care and successfully scaling up treatment (Chen and Hanvoravongchai 2005; Das and Hammer 2007; Das and Sohnesen 2007; Marchal, De Brouwere, and Kegels 2005; Schneider et al. 2006; Wouters et al. 2008). Weak and overloaded health systems threaten the quality of care and patient satisfaction, which can, in turn, seriously lessen the chances of successfully confronting AIDS (Wouters et al. 2008).

Quality of care and patient satisfaction influence care-seeking behavior and determine the demand for health services. If patients are dissatisfied with the quality of care they receive, they may not adhere to a treatment regimen or they may fail to attend follow-up visits (Mesfin et al. 2009; Wouters et al. 2008). For patients suffering from HIV/AIDS, in particular, adherence to a regimen and strict follow-up schedules play a central role in treatment success. Therefore, the quality of care and patient satisfaction underpin the success of public health policies in enhancing access to care, especially for policies that aim to increase access and improve adherence to ART.

In this chapter, we assess the quality of care received in a sample of health facilities delivering ART in Burkina Faso. Our analysis focuses on the quality of care based on structured interviews with outpatients.[1] We use multivariate regressions to explore the determinants of the quality of care, focusing on patients' wealth and the purpose of the visit—specifically, whether the visit was related to HIV.

Methods: Sampling and Survey

The sample was drawn to be representative of health facilities offering ART in Burkina Faso as of July 2006.[2] All health facilities with at least 100 registered HIV/AIDS patients were included in the sampling process. In total, the study comprises 43 health facilities, including 32 public health facilities, 10 run by associations of PLWHA or nongovernmental organizations (including 3 faith-based organizations), and 1 private clinic. In the analysis, we group health facilities into four categories: (1) public reference hospitals, including the Centres Hospitaliers Universitaires and the Centres Hospitaliers Régionaux; (2) public local health facilities, including the Centres Médicaux avec Antenne Chirurgicale and the Centres Médicaux; (3) associations and nongovernmental organizations, including facilities run by associations of PLWHA and faith-based organizations; and (4) private for-profit clinics. In each health facility, the manager and health providers were surveyed, with at least one health provider selected from the HIV/AIDS department.

We interviewed 10 randomly selected outpatients (5 from HIV/AIDS services and 5 from other services) present on the day of the survey in each health facility selected. Informed consent was obtained from every respondent prior to the interview. The survey covered basic sociodemographic and socioeconomic data, service used during the visit, direct and indirect costs associated with the visit, and satisfaction level with the service used. Respondents were asked 17 questions about the medical procedures performed during their visit. Table 7.1 includes the list of questions.

The score obtained for each question—that is, 1 if the procedure was performed or 0 if it was not—was assigned the same weight of 1/17 to normalize the quality index between 0 and 1, with 0 indicating the poorest quality of care and 1 indicating the highest.[3] We classify a patient as visiting for HIV-related services if he or she declared that the purpose of the visit was for a

Table 7.1 Frequency of Patients' Positive Answers on Whether Questions on Their Medical History Were Asked during the Visit to a Health Facility in Burkina Faso
Percentages

	Quality index component: Patients asked about	Total	Male	Female	P-value	HIV	Non-HIV	P-value
1	Beginning of current pain	80.9	83.6	79.2	(0.317)	73.0	89.3	(0.000)
2	Beginning of sickness	81.2	84.3	79.2	(0.238)	73.6	89.3	(0.000)
3	Presence of blood in sputum	32.7	32.1	33.0	(0.857)	38.2	26.8	(0.024)
4	Episode of breathing difficulties	29.5	32.8	27.4	(0.276)	29.2	29.8	(0.911)
5	Stitch	23.1	23.1	23.1	(0.996)	25.8	20.2	(0.217)
6	Night perspiration	31.2	27.6	33.5	(0.250)	41.0	20.8	(0.000)
7	Contact with coughing individuals	32.4	31.3	33.0	(0.746)	45.5	18.5	(0.000)
8	Weight loss	47.7	45.5	49.1	(0.521)	60.7	33.9	(0.000)
9	Prior pathologies, including HIV and tuberculosis	44.2	39.6	47.2	(0.165)	60.1	27.4	(0.000)
10	Asthma history	18.2	20.9	16.5	(0.303)	23.0	13.1	(0.017)
11	Is the patient currently under treatment?	59.0	61.2	57.5	(0.502)	57.9	60.1	(0.670)
12	Smoking history	17.3	33.6	7.1	(0.000)	20.8	13.7	(0.081)
13	Medicinal allergy	45.1	45.5	44.8	(0.897)	53.4	36.3	(0.001)
14	Other medical history	41.3	43.3	40.1	(0.557)	48.3	33.9	(0.007)
15	Patient's employment	53.8	56.0	52.4	(0.512)	59.6	47.6	(0.026)
16	Alcohol consumption history	30.3	36.6	26.4	(0.045)	33.7	26.8	(0.162)
17	Other question	7.8	11.2	5.7	(0.062)	5.6	10.1	(0.119)
	N	346	134	212		178	168	

Note: P-values of Pearson's Chi-2 test are in parentheses. HIV and non-HIV indicate whether or not the consultation was related to HIV.

follow-up on the evolution of HIV/AIDS or adherence to ART or if it was for HIV/AIDS counseling or voluntary testing. Therefore, our analysis concerns the impact of HIV-related services delivery. We do not focus on HIV-positive patients, since not all the patients visiting for these services were HIV-positive. Instead, our focus is on the type of service delivered.

We define up-front fees as any fees (legal or not) that the patient paid at the health facility before seeing a health professional. Thus our definition excludes the costs of both prescriptions and exams. Other external costs borne by the patient, such as transportation costs, are also excluded.

The analysis also controls for patients' wealth level. We measure wealth as a weighted index calculated from 14 variables. We use principal component analysis to choose weights for the wealth index because it has been shown to outperform alternative methods. The variables used include housing quality, access to water and electricity, and ownership of assets such as livestock, agricultural tools, household appliances, communication devices, and vehicles. For ease of interpretation, we normalize the wealth index between 0, representing the lowest level of wealth, and 1, indicating the highest level.

Data Analysis

We use the answers to 17 questions to construct a health care quality index from the patient's perspective. By asking more detailed questions, this approach offers more variations in their perceived quality of health care received than single questions on their satisfaction.[4] Indeed, exit interviews of patients have been widely used in both developed and developing countries to measure the quality of health care.

We first provide descriptive statistics of the characteristics of the health services received and the patients interviewed, distinguishing between patients coming for HIV/AIDS services and those coming for other services. Next, we use multivariate regression analysis to explore the quality of care as measured by the quality index, the determinants of up-front costs paid by patients, and the time spent at the health facility.

Our primary explanatory variables of interest are patient wealth and whether the consultation is related to HIV/AIDS. Nevertheless, we control for patients' sociodemographic variables, including education level, gender, and age. We use health facility fixed effects to control for the characteristics of health facilities. This allows us to remove effects idiosyncratic to each facility. Our focus is, therefore, on how resources are allocated within the same health facility between HIV/AIDS services and other services.[5]

Results

We examine how responses to each element of the exit interview (used to determine the quality index) vary by gender of the patient and by whether the patient visited the facility for HIV/AIDS services (table 7.2). Based on bivariate analysis, patients visiting for HIV-related services were more likely to have been questioned about their medical condition or history. However, most of the other types of visits were classified as "adult care"

Table 7.2 Summary Statistics for Patients Visiting Health Facilities in Burkina Faso

a. Means for continuous variables

Variable	Total (gender)				Total			Males			Females		
	Total	Males	Females	P-value	HIV	Non-HIV	P-value	HIV	Non-HIV	P-value	HIV	Non-HIV	P-value
Age (years)	35.369	39.107	33.014	(0.000)	34.632	36.145	(0.334)	37.620	40.025	(0.461)	33.427	32.405	(0.460)
	[0.663]	[1.207]	[0.723]		[0.702]	[1.142]		[1.609]	[1.680]		[0.719]	[1.446]	
Education (years)	4.295	4.252	4.322	(0.881)	4.126	4.473	(0.513)	3.020	5.012	(0.026)	4.573	3.952	(0.298)
	[0.270]	[0.470]	[0.328]		[0.340]	[0.425]		[0.517]	[0.678]		[0.423]	[0.518]	
Wealth index	0.370	0.314	0.405	(0.003)	0.363	0.378	(0.677)	0.287	0.331	(0.378)	0.393	0.423	(0.531)
	[0.015]	[0.024]	[0.018]		[0.019]	[0.023]		[0.030]	[0.034]		[0.023]	[0.030]	
N	346	134	212		178	168		52	82		126	86	

Note: Standard deviations are in brackets. P-values of means test are in parentheses. HIV and non-HIV represent whether or not the consultation was related to HIV.

Poverty, Inequality, and Evaluation

b. Frequencies for categorical variables

Variable	Total (gender)				Total (HIV-related visit)			Males			Females		
	Total	Males	Females	P-value	HIV	Non-HIV	P-value	HIV	Non-HIV	P-value	HIV	Non-HIV	P-value
Share (%)	100	38.7	61.3		51.5	48.6	(0.000)	38.8	61.2	(0.026)	59.4	40.6	(0.000)
N	346												
Marital status				(0.000)			(0.000)			(0.026)			(0.000)
Single	19.9	23.8	17.4		16.2	23.8		22.4	24.7		13.7	22.9	
Married or a couple	53.7	70.8	43.0		42.2	65.9		65.3	74.1		33.1	57.8	
Divorced or widowed	26.4	5.4	39.6		41.6	10.4		12.2	1.2		53.2	19.3	
N	337	130	207		173	164		49	81		124	83	
Occupation				(0.000)			(0.257)			(0.919)			(0.317)
Salaried employee	12.8	21.1	7.4		11.0	14.8		19.1	22.4		7.7	6.8	
Farmer, housewife, breeder	54.3	46.3	59.5		55.5	53.0		44.7	47.4		59.8	58.9	
Shopkeeper	22.0	17.1	25.3		25.0	18.8		19.1	15.8		27.4	21.9	
Other	10.9	15.4	7.9		8.5	13.4		17.0	14.5		5.1	12.3	
N	313	123	190		164	149		47	76		117	73	

Note: *P*-values of Pearson's Chi-2 test, which are in parentheses, apply to the overall distribution of each variable with regard to sex or the purpose of the visit. HIV and non-HIV represent whether or not the consultation was related to HIV. The difference in frequencies between HIV-related and non-HIV-related visits with regard to sex is significant (*P*-value = 0.000; not presented).

(164 consultations out of 346), which may or may not require as many investigations of the patient's condition and medical history. In addition to a difference in the health care quality index, patients visiting for HIV/AIDS services reported being more satisfied with the services received, except for waiting time (not shown).

In table 7.3, column 1, we regress the quality of health care on wealth and control variables using the quality index. Then in column 2, we include a

Table 7.3 Estimated Fixed Effects of Quality of Care in Burkina Faso

Variable	(1)	(2)	(3)	(4)
Up-front costs			−0.023	0.002
			[0.014]	[0.014]
HIV-related services * Up-front costs				−0.169
				[0.237]
Wealth index	−0.110	−0.035		
	[0.065]*	[0.075]		
HIV-related services		0.175		0.169
		[0.045]***		[0.029]***
HIV-related services * Wealth index		−0.032		
		[0.094]		
Years of education	−0.001	−0.001	−0.003	−0.002
	[0.003]	[0.003]	[0.003]	[0.002]
Female	0.007	−0.023	−0.003	−0.029
	[0.027]	[0.026]	[0.026]	[0.026]
Age	0.015	0.005	0.014	0.004
	[0.006]**	[0.006]	[0.006]**	[0.006]
Age squared	−0.015	−0.002	−0.014	−0.001
	[0.007]**	[0.007]	[0.007]**	[0.007]
Constant	0.129	0.218	0.121	0.227
	[0.120]	[0.115]*	[0.116]	[0.112]**
N	344	344	344	344
R-squared	0.51	0.56	0.51	0.56

Note: The dependent variable is the quality index. Robust standard errors are in brackets, clustered at the health facility level. Quality of care is the sum of 17 discrete variables (see table 7.1), normalized between 0 and 1. Wealth index is a 0 to 1 score. Regressions also include health facility fixed effects.
*p<.10 **p<.05 ***p<.01

Poverty, Inequality, and Evaluation

binary variable indicating whether the respondent visited the facility for HIV/AIDS services and the same variable interacted with wealth. We want to test if the quality of care varies between patients visiting for services related to HIV/AIDS and those visiting for other purposes and whether wealth plays a role in this relationship. In column 1, the estimated coefficient of the normalized wealth index is negative and statistically significant at the 10 percent level. In column 2, it is no longer significant. However, the coefficient on HIV/AIDS services is positive and significant at the 1 percent confidence level. To provide further evidence of the link between wealth and the quality of care, we look directly at the relation between up-front costs and health care quality in columns 3 and 4. The estimated coefficients are small and statistically insignificant at the 10 percent level.

In table 7.4, the dependent variable is up-front fees. In columns 1 and 2, we find a positive association between up-front fees and wealth. The estimated coefficient is statistically significant at the 1 percent level in each case. In column 2 we also include as independent variables HIV-related services and the same variables interacted with wealth. Both estimated coefficients are negative, but only the coefficient of the interaction term is significant at the 1 percent level. In column 3, we find a negative association between up-front fees and HIV-related services, and the estimated coefficient is significant at the 1 percent level.

In table 7.5, the dependent variable is waiting time. In column 1, we find a negative association between waiting time and wealth. The estimated coefficient is statistically significant at the 1 percent level. In column 2, we also include as independent variables HIV-related services and the same variables interacted with wealth. The estimated coefficient of wealth is still negative, but no longer significant at the 10 percent level. The coefficient of HIV-related services is positive and significant at the 5 percent level, while the coefficient of wealth interacted with HIV-related services is negative and significant at the 10 percent level.

Discussion

The bivariate analysis indicates that patients visiting a facility for HIV-related services are more likely to be asked about important elements of their medical condition or history than others (table 7.1). However, most of the other types of visits are classified as "adult care" (164 consultations out of 346), which may or may not require as many questions about the patient's condition and medical history. We do not have a sufficient level of detail about the consultation purposes to assess whether the difference between

Table 7.4 Estimated Fixed Effects of Up-front Costs in Burkina Faso
FCFA, thousands

Variable	(1)	(2)	(3)
Wealth index	0.705	0.980	
	[0.271]***	[0.308]***	
HIV-related services		−0.165	−0.640
		[0.188]	[0.114]***
HIV-related services * Wealth index		−1.175	
		[0.386]***	
Years of education	0.000	0.000	0.012
	[0.013]	[0.012]	[0.010]
Female	−0.132	−0.001	0.022
	[0.113]	[0.109]	[0.106]
Age	−0.022	0.011	0.017
	[0.024]	[0.024]	[0.024]
Age squared	0.027	−0.012	−0.022
	[0.029]	[0.029]	[0.028]
Constant	0.521	0.011	0.248
	[0.497]	[0.476]	[0.469]
N	344	344	344
R-squared	0.24	0.33	0.30

Note: Robust standard errors are in brackets, clustered at the health facility level. Up-front costs include all fees (legal or not) paid by the patient at the health facility before being received by a health professional. The definition excludes both prescription and exam costs. Other external costs borne by the patient such as transportation costs are also excluded. Wealth index is a 0 to 1 score. Regressions also include health facility fixed effects. FCFA = West African CFA franc.

*p<.10 **p<.05 ***p<.01

patients visiting for HIV versus non-HIV services is still significant for the consultations needing such medical history. In addition to a difference in the health care quality index, patients visiting for HIV-related services also reported being more satisfied with the services received, with the exception of waiting time (not shown).

Within the same health facility, level of wealth correlates negatively with the quality of care (table 7.3, column 1).[6] There is some evidence suggesting that patients visiting for HIV-related services receive higher-quality care. Comparing the results in column 2 to those in column 1 suggests that clients of HIV/AIDS services are less wealthy,[7] but receive relatively higher-quality care. The higher quality of care received by HIV/AIDS patients is confirmed

Poverty, Inequality, and Evaluation

Table 7.5 Estimated Fixed Effects of Waiting Time in Burkina Faso

Variable	(1)	(2)
Wealth index	−2.227	−1.145
	[0.735]***	[0.878]
HIV-related services		1.379
		[0.535]**
HIV-related services * Wealth index		−1.98
		[1.101]*
Years of education	−0.065	−0.068
	[0.035]*	[0.034]**
Female	0.455	0.369
	[0.307]	[0.311]
Age	0.022	−0.024
	[0.065]	[0.068]
Age squared	−0.015	0.048
	[0.077]	[0.081]
Constant	2.28	2.367
	[1.348]*	[1.358]*
N	339	339
R-squared	0.30	0.32

Note: Robust standard errors are in brackets, clustered at the health facility level. Wealth index is a 0 to 1 score. Regressions also include health facility fixed effects.

*p<.10 **p<.05 ***p<.01

by the multivariate results in table 7.3: on average, visiting a facility for HIV-related services increases the health care quality score by about .17 units.

However, in a cross-sectional study like ours, the finding that patients visiting for HIV services receive, on average, better-quality care than others does not imply that HIV services have a negative impact on other health services. Our empirical results could be observed in a context where the quality of the other services is improving, deteriorating, or remaining the same. Addressing this question would require a panel of health facilities before and after the introduction of antiretroviral services.

A relevant question is whether patients seeking HIV-related services pay a premium for the additional quality of care they receive. If health facilities are charging these patients more in return for quality of care, the cost might exclude relatively poor patients desiring to receive HIV-related services.

We investigate this question formally by exploring the correlations between up-front costs, on the one hand, and wealth and visiting for HIV/AIDS services, on the other hand (table 7.4). We find a strong correlation between wealth and up-front fees, with wealthier individuals paying more, on average, except when they are visiting for HIV/AIDS-related services.

Our analysis suggests that higher wealth is positively associated with higher up-front costs but not significantly correlated with quality of care. We find, however, that wealth is negatively and significantly correlated with waiting time at the health care center, especially for HIV/AIDS services. It is plausible that health facilities engage in price discrimination based on wealth. If health professionals form a belief about the wealth level of a patient at the time of the service (and they guess correctly, on average), then they could effectively discriminate between rich and poor patients and charge rich patients more. This finding is consistent with the result from Banerjee (1997), who finds that hospitals use waiting times as a screening device. It is therefore consistent with some type of price discrimination with regard to the health sector in Uganda. He finds that wealthier patients are more likely to pay higher bribes and that this is consistent with price discrimination by health care providers.

Conclusions and Policy Recommendations

Our results indicate that visiting for HIV-related services makes a difference in the overall quality of care, costs of care, and waiting time in health facilities in Burkina Faso. First, requiring HIV-related services guarantees a better quality of care, without having to pay more. However, requiring HIV-related services also means enduring a longer waiting time at the facility. That longer waiting time is shorter for wealthier individuals. These initial findings indicate that there is a difference in the treatment of patients depending on the purpose of their visit. Even if the better quality somehow compensates for the increase in waiting time, it is still concerning that a certain category of patients receives differential treatment.

These findings have two plausible explanations. First, HIV-related services might be different in nature from other health services. HIV/AIDS is a serious chronic disease that might require more attention from the health care provider than other medical conditions. The lack of detailed information on non-HIV/AIDS patients does not allow further exploration of this potential explanation. The government of Burkina Faso subsidizes antiretroviral treatment, which explains why out-of-pocket expenses are not higher for this upgraded service.

Second, HIV/AIDS services have benefited in recent years from more generous funding, provided to a large extent by external donors, than other health services. This could explain why the quality of care is higher (better equipment and supplies, more motivated health practitioners) and why up-front costs for patients are lower (if both the supply of drugs and the chain of service delivery are funded externally, it is easier for government to subsidize treatment). This could also explain the longer waiting time, as relatively better quality of care and low cost can lead to more crowded waiting rooms.

Whether these changes in HIV services have had an overall positive or negative impact on the delivery of other health services is still debated. On the one hand, the improvement of equipment and supply chains and the fact that many AIDS patients have turned from being terminally ill patients crowding inpatient services into chronic patients easier to manage as outpatients might have, as a positive spillover, benefited other health services. On the other hand, the influx of resources and money into HIV/AIDS services might have distorted incentives at both the facility and the provider levels and encouraged a neglect of other services. Our cross-sectional study does not allow for a clear-cut answer to this debate. Further investigation could address this type of question. However, we can conclude that it would be desirable for the quality of care in other services to reach at least the level attained in HIV/AIDS services and for the up-front costs to be reduced.

Our finding that wealth does not affect quality of care is reassuring with regard to equity. But we find that wealth is associated with lower waiting time for HIV-related services, even though wealthier patients do not pay more for those services (and for those services only). This suggests more subtle ways in which wealthier individuals enjoy a more comfortable experience while visiting health facilities. Although this type of preferred access is difficult to detect and correct, it goes against the principle of equity.

Annex 7A Robustness of Multivariate Analysis to an Alternative Definition of Health Care Quality Index

A potential concern is that the quality index may not be directly comparable across HIV and non-HIV patients. Presumably, a doctor who is interacting with a patient who has already been diagnosed with HIV should (and will) ask a different set of questions than one interacting with a patient with an unknown illness.[8] As a robustness check, we separate the questions that should be asked regardless of the condition of the patient from the questions that are more specific to HIV/AIDS. Based on the national health protocol in

Burkina Faso, questions 1 (beginning of current pain), 2 (beginning of sickness), 10 (asthma history), 11 (is patient currently under any treatment?), 12 (smoking history), 13 (is patient allergic to any medication?), 14 (other medical history), 15 (patient's employment), and 16 (history of alcohol consumption) in table 7.1 should be asked of any patient, regardless of his or her condition. Questions 8 and 9 (weight loss and prior pathologies, including HIV and tuberculosis, respectively) are systematically asked of patients coming to the health facility for HIV/AIDS–related reasons. We calculate two different health care quality indexes based on these sets of questions.[9]

The regression results using these different indexes are reported in table 7A.1 for the HIV/AIDS–specific questions—that is, questions 8 and 9—and table 7A.2 for the standard questions. The estimated coefficients in both tables support qualitatively the findings reported in table 7.3 that the health care quality index is higher for HIV/AIDS patients. It is apparent that HIV/AIDS patients have, on average, a higher health care quality index, whether the quality index uses only the questions that are asked of each patient, regardless of his or her condition (table 7A.2) or the questions that are asked specifically of HIV/AIDS patients (table 7A.1). While the results in table 7A.1 are to be expected, the results in table 7A.2 confirm the results in table 7.3 and indicate that they are robust since they persist when we focus on the questions that should be asked of all patients.

Table 7A.1 Estimated Fixed Effects of Health Care Quality Index Based on HIV/AIDS–Specific Questions in Burkina Faso

Variable	(1)	(2)	(3)	(4)
Up-front costs			−0.086	−0.03
			[0.031]***	[0.021]
HIV-related services * Up-front costs				−0.021
				[0.463]
Wealth index	−0.282	−0.219		
	[0.134]**	[0.155]		
HIV-related services		0.312		0.375
		[0.103]***		[0.076]***
HIV-related services * Wealth index		0.186		
		[0.204]		
Female	−0.001	−0.002	−0.007	−0.005
	[0.006]	[0.005]	[0.005]	[0.004]

(continued next page)

Table 7A.1 (continued)

Variable	(1)	(2)	(3)	(4)
Years of education	0.112	0.039	0.085	0.032
	[0.061]*	[0.049]	[0.060]	[0.049]
Age	0.043	0.02	0.044	0.021
	[0.012]***	[0.010]*	[0.012]***	[0.010]**
Age squared	−0.05	−0.022	−0.051	−0.022
	[0.014]***	[0.012]*	[0.015]***	[0.012]*
Constant	−0.324	−0.079	−0.37	−0.143
	[0.244]	[0.212]	[0.253]	[0.214]
N	339	339	344	344
R-squared	0.42	0.54	0.44	0.54

Note: Robust standard errors are in brackets. Quality of care is based on questions 8 and 9 in table 7.1, normalized between 0 and 1. Wealth index is a 0 to 1 score. Regressions also include health facility fixed effects.

*$p<.10$ **$p<.05$ ***$p<.01$

Table 7A.2 Estimated Fixed Effects of Health Care Quality Index Based on Non-HIV/AIDS–Specific Questions in Burkina Faso

Variable	(1)	(2)	(3)	(4)
Up-front costs			0.001	0.021
			[0.008]	[0.013]
HIV-related services * Up-front costs				−0.263
				[0.206]
Wealth index	−0.109	−0.016		
	[0.061]*	[0.074]		
HIV-related services		0.156		0.130
		[0.067]**		[0.056]**
HIV-related services * Wealth index		−0.123		
		[0.098]		
Female	−0.031	−0.050	−0.039	-0.060
	[0.032]	[0.032]	[0.032]	[0.032]*
Years of education	0.002	0.002	−0.001	0.000
	[0.003]	[0.003]	[0.003]	[0.003]
Age	0.007	−0.001	0.007	−0.001
	[0.006]	[0.007]	[0.006]	[0.007]

(continued next page)

Table 7A.2   (continued)

Variable	(1)	(2)	(3)	(4)
Age squared	−0.005	0.004	−0.006	0.004
	[0.007]	[0.008]	[0.007]	[0.008]
Constant	0.373	0.419	0.341	0.426
	[0.136]***	[0.133]***	[0.133]**	[0.132]***
N	339	339	344	344
R-squared	0.54	0.56	0.54	0.57

Note: Robust standard errors are in brackets. Quality of care is an average of nine discrete variables on questions 1, 2, 10, 11, 12, 13, 14, 15, and 16 in table 7.1, normalized between 0 and 1. Wealth index is a 0 to 1 score. Regressions also include health facility fixed effects.

*p<.10 **p<.05 ***p<.01

Notes

1. Simple correlations indicate that self-reported satisfaction levels are highly correlated with the quality index. These simple correlations are available from the authors upon request.

2. The universe from which the sample is drawn includes all health facilities that offered ART and had at least 100 patients on their waiting list. The sample is representative of these health facilities.

3. We use equal weights in order to avoid assigning arbitrary weights to some questions. The normalization between 0 is for convenience only; it does not influence our findings. The quality index is ordinal in nature, not cardinal.

4. The quality index is different from the vignette score since the former focuses on exit patients and the latter asks questions directly of health care providers (for example, Baltussen and Ye 2006; Das, Hammer, and Leonard 2008; Wouters et al. 2008).

5. A related question that we do not address is whether health facilities that offer HIV/AIDS treatment offer better treatment to HIV/AIDS patients. To the extent that HIV/AIDS treatment is associated with the facility's equipment level, this question would address the allocation of resources at the health sector level, which is beyond the scope of this chapter.

6. In annex 7A, we provide some evidence that these findings are robust to alternative measures of the quality index.

7. The results in table 7.2 show that patients visiting for HIV services are slightly less wealthy, but the difference in wealth is not significant.

8. For instance, it makes sense to ask an HIV patient about "blood in the sputum" to check for opportunistic tuberculosis infection, but it makes no sense to ask this to a patient who has come in with, say, a headache. Therefore, it is not at all surprising that this question is asked more often of HIV patients than non-HIV patients.

9. One potential limitation of this approach is the extent to which patients are able to recall accurately the questions that doctors ask. For our purpose, this may not be a problem if the recall bias is the same for HIV and non-HIV patients, but there might be reason to believe that the measurement error in this case is correlated with the sickness—HIV patients, for instance, may be more distressed and therefore less likely to remember questions accurately.

References

Baltussen, R., and Y. Ye. 2006. "Quality of Care of Modern Health Services as Perceived by Users and Non-Users in Burkina Faso." *International Journal for Quality in Health Care* 18 (1): 30–34.

Banerjee, A. V. 1997. "A Theory of Misgovernance." *Quarterly Journal of Economics* 112 (4): 1289–332.

Chen, L., and P. Hanvoravongchai. 2005. "Editorial: HIV/AIDS and Human Resources." *Bulletin of the WHO* 83: 243–44.

Das, J. and J. Hammer. 2007. "Location, Location, Location: Residence, Wealth, and the Quality of Medical Care in Delhi, India." *Health Affairs* (Millwood) 26(3): w338–51.

Das, J., J. Hammer, and Kenneth Leonard. 2008. "The Quality of Medical Advice in Low-Income Countries." *Journal of Economic Perspectives* 22 (2): 93–114.

Das, J., and T. P. Sohnesen. 2007. "Variations in Doctor Effort: Evidence from Paraguay." *Health Affairs* (Millwood) 26 (3): w324–37.

Fowler, R. A., N. K. Adhikari, and S. Bhagwanjee. 2008. "Clinical Review: Critical Care in the Global Context; Disparities in Burden of Illness, Access, and Economics." *Critical Care* 12 (5): 225.

Mapunjo, S., and D. P. Urassa. 2007. "Quality Standards in Provision of Facility-Based HIV Care and Treatment: A Case Study from Dar es Salaam Region, Tanzania." *East African Journal of Public Health* 4 (1): 12–18.

Marchal, B., V. De Brouwere, and G. Kegels. 2005. "Viewpoint: HIV/AIDS and the Health Workforce Crisis: What Are the Next Steps?" *Tropical Medicine and International Health* 10 (4): 300–04.

Mesfin, M. M., J. N. Newell, J. D. Walley, A. Gessessew, T. Tesfaye, F. Lemma, and R. J. Madeley. 2009. "Quality of Tuberculosis Care and Its Association with Patient Adherence to Treatment in Eight Ethiopian Districts." *Health Policy Plan* 24 (6): 457–66.

O'Donnell, O. 2007. "Access to Health Care in Developing Countries: Breaking Down Demand-Side Barriers." *Cadernos de Saúde Pública* 23 (12): 2820–34.

Schneider, H., D. Blaauw, N. Chabikuli, and J. Goudge. 2006. "Health Systems and Access to Antiretroviral Drugs for HIV in Southern Africa: Service Delivery and Human Resources Challenges." *Reproductive Health Matters* 14 (27): 12–23.

UNAIDS (United Nations HIV/AIDS Program). 2008. "Report on the Global AIDS Epidemic." UNAIDS, Geneva.

——. 2013a. "Fast-Track: Ending the AIDS Epidemic by 2030." UNAIDS, Geneva.

———. 2013b. "Report on the Global AIDS Epidemic." UNAIDS, Geneva.

———. 2014. "The Cities Report (UNAIDS Outlook 2014)." UNAIDS, Geneva. http://www.unaids.org/sites/default/files/media_asset/JC2687_TheCitiesReport_en.pdf.

WHO (World Health Organization). 2015. Global Health Observatory (GHO) data. http://www.who.int/gho/hiv/en/.

Wouters, E., C. Heunis, D. van Rensburg, and H. Meulemans. 2008. "Patient Satisfaction with Antiretroviral Services at Primary Health-Care Facilities in the Free State, South Africa: A Two-Year Study Using Four Waves of Cross-Sectional Data." *BMC Health Services Research* 8 (October 9): 210.

Zere, E., M. Moeti, J. Kirigia, T. Mwase, and E. Kataika. 2007. "Equity in Health and Healthcare in Malawi: Analysis of Trends." *BMC Public Health* 7 (May): 78.

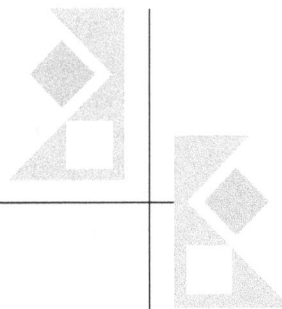

CHAPTER 8

A Portfolio Approach to Evaluation: Evaluations of Community-Based HIV/AIDS Responses

Rosalía Rodriguez-García

Introduction

The new strategy of the World Bank Group, unveiled at the 2013 Annual Meetings on October 12, calls for greater efficiency in operations, while moving definitively from a project mentality to a development solutions culture embedded in sharing knowledge and evidence of what works and how to deliver it. The World Bank Group proposes to transform itself from a "knowledge institution" into a "solutions institution" in order to achieve the goals of ending extreme poverty and promoting shared prosperity.[1] Furthermore, the strategy calls for systematically supporting clients in delivering customized solutions that integrate knowledge and financial services and that encompass the complete cycle from policy design through implementation to evaluation of results (World Bank 2013, 1).

Rosalía Rodriguez-García has retired from the World Bank.

The multistudy evaluation or evaluation portfolio described in this chapter was completed as the new strategy was being shaped.[2] Yet how the evaluation was planned, designed, implemented, and managed fits squarely within the core values of client engagement, knowledge sharing, and evidence building for policy and program applications. This evaluation of the results achieved by community responses to human immunodeficiency virus (HIV)/acquired immune deficiency syndrome (AIDS) includes country-level evaluations in addition to overarching desk studies. The term evaluation portfolio refers to the set of 17 studies conducted as part of the evaluation. Each study in isolation illuminates a slice of the phenomena of interest; taken together, they provide a body of evidence that documents effects that are common to the community response to HIV/AIDS in varying contexts.

The Global Context of Community Engagement in HIV/AIDS

The Millennium Declaration adopted in 2000 produced a historic international compact to improve human development outcomes and achieve the Millennium Development Goals (MDGs). Two MDGs are concerned directly with HIV/AIDS: (1) to halt and begin to reverse the spread of HIV and achieve universal access to treatment and (2) to provide assistance to children orphaned by HIV/AIDS. Three other MDGs are related indirectly to HIV/AIDS: (1) to halve the proportion of persons whose income is less than US$1 a day, (2) to ensure that girls and boys have equal access to all levels of education and complete a full course of primary schooling, and (3) to reduce maternal and under-five child mortality (United Nations 2000).

During the past decade, considerable progress has been made toward reducing poverty and hunger, combating disease and child mortality, promoting gender equality, expanding education, and building global partnerships for development. Many of the achievements, however, have been based on improvements made in national averages, which can hide wide disparities among regions and within countries (Bamberger and Segone 2011). In HIV/AIDS, these disparities hamper progress toward reaching the three zeros—zero new HIV infections, zero discrimination, and zero AIDS-related deaths (UNAIDS 2012)[3]—and pose a significant obstacle to the attainment of decent work and livelihoods for millions of persons living with HIV or affected by the epidemic (ILO 2010, 2012).

Communities were at the forefront of the global response to the spread of HIV/AIDS from the beginning. As the epidemic unfolded, communities organized themselves to care for those in need (UNAIDS 2006). Later, as public hospitals became overwhelmed by the burden of HIV, civil society organizations also took on responsibility for health care (UNAIDS 2006, 209).[4] Since then, civil society organizations and community groups have been instrumental in accessing and empowering marginalized populations and people living with or affected by HIV. Civil society has also contributed to developing innovative approaches to the uptake and delivery of services (UNAIDS 2006). In this evaluation portfolio, we use the term "community response" to encompass the combination of purposeful actions taken by communities and civil society organizations (CSOs) to address HIV/AIDS, including the provision of goods and services.[5]

Civil society groups working on HIV/AIDS have become a rich network of organizations around the world, working along the entire continuum of HIV prevention, care, treatment, and support (Rodriguez-García et al. 2011). In the past decade, some large technical organizations have become major actors in the AIDS response, often delivering substantial services and products to the population—such as distributing condoms, supporting treatment, or providing care, either directly or through smaller organizations in their networks. As a result of their different roles, civil society organizations exist in many forms, ranging from support groups or associations of mainly volunteer workers to larger organizations (Taylor 2010; see box 8.1).

As a result of the increased demand for their services and expansion in their funding, CSOs have become a mainstay of the AIDS response. At this stage, nobody questions that civil society is a vital actor in international development in general and in HIV/AIDS in particular. However, as early as 2005, a review of World Bank assistance for control of HIV/AIDS conducted by the World Bank Independent Evaluation Group (called the Operations Evaluation Department at the time) found results of community-based investments elusive and our understanding of civil society groups wanting (IEG 2005).

The global response to HIV/AIDS has been remarkable. Global resources available for HIV in low- and middle-income countries rose from about US$1.6 billion in 2001 to almost 16 billion by 2009 (UNAIDS 2011a, 30). Funding from domestic public sources in these countries grew by more than 15 percent between 2001 and 2011, supporting more than 50 percent of the global response. Bilateral donors, banks, and philanthropy contributed about 25 percent, and the U.S. government and the Global Fund together accounted for 25 percent of contributions or US$5.5 billion in disbursements (UNAIDS 2012).

The annual funding analysis conducted by the Kaiser Family Foundation and UNAIDS found that donor governments disbursed US$7.86 billion toward the AIDS response in low- and middle-income countries in 2012, essentially unchanged from the US$7.63 billion level in 2011 after adjusting for inflation. Donor government funding for HIV/AIDS has stayed at about the same level since 2008—a plateau that mirrors a similar trend in development assistance more generally, reflecting the economic and fiscal constraints of the post-financial-crisis period (Kaiser Family Foundation 2013). Although the financial landscape has changed in the last five years and funding for HIV/AIDS has reached a plateau, the total amount of resources that are committed and disbursed remains substantial (figure 8.1).

By 2011, more than 8 million people living with HIV were receiving treatment, a 20 percent increase from 2010, reaching more than half of those infected. Of the estimated 1.5 million pregnant women living with HIV in 2011, 57 percent were receiving treatment to prevent mother to child transmission, up from 48 percent in 2010, and 34.2 million people were living with HIV, more than ever before (UNAIDS 2012, 18). The HIV epidemic is shifting from a death sentence to a chronic disease.

This shift in the evolution of the epidemic since the 1980s and 1990s and the many advances in HIV/AIDS prevention, treatment, care, support, and mitigation have given the international community a sense that the MDG of halting new HIV infections is within reach. With this certainty came recognition that this goal cannot be achieved without reaching out to the populations most at risk, who are driving the current phase of the epidemic, and

Figure 8.1 Donor Government Commitments and Disbursements for HIV/AIDS, 2002–12
US$ (billions)

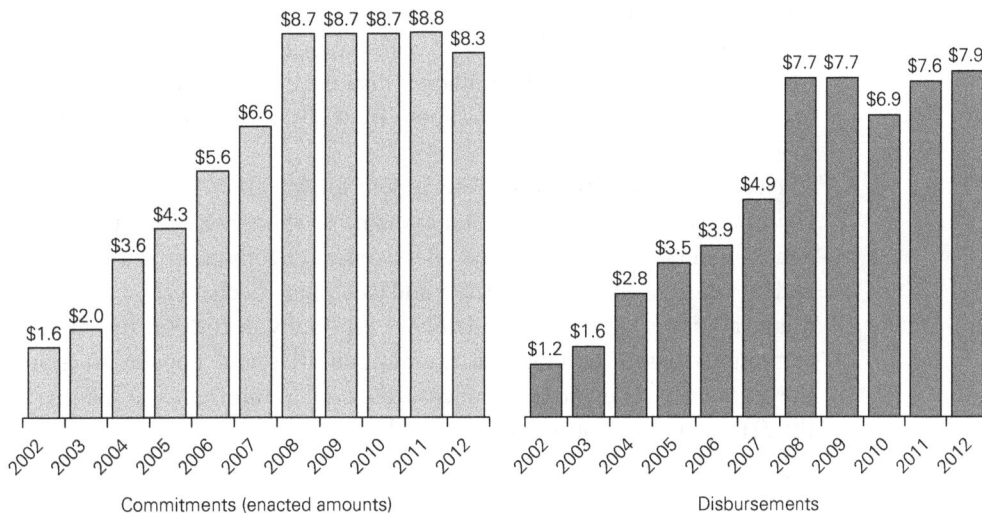

Commitments (enacted amounts)   Disbursements

Source: Kaiser Family Foundation 2013.

those lost to treatment. Community involvement has been identified as a "critical enabler" of an effective HIV/AIDS response; to succeed, communities, civil society, people living with HIV/AIDS (PLWHA), and those affected by the epidemic must be critical partners in these efforts (Schwartlander et al. 2011).

Although communities leverage their own resources, as this evaluation portfolio shows, civil society organizations depend to a great extent on funding from outside their communities. For instance, the CBOs surveyed in Kenya and Nigeria are heavily dependent on direct external funding. In Kenya, funding provided directly by donors to small CBOs amounted to 46 percent of CBO resources. In Nigeria, the corresponding share was 33 percent. In both cases, the dependence on external financing was higher, as some of the funds obtained through national funding channels were also provided by external donors (Bonnel et al. 2013, xiv). A study of 400 CSOs surveyed in Southern Africa shows that spending increased threefold from 2001 to 2006 (Birdsall and Kelly 2007). This means that, in many cases, external funding does reach civil society and community-based organizations.

Globally, this translates into a significant amount of funding for the community response. The financial flows analysis conducted as part of this evaluation portfolio shows that, in total, the four donors most actively involved in the AIDS response—the U.K. Department for International

Development (DFID), the Global Fund, the U.S. President's Emergency Plan for AIDS Relief (PEPFAR), and the World Bank—provided, on average, at least US$690 million a year for CSOs (NGOs, CBOs, and FBOs) during the 2003–09 period (Bonnel et al. 2013, xiii). The Global Fund alone estimates that one-third of the US$910 million it disbursed for HIV, tuberculosis, and malaria from 2002 to 2010 was spent by CSOs, or about US$300 million (Global Fund 2011; see table 8.1).[6]

Needless to say, the level of investment for the HIV/AIDS response and civil society has brought with it a mandate to show results on the ground and to understand the reach and effectiveness of community-based actions and services.[7] Although civil society and CBOs have been receiving increased financial support from major aid donors, especially since 2000, the effects of community-based activities on the communities and population groups they serve have been largely unmeasured, even as international funding for the HIV/AIDS response has been scaled up, partly with the intention of supporting community groups. The relevancy of this portfolio evaluation is

Table 8.1 Summary of Donor Funding of Civil Society Organizations (CSOs)

Donor	Proxy for the funding of community responses to AIDS	Period	Available funding for national AIDS responses per year (US$)	Average funding per year for CSOs (US$)
World Bank	Share of CSO funding in multisectoral AIDS projects applied to all Bank projects for HIV/AIDS	June 2003–December 2010	262 million	100 million (indirect funding)
Global Fund	CSO expenditures	2002–10	910 million	300 million (direct and indirect funding)
PEPFAR (United States)	Estimated funding for nonclinical activities reaching national CSOs	June 2003–December 2010	2.1 billion	230 million (mostly direct funding)
DFID (United Kingdom)	Estimated funds to CSO first-line recipients with AIDS as a major project or significant priority	2004/05–2008/09 (five years)	590 million	60 million (mostly direct funding)
Total		Average in 2004–09	3.8 billion	At least 690 million

Source: Bonnel et al. 2013, 11, using data from the World Bank and Global Fund database and data from the International HIV/AIDS Alliance database for Department for International Development (DFID) and U.S. President's Emergency Plan for AIDS Relief (PEPFAR).

Poverty, Inequality, and Evaluation

reinforced by the fact that community engagement is one of the three or four major pillars in the majority of national HIV/AIDS strategies and response plans.

It is against this backdrop—the need for evidence on the results of investments—that this evaluation of the community response to HIV/AIDS was conceptualized. The evaluation portfolio was implemented from 2009 to 2012 through a partnership between the United Kingdom's DFID and the World Bank, with the U.K. Consortium on AIDS and International Development (U.K. Consortium) as a strategic civil society partner.[8]

The partners acted with autonomy as knowledge brokers and facilitators. They were structurally independent of corporate mandates, as they did not evaluate corporate programs. This partnership met the U.K. Audit Commission criteria (Rodriguez-García 2013, 13),[9] which defines a partnership as a joint working relationship, where the partners:

- Are otherwise independent bodies;
- Agree to cooperate to achieve a common goal;
- Create a new process to achieve this goal;
- Plan and implement a joint program; and
- Share relevant information, risks, and rewards.

Why a "Portfolio Approach"

The study of social issues in real-world situations is complex. With this complexity in mind, the evaluation applied a dual lens, looking at the specific and the collective. At the micro level, it examined the results achieved in specific countries in specific areas; at the macro level, it examined issues with broader applicability such as funding flows. In a "portfolio approach," the specific parts (that is, community evaluations) and the collective components (that is, survey of CBOs in a large global network) intertwine, yielding more and stronger knowledge. In a portfolio approach, the whole is more than the sum of the parts.

The portfolio approach was designed to capture a wide diversity of contexts and processes. This approach also mixed quantitative, qualitative, and financial data to capture and interpret evidence from a range of perspectives to establish statistically and programmatically reliable results (Cook and Seymour 2013). The evaluation portfolio comprised 17 studies, including country-specific evaluations (Burkina Faso, India, Kenya, Lesotho, Nigeria, Senegal, South Africa, and Zimbabwe), secondary analysis of data, desk surveys, and desk studies. Synthesis of the evaluation portfolio enabled evaluators to look across interventions addressing similar issues or themes to identify commonalities or corroborate differences. This approach was relevant, as the evaluation sought to discover the overall effectiveness of broad interventions (Morra Imas and Rist 2009).

Planning and implementation of the evaluation were guided by eight principles:

- *Selectivity*. Be selective; not every single aspect of the phenomenon can be or should be evaluated in every country.
- *Ethics*. Adopt a protocol for each country evaluation that meets the standards of national ethical review boards and addresses issues pertaining to the protection of human subjects, data confidentiality, and informed consent.
- *Methods*. Use a mixed-method approach, keeping the evaluation as rigorous and robust as possible, applied by an interdisciplinary group of researchers and evaluators. In this way the evaluation would benefit from triangulation of methods, sources, evaluators, and analysis.
- *Implementation*. Phase in implementation, allowing time for on-the-road adjustments and paying attention to evaluation management to ensure quality and progress at a reasonable speed.
- *Data*. Analyze existing data if they are current and of high quality. In addition to data mining, collect primary data—quantitative, qualitative, and financial. Conduct synthesis and triangulation analysis.
- *Partnerships*. Establish partnerships and a transparent consultative process with experienced researchers, civil society, and development partners.
- *Local ownership*. Work closely with local AIDS or health authorities, civil society, and engaged local talent. Consult and validate findings with national authorities and stakeholders.
- *Utilization*. Promote purposeful dissemination and apply findings at the institutional, global, and local levels.

The working principles of the evaluation attempted to overcome some of the potential limitations of the evaluation approach. In theory, one could wish to study all aspects of the community response in every country affected by the HIV/AIDS epidemic. In practice, this was not possible—or desirable—as the logistical implications would have been overwhelming. Instead, the chosen approach was to evaluate community responses and community interventions representing different community response typologies. The difficulty involved in evaluating a complex set of activities with various dimensions was another challenge. To address it, the country evaluations relied on a combination of data that sheds light on different aspects of a particular community response. A process of expert review and consultation was instrumental in managing the limitations of the approach.

Objectives

The evaluation sought to document in a robust and rigorous way the results achieved by the community response to HIV/AIDS. Key clusters of questions were asked:

1. Does the flow of funds to communities contribute to the local community response and thereby to the national response to HIV/AIDS?
2. Do community responses result in improved knowledge and behavior?
3. Do community responses result in increased access to and use of services?
4. Do community responses result in observable social transformation?
5. Can these factors combine to decrease HIV incidence and improve HIV/AIDS–related health?

Design and Framework

To address the highly contextual nature of community-level work, the evaluation used a mixed-method, multiple-country approach, while preserving the rigor of the exercise. The mixed-method design of the evaluation portfolio was guided by the program theory of change. The term "theory of change" describes the set of assumptions that explain both the small steps that lead to long-term goals and the connections between program activities and outcomes that occur at each step of the way (Weiss 1995). Weiss hypothesizes that a key reason why complex programs are so difficult to evaluate is that the assumptions that inspire them are poorly articulated. She argues that the stakeholders of complex community initiatives typically are unclear about how the change process will unfold and therefore give little attention to the early and mid-term changes that need to happen in order to reach a longer-term goal. Operational definitions are summarized in box 8.2.

Program theories of change are often represented graphically through a logic model. The results logic model is widely used because "it is the simplest and clearest model to outline the theory of change in the operational context of development programs" (Gertler et al. 2011, 25). Figure 8.2 presents a simplified linear logic model describing a pathway from community inputs toward HIV/AIDS impacts at the macro level. It lays out the sequence of outcomes that are hypothesized to occur as the result of the community response to HIV/AIDS.

Figure 8.2 summarizes a much more complex pathway of the assumed relationships from inputs to impacts. Given the complex reality within which HIV/AIDS programs operate, a program theory of change in the context of

Box 8.2 Operational Definitions

Communities can be described as sharing:

- *A cultural identity* (a group that shares common characteristics or interests). For example, a group could include people living with HIV, men who have sex with men, and sex workers.
- *A geographic sense of place* (a group in a location or an administrative entity). For instance, a community can be defined as a collection of household units brought together by common interests or made up of a certain number of units (that is, in Kenya, at least 5,000 people or 100 households) living in the same geographic area.

The *community response* refers to the combination of actions and steps taken by communities, including the provision of goods and services, to prevent or address a problem to bring about social change. Community responses can be characterized by (a) types and structures of implementing organizations; (b) types of implemented activities or services and beneficiaries; (c) actors involved in and driving the response; (d) contextual factors influencing the response; (e) the extent of community involvement in the response; and (f) the extent of wider partnerships and collaborative efforts.

Social transformation is defined as the process by which society, organizations, and individual change happens, such as changes in behaviors or cultural norms and perceptions as a direct or indirect result of community action.

Civil society refers to a wide variety of organizations, including community-based, nongovernmental, and faith-based organizations, academia, think tanks, trade unions, women's groups, and others.

Source: Rodriguez-García et al. 2011.

this research provides only broad parameters for understanding the expected results. One key reason is that "complex interventions present the greatest challenge for research and for the utilization of findings because the path to success is so variable and it cannot be articulated in advance" (Rogers 2008, 31). Accordingly, the causal-logic theory of change was specified further for each site evaluation.

A logic model usually includes three main components: program cycle, contextual factors, and sociocultural characteristics (Bamberger and Segone 2011). All of these components were considered in the design of the evaluation and the analysis of findings, although figure 8.2 shows five fundamental stages in the program cycle in more detail (box 8.3).

Figure 8.2   A Logic Model of the Program Theory of Change: Linking Community Response Inputs to HIV/AIDS–Related Impacts

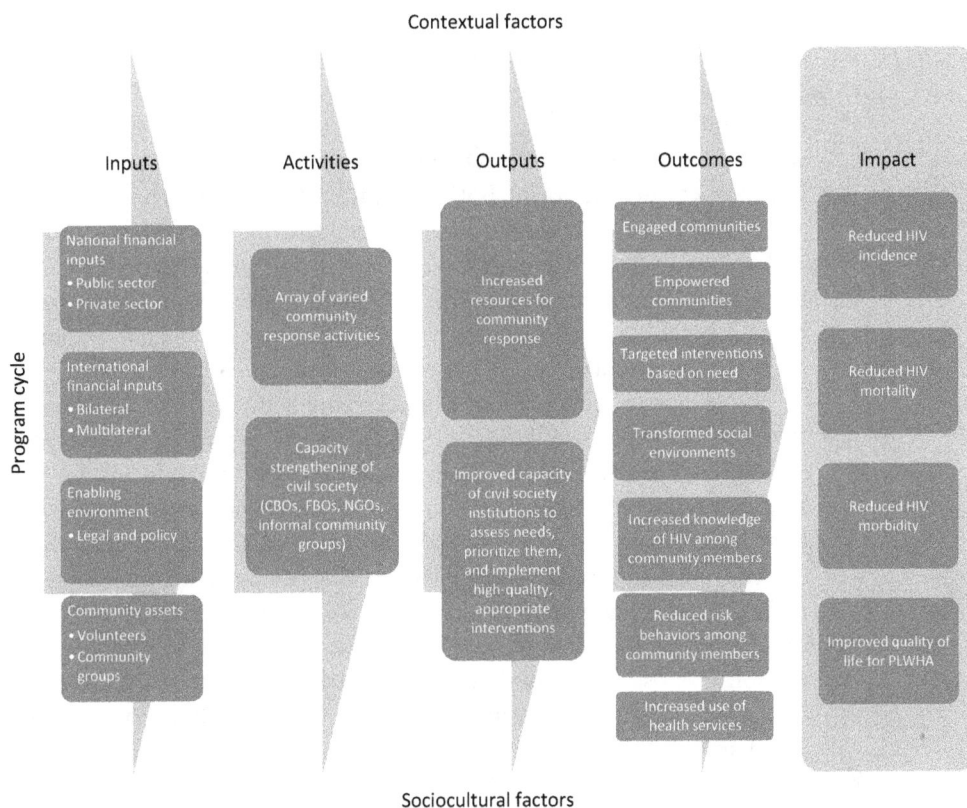

Contextual factors

| Inputs | Activities | Outputs | Outcomes | Impact |

Sociocultural factors

Source: Adapted from Rodriguez-García, Bonnel, et al. 2013, 111.

Note: CBO = community-based organization; FBO = faith-based organization; NGO = nongovernmental organization; PLWHA = people living with HIV/AIDS.

Box 8.3   Three Main Components of a Logic Model

- The major *phases in the program cycle*—inputs, processes, outputs, outcomes (shorter-term and longer-term outcomes) and impacts—that define the major social protection elements at each stage
- The *contextual factors* (sociopolitical, economic, institutional or operational, and the natural environment) that affect implementation
- The *sociocultural characteristics* of the target populations (people living with HIV/AIDS) that affect implementation and outcomes

Source: Adapted from Bamberger and Segone 2011, 43–44.

Methodology: A Mixed-Method Approach

Traditionally, the term "mixed methods" has referred to combining quantitative and qualitative data to answer evaluation questions. Two primary schools of thought provide different—albeit, complementary—views of the mixed-method approach. For some, mixed method is a sort of research in which the investigator collects and analyzes data, integrates the findings, and draws inferences using both qualitative and quantitative approaches and methods in a single study or program of inquiry (Tashakkori and Teddlie 2010). For others, mixed method is a form of inquiry that looks more broadly at the social world, in which multiple ways of observing and making sense of phenomena and multiple views of what is important coexist (Greene 2007).

The evaluation portfolio combined and applied these views and went a step further by also using different designs to answer specific questions in diverse contexts (table 8.2). Thus the design and methodology for each study varied across countries as a function of the specific research questions to be studied and the context. Some studies used an experimental design (for example, randomized control trial) with individual, household, or community randomization. Some studies were quasi-experimental, using repeated cross-sectional surveys and matching methods to establish comparison groups. The experimental and quasi-experimental studies used robust methods for establishing a "counterfactual" asking, "What would have happened to a similar group of people in the absence of the community intervention?"

Two studies applied secondary analysis. One analyzed recent Demographic Health Survey (DHS) data (Lesotho), and another analyzed new data for an in-depth state-level analysis (Nigeria). In addition, there were two systematic reviews of evidence—one on orphans and vulnerable children and one on a typology of community responses and an analysis of cost structure of CBO budgets—plus two cross-cutting studies on financial flows (data collected from donors and from CBOs through a global survey). Desk studies reviewed existing documentation as well as new survey data to inform and complement the country evaluations. Using several methods mitigated the limitations of any particular method, and each method provided more value when used in a mixed-method approach, yielding information that is more coherent, reliable, and useful than is provided in single-method studies (Adato 2012).

Experimental designs are generally viewed as the most rigorous method in sciences. By randomly allocating the interventions among

Table 8.2 Evaluation Portfolio: Focus and Methodologies by Study

Country evaluation	Focus	Method of analysis	Collection of primary data
Burkina Faso	Impact of community prevention activities on knowledge, prevention behavior, and stigma	Quasi-experimental: exposure to a national program as an instrumental variable for community group participation	Yes
India (Karnataka)	Impact of mobilization and empowerment among female sex workers on reduced risk and vulnerability	Quasi-experimental and qualitative: propensity score matching, multivariate logistic regression, and case studies	Yes
India (Andhra Pradesh)	Impact of community collectivization among female sex workers and high-risk men (men who have sex with men and transgender individuals) on behaviors such as condom use and treatment of sexually transmitted infections	Multivariate regression, computation of odds ratios	Yes
Kenya	Funding and activities of CBOs and the impact of strong community response on knowledge, behavior, and service uptake	Quasi-experimental quantitative and qualitative: cluster propensity score matching and key informant interviews	Yes
Kenya (home-based counseling and testing)	Ability to implement home-based testing in the presence of stigma and impact of testing effort on community leader and member stigma	Randomized control trial	Yes
Lesotho	Relationship between HIV/AIDS stigma and preventive behaviors: uptake of services and testing	Multivariate analysis with linear regression; probit model	No
Nigeria	Funding and activities of CBOs and the impact of strong community response on knowledge, behavior, and service uptake	Quasi-experimental quantitative and qualitative: cluster propensity score matching and key informant interviews	Yes
Nigeria	State-level secondary analysis to understand funding and activities of CBOs and evaluate the impact of strong community response on knowledge, behavior, and service uptake	Multivariate regression	No

(continued)

Table 8.2 (continued)

Country evaluation	Focus	Method of analysis	Collection of primary data
Senegal	Impact of social mobilization on counseling and testing uptake (comparing peer mentoring to traditional sensitization)	Randomized control trial	Yes
South Africa	Impact of peer support and nutrition supplementation on treatment adherence	Randomized control trial	Yes
Zimbabwe	Impact of grassroots community group membership on behavior, service use, and HIV incidence	Longitudinal prospective data from biomedical and behavioral surveys with statistical associations likely to be causal	Yes
Zimbabwe	Impact of social spaces and social networks in HIV outcomes	Meta-qualitative analysis	Yes
Studies			
Typology of community response		Desk study	No
Cost structure of CBO budgets in Kenya		Field study	No
Funding mechanisms		Survey and desk study	Yes
Orphans and vulnerable children		Systematic review	No
CBO resources and expenditures in Kenya, Nigeria, and Zimbabwe		Field study	Yes

Source: Rodriguez-García, Wilson, et al. 2013, S10.

Note: CBO = community-based organization.

beneficiaries, this method creates comparable treatment and provides for control groups that allow the identification of causal factors.[10] This design was applied in Kenya to assess the impact of home-based counseling and testing, in Senegal to evaluate the effects of different sensitization techniques for HIV counseling and testing, and in South Africa to evaluate the impact of peer support in adherence to a schedule of clinic visits for antiretroviral treatment.

Quasi-experimental designs were applied in seven country studies: Burkina Faso, India (two studies), Kenya, Nigeria (two studies), and Zimbabwe. A limitation of quasi-experimental methods is that they can confirm an association, but they cannot establish statistical causality between an intervention and its effects. However, they offer the major advantage of being able to evaluate broad programs rather than only specific program components.

To overcome the limitations of quasi-experimental studies, the country evaluations included comparison groups and randomly selected households within communities. The selection of communities was based on criteria. The "community study groups" were determined by "intensity"—that is, the number of CBOs per 100,000 population. The evaluations were designed so that the same intervention or activities would be evaluated in several sites. This allowed the evaluations to reach a somewhat stronger conclusion. When an intervention in one site was found to be associated with a similar outcome in another site, there was a stronger likelihood that the association was not purely coincidental.

Additional information on the community response was provided by *qualitative studies and analysis of CBO budgets*. In Kenya and Nigeria, the evaluations included four components: (a) a household survey, (b) in-depth interviews with CBO staff members and key informants from community groups, (c) in-depth interviews with key informants in study communities, and (d) funding allocation data collected from CBOs. In Zimbabwe, two in-depth qualitative analyses of community responses, including the role of social networks, provided information on the pathways through which behavioral changes were taking place. In India, a background study reported the process by which communities of female sex workers (FSWs) and men that have sex with men and transgender individuals (MSM/Ts) became empowered, leading to improved HIV/AIDS–related health outcomes. Additional information on the resources mobilized by CBOs came from a three-country analysis of funding flows and resource allocation in Kenya, Nigeria, and Zimbabwe.

In this type of mixed-method approach, the weakness of one method or design is offset by the strengths of another, thereby supporting the corroboration of findings, enhancing the integrity of the findings, and improving the breadth and depth of our understanding of the social world in which the community response takes place. In this evaluation portfolio, the mixed-method rationale reflects both a philosophy and a research design orientation.

A common limitation of previous analyses of community-based programs has been their project-only orientation and their small sample size. To ensure that the results are robust, the studies used as large a sample as possible, taking into consideration the method selected, the size of the population of interest, the desired level of confidence, and the desired level of precision, as recommended by Morra Imas and Rist (2009, 364; see table 8.3).

Table 8.3 Sample Sizes in the Evaluation Portfolio

Country	Survey sample size
Burkina Faso	44,417 individuals from 8,496 households (nationally representative data from the 2007 Questionnaire on Basic Welfare Indicators)
India (Karnataka)	6,449 = 1,750 FSWs (2010 Behavioral Tracking Survey) and 4,699 FSWs (2005, 2009 Integrated Behavioral and Biological Assessment)
India (Andhra Pradesh)	7,103 = 3,557 FSWs and 3,546 MSM/Ts in five districts (2010–11 cross-sectional survey, Behavioral Tracking Survey)
Kenya	4,378 individuals from 2,715 randomly selected households in 14 communities
Kenya (home-based counseling and testing)	2,700 randomly selected households in 35 randomly selected sites
Lesotho	20,833 = 14,719 women and 6,114 men (nationally representative data of men and women of reproductive age from 2004, 2009 Lesotho DHS)
Nigeria	5,376 randomly selected households in 28 communities
Senegal	156,178 HIV tests over 15 months in 52 health districts
South Africa	648 PLWHA (four groups of 216 randomly selected individuals on antiretroviral therapy)
Zimbabwe	16,280 = 9,600 women and 6,680 men (four rounds with 2,400 women and 1,670 men each) in 200 communities
Zimbabwe (qualitative study)	553 informants; 168 in-depth interviews; 60 focus groups
Kenya, Nigeria, Zimbabwe	126 CBOs or NGOs; field survey for funding analysis
Southern Africa	400 CSOs; secondary analysis
Global survey	146 CSOs; electronic survey for funding analysis

Source: Adapted from Rodriguez-García, Bonnel, et al. 2013, 110.

Notes: CBO = community-based organization; CSO = civil society organization; DHS = Demographic and Health Survey; FSW = female sex worker; MSM/T = men who have sex with men and transgender individual; NGO = nongovernmental organization; PLWHA = people living with HIV/AIDS.

Implementing the Evaluation Portfolio: A Phase-in Approach

The evaluation portfolio was implemented by a core team aiming at quality assurance, efficiency, and accountability. The design of the evaluation involved several phases. In the first stage (2008), the overall concept note was reviewed through a broad process of stakeholder consultation involving national experts, development partners, and civil society. The design of the evaluation was further revised in 2009 during the second phase, focusing on individual country-level evaluations and the preparation of an evaluation protocol, which was informed by several desk studies. Country-level evaluations started in 2010 and continued throughout 2011 until mid-2012. Desk studies were conducted, and data were triangulated with the country evaluations as available (figure 8.3).

Figure 8.3   Design and Implementation of the Evaluation, 2008–13

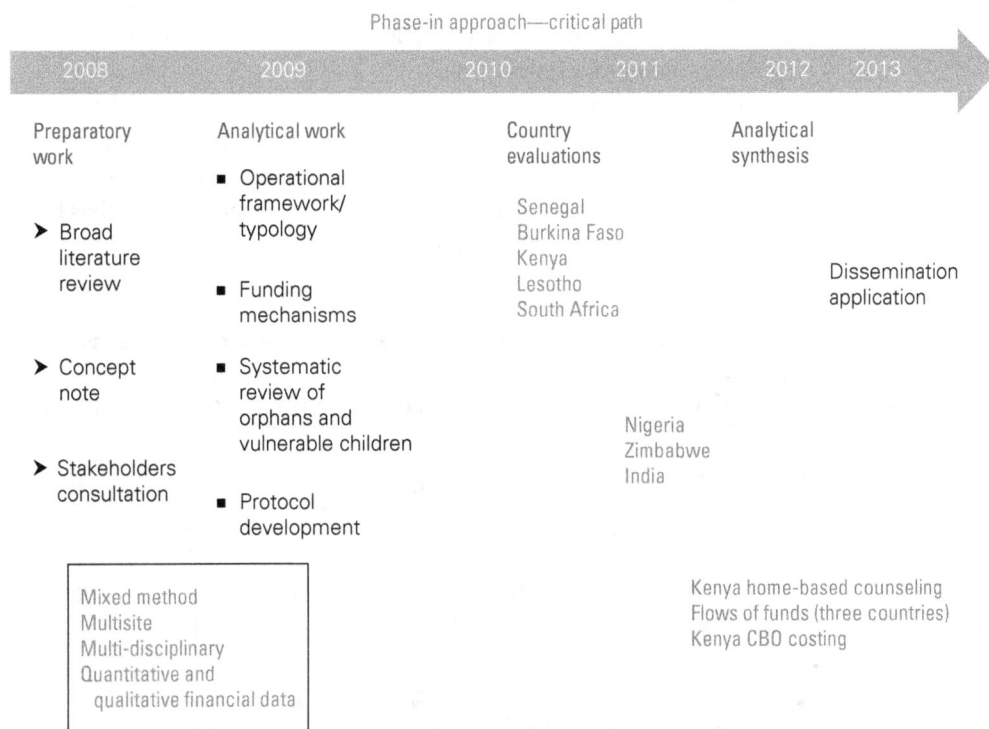

Phase-in approach—critical path

2008   2009   2010   2011   2012   2013

Preparatory work

➤ Broad literature review

➤ Concept note

➤ Stakeholders consultation

Analytical work

- Operational framework/ typology

- Funding mechanisms

- Systematic review of orphans and vulnerable children

- Protocol development

Country evaluations

Senegal
Burkina Faso
Kenya
Lesotho
South Africa

Nigeria
Zimbabwe
India

Analytical synthesis

Dissemination application

Mixed method
Multisite
Multi-disciplinary
Quantitative and
   qualitative financial data

Kenya home-based counseling
Flows of funds (three countries)
Kenya CBO costing

Sources: Rodriguez-García 2013, 13; Rodriguez-García, Bonnel, et al. 2013, 107; Rodriguez-García, Wilson, et al. 2013, S9.
Note: CBO = community-based organization.

Validation and information sharing began at the local and country levels as soon as the findings of the first studies and evaluations were available in 2011. This approach created a stream of knowledge at the national and global levels that informed the response to HIV/AIDS well before the end of the overall exercise. The overall synthesis of the evaluation portfolio was completed in late 2012.

Overview of Findings

Dimensions and Funding of the Community Response

To capture the diversity of communities, the country evaluations looked at different types of entities. In Burkina Faso, the focus was on households (*geographic* communities). In India, two evaluations focused on communities of FSWs and MSM/Ts (*identity* communities). In Zimbabwe, the focus was on grassroots organizations (rotating credit clubs, farmers' associations, youth clubs, and so on) that constituted different communities. In Kenya and Nigeria, the evaluation looked at CBO activities in their catchment areas (*geographic* communities; table 8.4).

Community groups and community-based organizations tend to originate within communities and work in the communities they represent. They reflect local ways of forming groups and interacting with local leaders, and they draw on local resources. Community group membership has been found to be associated with reduced stigma, improved access to some

Table 8.4   Dimensions of the Community Response Analyzed in the Country Evaluations

Dimension	Burkina Faso	Kenya HBCT	India	Kenya, Nigeria	Lesotho	Senegal	South Africa	Zimbabwe
Most informal								
Households	●				●			
Community initiatives		●	●				●	●
CBOs, FBOs			●	●		●		●
NGOs		●						
Most formal								

Source: Rodriguez-García, Bonnel, et al. 2013, 31.

Note: CBO = community-based organization; FBO = faith-based organization; HBCT = home-based counseling and testing; NGO = nongovernmental organization.

Table 8.5 Community Groups in Manicaland, Eastern Zimbabwe

Group	Description
Church group	Members from the same congregation meet outside of regular church worship times. They engage in Bible study, discuss marital issues, and participate in community outreach, particularly helping families in need (such as those with sick members or orphans).
HIV/AIDS group	This loose term applies to a variety of groups, including post-HIV-test clubs (mostly people living with HIV/AIDS), HIV-ART support groups (often organized by clinics), youth groups, peer education groups, home-based care groups (members go house to house, helping families with sick relatives, doing chores, bathing the sick, and sometimes collecting pills from the clinic).
Burial society	Members contribute small sums of money to a central fund to cover basic funeral expenses for themselves and other members. Members commit to organizing proper burials for one another and often sing at funerals. They generally meet monthly.
Rotating credit society	Members contribute to a central fund and, when they reach a certain amount, the money is shared for income-generating projects, such as buying seeds. Members borrow at the same interest rate, and loans can be made to nonmembers at a higher rate.
Women's group	The group is generally linked to government women's empowerment initiatives and is supported by government income-generating grants.
Sports group	Clubs are generally all-male. They organize tournaments, generally soccer, against other regions.
Youth group	Groups are often organized by political parties or teachers. They seek to develop leadership skills and provide recreation for youth (often into their 20s—the end of youth, which is often determined by age of marriage)
Cooperative	Cooperatives are becoming less common in the region. They are generally linked to income generation.
Farmers' group	Farmers, both male and female, meet monthly to plan crops, discuss weather patterns and new technologies, share labor, and access nongovernmental organization assistance (for example, a beekeeping group).

Source: Campbell et al. 2013, S115.

Note: ART = antiretroviral therapy.

services, and even decreased HIV incidence, particularly among women (Campbell et al. 2013). Table 8.5 shows the variety of community groups found in Zimbabwe.

CBOs are typically small and rely heavily on volunteers to fulfill their mission or to deliver services (table 8.6). More often than not, volunteers are a critical resource without which many of the observed community-based results could not have been produced. In contrast, NGOs and FBOs may deliver various services to local communities as implementers of donor- or government-funded programs. They are usually larger than CBOs and have

Table 8.6 Value of Unpaid Volunteers as a Percentage of CBO or NGO Budgets in Kenya, Nigeria, and Zimbabwe

Indicator of value	Kenya	Nigeria	Zimbabwe
Number of volunteers per CBO or NGO	21	58	196
Value of unpaid volunteers' free labor as a % of CBO or NGO budgets	40	48	69

Source: Rodriguez-García, Wilson, et al. 2013, S12, using data from Krivelyova et al. 2013, S20–29.
Note: CBO = community-based organization; NGO = nongovernmental organization.

a more formal institutional structure that helps them to meet the fiduciary, reporting, and monitoring requirements of their funders. An average CBO in the sample (n = 126) received annually US$10,300 in Kenya and US$16,300 in Nigeria, compared to US$72,100 in Zimbabwe. A plausible explanation for this difference is that CBOs in Zimbabwe tend to be larger than CBOs in the other countries and perhaps better able to mobilize resources. About 69 percent of total funds reported by the sampled CBOs came from international sources, one-third of which was from multilateral organizations (Krivelyova et al. 2013).

Highlights

The evaluation of the community response to HIV/AIDS found that communities can be effective in addressing the HIV epidemic by improving their knowledge, increasing their access to and use of services, decreasing risky behaviors, supporting social transformation, and improving health outcomes by decreasing the incidence of sexually transmitted infections (STIs; see box 8.4).

Impact on Knowledge: Systematic and Targeted Community-Level Activities Can Increase Knowledge

In Kenya's Western and Nyanza provinces, the evaluation found that systematic outreach programs targeted to specific population groups and public meeting places increased HIV knowledge. Community members in the study communities had almost 15 times higher odds than respondents in the comparison communities of knowing that using a condom reduces the chance of becoming infected with HIV (odds ratio [OR] = 14.67; 95 percent confidence interval [CI] = 10.58–20.35), and more than 9 times higher odds of knowing that having one uninfected partner reduces the chances of HIV transmission (OR = 9.26; 95 percent CI = 5.29–16.22; Riehman et al. 2013).

In Senegal, well-targeted community activities had an impact. There is causal evidence that peer support resulted in an increase of 80 percent uptake of HIV testing and an increase of 110 percent pickup of test results as compared to traditional community activities providing general HIV/AIDS information (Arcand et al. 2010).

Since the beginning of the epidemic, nearly all countries have used some form of mass communication to increase knowledge. Invariably, CBOs mentioned increasing the level of awareness and knowledge as their main achievement. The traditional approach to broad types of informational activities was perhaps needed more in the earlier period of the epidemic. As general knowledge of HIV/AIDS became more widespread, targeted interventions became more likely to achieve results, whether to introduce a new program, scale up an existing one, or generate demand for specific services.

From Knowledge to Risk Reduction: Empowerment, Intensity of Community Mobilization, and Regular Participation in Community Groups Can Change Social Norms That Influence Behavior

Standard behavioral interventions are often based on models of cognitive behavior that assume that people will change their behavior if they are fully informed. Yet there are many examples of countries where, despite high knowledge about HIV, little behavioral change has taken place. In such contexts, empowerment, strong community mobilization, and involvement in community groups may provide the levers for changing the norms and social values that influence individual behavior.

In India, two studies carried out for this evaluation portfolio—one in Karnataka and one in Andhra Pradesh—found evidence that empowerment of groups at high risk of infection, such as female sex workers and men who have sex with men and transgender individuals, produced positive results. In Karnataka, peer group membership was associated with reduced HIV-related risk and vulnerability among FSWs (Bhattacharjee et al. 2013). In Andhra Pradesh, peer group membership was associated with consistent use of condoms with occasional clients (adjusted odds ratio [aOR] = 1.3; 95 percent CI = 1.1–1.7) and with regular clients (aOR = 1.4; 95 percent CI = 1.1–1.9). Among MSM/Ts, participation in community events was associated with consistent use of condoms with paying partners (aOR = 3.3; 95 percent CI = 2.1–5.2) and nonpaying partners (aOR = 2.7; 95 percent CI = 2.0–3.6; Saggurti et al. 2013).

The evaluation in Zimbabwe showed that community group membership can have strong protective effects, provided that (a) groups actively and frequently discuss HIV/AIDS–related issues and that (b) there is strong interpersonal communication about AIDS-related deaths or personal experiences. An analysis based on a longitudinal study of community groups in the region of Matabeleland, Zimbabwe, which started in 1998, revealed that the community response to HIV, in the form of widespread female participation in community groups, appears to have played an important part in Zimbabwe's HIV decline. In the 1990s–2000s period, women who were community group members were quicker to adopt safer sexual behavior and experienced a lower rate of infection than other women. Although women who participate in community groups are significantly more likely to reduce their risky behavior, the impact for men is much smaller (Gregson et al. 2013).

The effects of the community response on behaviors, although weaker, were also found in Burkina Faso, Kenya, and Nigeria. In Kenya, study group respondents had four times higher odds of reporting consistent condom use with all sex partners in the last 12 months (OR = 4.09; 95 percent CI = 1.74–9.19; see Riehman et al. 2013, 67–77) and in Burkina Faso, condom use with one partner or the second one was twice as high for those who attended community prevention activities (Rodriguez-García, Bonnel, et al. 2013, 67–71).

These results notwithstanding, the effects of the community response, although statistically significant in terms of the protective effects of group membership, cannot be guaranteed. Effects in Zimbabwe, for instance, differed across groups, between men and women, and over time: group participation was more effective in the earlier stage of the epidemic (1998–2003) than later (2003–08) and among women than men. Fewer men than women participated in community groups, which points toward the need for interventions that focus on men in HIV prevention programs.

From Behavioral Change to Utilization of Services: The Community Response Can Increase the Demand for Services among Groups at High Risk of Infection, among Women, and in Rural Areas

In Andhra Pradesh, India, the prevalence of HIV and sexually transmitted infections is high among FSWs. This evaluation found that the proportion of FSWs and MSM/Ts who reported visiting a government health facility for STI treatment was significantly higher among those with a medium level of collectivization (measured by participation in community public events) than among those with a low level of collectivization. The proportion of FSWs visiting a health care facility rose from 42.4 to 60.4 percent. MSM/Ts who participated in any community public event were significantly more likely to report the use of services from government health facilities than those who did not participate (59 versus 38 percent; aOR = 2.5; 95 percent CI = 2.0–3.1; see Saggurti et al. 2013, S63). FSWs who reported high levels of collective efficacy (measured by a belief in their power to achieve change) were more likely to report seeking STI treatment from government health facilities (59.8 versus 32.1 percent; aOR = 3.3; 95 percent CI = 2.1–5.1; Saggurti et al. 2013, S59).

Positive effects of community response on access to and use of services were observed in Nigeria, although only in rural areas. CBOs were involved in providing a variety of services: treatment (antiretroviral therapy and treatment of opportunistic infections), care (home-based care and home visits), and support (financial, material, and psychological support). The effects of CBO engagement were most noticeable in rural areas: an increase of 1 in the number of CBOs per 100,000 people was associated with a twofold increase in the odds of reporting the use of prevention services in rural areas and a 64 percent increase in the odds of reporting access to treatment. This finding was stronger in rural communities, where 44 percent were aware of any service, 48 percent were aware of prevention services, and 31 percent were aware of treatment services, compared to 19, 26, and 16 percent, respectively, in urban communities (Kakietek et al. 2013, S81).

The evaluation portfolio also found that broad community involvement (members but also leaders) in HIV/AIDS programs can increase the demand for services and overcome the adverse effects of stigma (causal relation). In Kenya, the evaluation of a community-wide, home-based counseling and testing (HBCT) campaign found that large-scale HIV testing can be implemented successfully in the presence of stigma, most likely because of its "whole community approach." By avoiding the need for individuals to single themselves out to seek testing, HBCT can blunt the impact of stigma on testing uptake. As a result, HBCT increased the probability of being tested for HIV by about 70 percent for individuals who were initially living in one of the treatment locations. Furthermore, HBCT reached people who had never had an HIV test: the percentage of people who were tested rose from 64 percent in the control groups to 95 percent in the treatment areas, a 31 percentage point gain, and no negative relationship was found between reported stigma and levels of testing (Low et al. 2013, S100).

Often, blocks to health services use are related to the lack of adequate supply of services, legal environment, and stigma. For instance, in Benin a program analysis of HIV/AIDS interventions for sex workers underscored the importance of effective implementation of STI services, which by 2006 had resulted in an increase in consistent condom use by FSWs from 39 to 86.2 percent and a decline in gonorrhea prevalence from 5.4 to 1.6 percent. However, subsequently, decreases in resources resulted in a decrease in the coverage of community-based services and lack of commodities such as condoms for sex workers. This reversed some of the previous gains (Semini et al. 2013).

The legal environment affects mostly FSWs, MSM/Ts, and drug users. For instance, sex work is not criminalized in India, and there are legal bases on which to fight abuse and discrimination of sex workers. The challenges of a discriminatory legal environment are compounded by stigma. In many countries, stigma represents a significant barrier to service access and uptake for PLWHA in general and sex workers and MSM/Ts in particular, as seen in India and Lesotho. In India, the perception among MSM/Ts that they are stigmatized by health providers hampered their use of health facilities. In Lesotho, the evaluation found a decline in stigmatizing attitudes among men and women between 2004 and 2009; however, stigma remains, being negatively associated with education, wealth, and age, but positively associated with Catholic religion for women and traditional circumcision for men (Corno and deWalque 2013).

These findings are supported by other studies. Evidence from the People Living with HIV Stigma Index (PSI)[11] found that in Rwanda 53 percent of people living with HIV who participated in the study had been verbally abused and 33 percent of Zambian, 20 percent of Rwandese, and 25 percent of Colombian study respondents had experienced physical violence (UNAIDS 2012). Data from the 2011 PSI in the Asia-Pacific region on loss of employment found that in the nine countries stigma and discrimination were the key factor—or had played a part—in respondents' loss of employment or income (16–50 percent) and lack of opportunity to work (9–38 percent; UNAIDS 2011b).

These findings point to the potential role that FBOs and CBOs can play in developing innovative strategies to break the barriers that prevent people living with HIV/AIDS and vulnerable populations from accessing health services. There is also need to raise awareness among FSWs and MSM/Ts that STIs are often asymptomatic and that they need to access and use health services.

Positive factors in the use of health services are mentoring and peer support. This was found in the case of both peer mentoring for home-based care and treatment in Senegal and peer support for adherence to antiretroviral treatment in South Africa. In Senegal, the evaluation found strong causal evidence that, when compared to unfunded traditional social mobilization activities, peer mentoring doubled the number of individuals attending pre-HIV test counseling and those being tested. Mentoring also increased the number of individuals receiving their test results—by about 120 percent ($p < .1$; Arcand et al. 2010). In addition, peer mentoring was effective in changing the behavior of individuals who tested positive. The number of HIV-positive individuals whose partners were tested ($p < .1$) rose by about 60 percent compared to traditional sensitization activities.

There is also evidence that peer support increases the timeliness of scheduled hospital visits for antiretroviral treatment in Free State, South Africa. Antiretroviral therapy clients who were visited twice weekly at their homes by a peer had statistically significant shorter delays in their scheduled clinic visits than those who did not receive such peer support (−15.8 days; $p < .05$; 95 percent CI = 2.4–29.1; Rodriguez-García, Bonnel, et al. 2013, 122).

From Use of Services to Better Health Outcomes: Empowerment of FSWs and Community Group Membership Can Improve Biological Outcomes

One of the most desired impacts of community responses are those that show statistically significant biological outcomes. The evaluation portfolio found this impact in two different epidemiological settings. The study in Karnataka, India, found that community group membership compared to nonmembership was associated with lower prevalence of STIs among FSWs: chlamydia and gonorrhea (5.2 versus 9.6 percent; $p < .001$) and syphilis (8.2 versus 10.3 percent; $p < .05$; Bhattacharjee et al. 2013).

There was less evidence that community group membership affected HIV prevalence among FSWs. HIV prevalence was lower among FSWs who were community group members, but the difference was not statistically significant. This may reflect, in part, the composition of the group of FSWs in Karnataka. Most of the women in the survey had been sex workers for some time, and infection might have occurred earlier with their initiation into sex work. Unless FSWs become members of an empowered or empowering group soon after they begin sex work, the social mobilization of FSWs may not translate rapidly into lower HIV prevalence among them. However, social mobilization would still protect the broader population as a result of the increased use of condoms.

Zimbabwe is one of the few Sub-Saharan African countries for which there is compelling evidence of a sustained decline in HIV prevalence driven by lower levels of risky behavior (Gregson et al. 2010). This has been attributed to changes in sexual behavior as a result of individuals' personal observation of AIDS-related deaths and interpersonal communications about HIV/AIDS, which played a key role in transmitting information (Halperin et al. 2011). Evidence from this evaluation suggests that group membership, specifically, played an important role in the decline of national HIV prevalence by creating opportunities for critical dialogue about HIV/AIDS (Campbell et al. 2013). Participation in a community group was associated with reduced HIV incidence for women (aIRR = 0.64; 95 percent CI = 0.43–0.94) during the period 1998–2003 (Gregson et al. 2011). These findings suggest that (a) a dose effect was in play for the decline in HIV incidence in the 1998–2003 period, when the response to HIV/AIDS was strong, but (b) the effect of group membership disappeared in the subsequent period (2003–08; Halperin et al. 2011; Gregson et al. 2013). Thus the link between community efforts and HIV incidence is inconclusive.

From Community Response to Social Changes: The Community Response Can Foster Social Changes, but These Are Affected by Gender and a Country's Policies

The community response can foster social changes among groups that are severely affected by the HIV epidemic. In India, for instance, the evaluation found a strong association between empowerment of FSWs and MSM/Ts and social change. Being a member of a sex worker community group in Karnataka was associated with access to social entitlements such as receiving one identification document (67.7 versus 61.6 percent; $p < .05$), reduced violence (19.7 versus 28.2 percent; $p < .001$), and reduced police coercion (88.5 versus 82.3 percent; $p < .001$; Bhattacharjee et al. 2013).

However, the effects of community programs are gender sensitive, supporting the need to implement different types of programs for men and women. Examples include the following: prevention programs in Burkina Faso affect men and women differently with regard to knowledge of HIV, awareness of antiretroviral treatment, and stigma toward infected persons. In Senegal, peer mentoring had strong effects on men's HIV testing and counseling, while standard forms of community mobilization were more effective for women. In Zimbabwe, group membership was found to be more beneficial for women than for men.

The country's context and government policies toward commercial sex work and men who have sex with men can make great differences. In India, sex work is illegal, but it is not a criminal offense. This opened the door to a dialogue with the police, which resulted in less police violence. In contrast, stigma attached to MSM/Ts and the existence of a repressive environment generally prevented MSM/Ts from accessing health services. In Kenya, key informants perceived declines in violence against women as linked primarily to changes in national policies (such as the introduction of free primary education and the adoption of legislation protecting women from violence). In Nigeria, increased awareness, social consequences for the perpetrators, and the influence of government, NGOs, and other local organizations were often cited as reasons for the decline in domestic violence.

Discussion of Findings and Implications

The evaluation portfolio found that community responses can increase knowledge, change behaviors, increase the demand for and uptake of health services among groups at high risk of infection, and affect STI incidence. Dedicated support from community members, such as peer mentoring, appears more effective than less-personalized approaches. However, stigma and a repressive environment remain major hurdles to achieving "zero new HIV infections" (UNAIDS 2012). Fostering broad involvement of community members *and* leaders may be able to overcome the discouraging impact of stigma by ensuring that no individual is singled out. Organized groups such as home-based care alliances and AIDS caregivers' networks are more important than ever as agents of community development and service delivery. They can provide a bridge between facility-based care and communities (Rodriguez-García, Wilson, et al. 2013). These findings support a recent systematic review of treatment programs in Sub-Saharan Africa, which found that, on average, only 70 percent of people receiving antiretroviral therapy from specialist clinics were still receiving treatment after two years as compared to a community treatment model implemented in Mozambique, which resulted in 97.5 percent of people still on treatment after 26 months (UNAIDS 2012, 59).

Findings that were not statistically significant might otherwise be programmatically significant. For instance, in Nigeria decision makers pondered why condom use was reportedly low in a country with a high level of

Figure 8.4 Focus of CBO Activities in Kenya and Nigeria

percentage of interviewed CBOs engaged in different prevention activities in Nigeria and Kenya

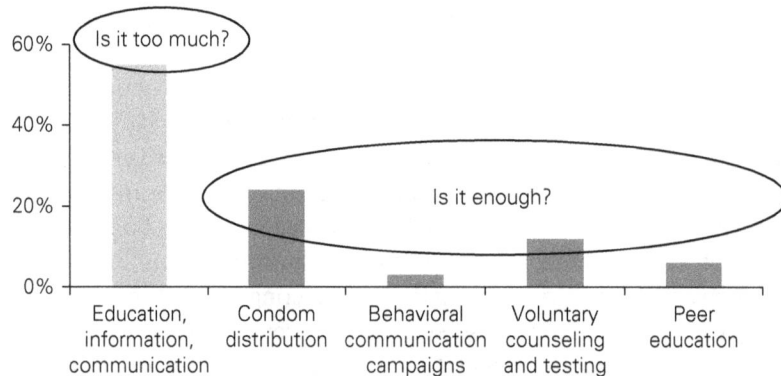

Note: CBO = community-based organization.

HIV knowledge (more than 90 percent) and a strong national program of condom distribution. While recognizing methodological issues that could be at play, this particular finding generated a useful policy and program dialogue at the country level. However, these findings raised the issue of why and whether CBOs provide the needed services to their catchment areas (figure 8.4). Another example is provided by India, where the incidence of STIs among MSM/Ts was found not to be statistically significant. However, it was programmatically significant. In this case, real and perceived stigma by these groups decreased their use of services, and therefore, very few were tested for STIs.

Communities continue to be a crucial component of HIV/AIDS strategies. In "Treatment 2.0," UNAIDS recognizes that strengthening community mobilization is crucial. Community-based approaches provide opportunities for socialization that can improve the ability of populations at high risk of HIV (drug users, men who have sex with men, sex workers) to access HIV services, to benefit from antiretroviral therapy, and to prevent new infections (UNAIDS 2010). However, the evidence from this evaluation portfolio indicates that complex pathways are at play between inputs and measurable results at the community level and that results depend substantially on the population groups, gender, country context, geographic location, and overall policy-legal environment in the country.

There are implications for policy and programming. Without diminishing the important role that UNAIDS and the global community give to and expect from communities, the reality is that communities cannot do everything. First, national stakeholders can play a critical role by helping communities to understand their epidemics and identify priorities for their catchment areas. Second, program designers need to be savvy about what CBOs and other community actors such as caregivers can realistically achieve and support their ability to achieve specific results in areas where community groups and CBOs might have comparative advantages and be able to deliver valuable services. Implementation of a combination of prevention, biomedical interventions, or social support programs would benefit by including specific roles for and expected results from community groups (that is, caregivers), thereby helping to relieve the shortage of health care professionals that exist in many high-HIV-prevalence, low-income countries. Finally, this shift toward greater specificity in community approaches should be achieved through a process of collaboration and consultation with the interested and affected communities (Rodriguez-García, Bonnel, et al. 2013).

The findings of this evaluation portfolio are supported by other major evaluations such as the recent evaluation of the Avahan Program (the India AIDS Initiative of the Bill and Melinda Gates Foundation), which assessed the role of community mobilization and structural interventions in HIV prevention, finding that community participation, structural interventions, and organizational development activities, coupled with access to services, lead to improved outcomes (Rodriguez-García and Bonnel 2012).

The consultative nature of the process was a catalyst for quality and relevance. The design and implementation of this evaluation portfolio benefited from the significant collaboration among three partners: the World Bank, the U.K.'s DFID as a critical partner and co-funder, and the U.K. Consortium on AIDS and International Development as a strategic civil society partner.

The meaningful engagement of civil society through the U.K. Consortium and its 80 global members, all of which are CSO networks themselves, proved worthwhile. The U.K. Consortium contributed to and facilitated key aspects of the evaluation. It facilitated the sharing of critical information, helped to ensure meaningful engagement of CSOs at the local, national, and global levels, and created a critical feedback loop for expert consultation. In its own words, "The UK Consortium brought to the partnership a strong civil society voice rooted in a 25-year history of democratic and inclusive engagement and skill for pulling together people from very diverse backgrounds" (Simms 2013, S2).

Dialogue with national and local AIDS authorities and stakeholders shaped the country-based evaluation approach, identified potential

> **Box 8.5 Lessons Learned from What We Decided Not to Do**
>
> 1. *Not establish a formal "static" advisory group.* Flexibility was preferred for a deeper engagement of national and international specialists in advisory roles.
> 2. *Not select consultation participants based on narrow criteria of experience and skills.* To leverage their skills, different specialists, partners, CSOs, and development agency representatives were selected to participate in specific consultations according to the themes discussed.
> 3. *Not schedule regular meetings but communicate often around concrete issues.* The use of technologies allowed for real-time feedback and enabled a more agile, iterative, and adaptive approach to the consultation process.
>
> *Source:* Rodriguez-García 2013, 13.

bottlenecks, and oversaw the development of evaluation protocols and their presentation to national ethics committees. Teams of evaluators and researchers included national specialists. Their role as peer reviewers of each other's studies leveraged the experience of these teams. Sustained throughout the three to four years of the partnership, these efforts helped to strengthen the design and focus of the evaluations and created an enabling platform for the validation and use of findings. In this evaluation portfolio, the consultative process was successful because it was deliberate, purposeful, and sustained, and the three key partners were equally committed (box 8.5).

Concluding Remarks

This evaluation portfolio provides robust evidence of the many contributions that community responses have made to the national and global HIV/AIDS response in many contexts and circumstances. Nonetheless, there are limitations. This portfolio of studies does not provide a definitive answer to the effects of community responses on knowledge, behavior changes, use of HIV/AIDS and health services, social changes, or biological outcomes. Further intervention-specific studies in selected community contexts would be helpful to corroborate or add robustness to the findings where this evaluation found mixed evidence, such as the role of perceived and real stigma in accessing and using services or factors affecting adherence to treatment.

The findings do indicate that investments in communities have produced results and that these results have contributed to the desired outcomes of the global response to HIV/AIDS. Importantly, the findings of this evaluation portfolio do not support a one-size-fits-all design of community responses; they do support the tenet that community responses have a critical role to play in holding to account and complementing broader efforts delivered by government, private sector providers, NGOs, and donors. In addition, several issues warrant further attention, as Cook and Seymour (2013, S2-6) suggest:

- Temporal changes in the dynamics of the epidemic and the contexts in which communities operate need to be better reflected in the evolving objectives of the community response and the flexibility of funding.
- The critical importance of gender differences needs to be better understood programmatically.
- The assumptions that the community response always has positive impacts need to be challenged more systematically.
- Expectations of what the community response can deliver need to be realistic and to recognize that there may be limitations to what can be delivered.
- The community response needs to be linked more explicitly with the national response, which might be a way to improve effectiveness, focus, and comparative advantage.

In terms of the methodological approach, this portfolio of 17 studies supports the appropriateness of applying a mixed-method approach to complex evaluations. The value of the portfolio approach is that it maximizes the usefulness of each individual study when viewed in the context of the findings of other studies in the same portfolio—parts of the whole. Each single study provides only a partial view of how communities shape the local response to HIV/AIDS. Taken together, however, these 17 studies paint a more comprehensive picture of the results of the community response in different contexts. Hence, the evaluation portfolio approach provides a robust body of evidence, showing, in this case, that investing in communities achieves results.

Notes

1. Specifically, the new strategy aims to reduce the percentage of people living on less than US$1.25 a day to 3 percent by 2030 and to foster income growth of the bottom 40 percent of the population in every developing country.

2. This chapter borrows from three major publications on the results of this multistudy evaluation portfolio led by the author of this chapter: Bonnel et al. (2013); Rodriguez-García, Bonnel, et al. (2013); Rodriguez-García, Wilson, et al. (2013, S7–19).

3. UNAIDS brings together the resources of its Secretariat (based in Geneva) and 11 organizations in the United Nations system organizations: the International Labour Organization; United Nations Development Programme; United Nations Educational, Scientific, and Cultural Organization; United Nations High Commission for Refugees; United Nations Children's Fund; United Nations Population Fund; United Nations Office on Drugs and Crime; United Nations Women; the World Bank; the World Food Program; and the World Health Organization. See http://www.unaids.org/en/aboutunaids/unaidscosponsors/.

4. For UNAIDS, civil society is made up of ordinary citizens who organize themselves outside of government and the public service to deal with specific issues and concerns that the regular government process cannot address by itself. Societies function more effectively when the state and its citizens engage openly on how policies are formulated and implemented (UNAIDS 2006, 202).

5. For detailed discussion of the typology of community responses, see Rodriguez-García et al. (2011).

6. Different agencies define civil society organizations in different ways. For instance, the Global Fund includes academic organizations and think tanks.

7. Effectiveness in this context refers to the extent to which community-based programs and actions have achieved their objectives under normal conditions in their real-life setting.

8. The U.K. Consortium is a network of more than 80 not-for-profit, faith-based, and academic agencies based in the United Kingdom, with strong links to governments, international and multilateral agencies, and civil society networks. See www.aidsconsortium.org.uk.

9. For U.K. partnership criteria, see http://www.goodpracticeparticipate.govt.nz /levels-of-participation/collaborative-processes-and-partnerships/index.html.

10. Random allocation ensures that no systematic differences between intervention groups in factors, known and unknown, may affect the outcome. Other study designs, including quasi-experimental studies, can detect associations between an intervention and an outcome, but they cannot rule out the possibility that the association was caused by a third factor linked to both interventions.

11. The PSI is a research tool used to capture data on the experiences and perceptions of HIV-positive persons regarding stigma and discrimination. See http://www.stigmanindex.org.

References

Adato, M. 2012. "Combining Quantitative and Qualitative Methods for Program Monitoring and Evaluation: Why Are Mixed-Method Designs Best?" In *Building Better Policies,* edited by G. Lopez-Acevedo, P. Krause, and K. MacKay, 151–63. Washington, DC: World Bank.

Arcand, J., P. A. Diallo, C. Sakho, and N. Wagner. 2010. "HIV/AIDS Sensitization, Social Mobilization, and Peer-Mentoring: Evidence from a Randomized Experiment in Senegal." A research report for Evaluation of the Community Response, World Bank, Washington, DC.

Bamberger, M., and M. Segone. 2011. "How to Design and Manage Equity-Focused Evaluations." United Nations Children's Fund, New York.

Bhattacharjee, P., R. Prakash, P. Pillai, S. Isac, M. Haranahalli, A. Blanchard, J. Shahmanesh, M. Blanchard, and S. Moses. 2013. "Understanding the Role of Peer Group Membership in Reducing HIV-Related Risk and Vulnerability among Female Sex Workers in Karnataka, India." AIDS Care 25 (S1): S46–54. http://dx.doi.org/10.1080/09540121.2012.733334.

Birdsall, K., and K. Kelly. 2007. "Pioneers, Partners, Providers: The Dynamics of Civil Society and AIDS Funding in Southern Africa." Centre for AIDS Development, Research and Evaluation CADRE/Open Society Initiative for Southern Africa, Johannesburg.

Bonnel, R., R. Rodriguez-Garcia, J. Olivier, Q. Wodon, S. McPherson, K. Orr, and J. Ross. 2013. Funding Mechanisms for Civil Society: The Experience of the AIDS Response. Washington, DC: World Bank.

Campbell, C., K. Scott, M. Nhamo, C. Nyamukapa, C. Madanhire, M. Skovdal, L. Sherr, and S. Gregson. 2013. "Social Capital and HIV Competent Communities: The Role of Community Groups in Managing HIV/AIDS in Rural Zimbabwe." AIDS Care 25 (1): S114–22. http://dx.doi.org/10.1080/09540121.2012.748170.

Cook, A. E., and A. Seymour. 2013. "DFID Commentary on the Evaluation of the Community Response to HIV and AIDS." AIDS Care 25 (S1): S4–6. http://dx.doi.org/10.1080/09540121.2012.714458.

Corno, L., and D. de Walque. 2013. "Socioeconomic Determinants of Stigmatization and HIV Testing in Lesotho." AIDS Care 25 (S1): S108–13. http://dx.doi.org/10.1080/09540121.2012.736937.

Gertler, P., S. Martinez, P. Premand, L. Rawlings, and C. Vermeersch. 2011. Impact Evaluation in Practice. Washington, DC: World Bank.

Global Fund. 2011. Making a Difference: Global Fund Results Report 2011. Geneva: Global Fund.

Greene, J. C. 2007. Mixed Methods in Social Inquiry. San Francisco: Jossey-Bass.

Gregson, S., E. Gonese, B. Hallett, N. Taruberekera, J. W. Hargrove, E. L. Corbett, R. Dorrington, S. Dube, K. Dehne, and O. Mugurungi. 2010. "HIV Decline due to Reductions in Risky Sex in Zimbabwe? Evidence from a Comprehensive Epidemiological Review." International Journal of Epidemiology 39 (5): 1311–23.

Gregson, S., P. Mushati, H. Grusin, M. Nhamo, C. Schumacher, M. Skovdal, and C. Campbell. 2011. "Social Capital and Women's Reduced Vulnerability to HIV Infection in Rural Zimbabwe." Population and Development Review 37 (2): 333–59.

Gregson, S., C. Nyamukapa, C. Schumacher, S. Magutshwa-Zitha, M. Skovdal, R. Yekeye, L. Sherr, and C. Campbell. 2013. "Evidence for a Contribution of the Community Response to HIV Decline in Eastern Zimbabwe?" AIDS Care 25 (S1): S88–96. http://dx.doi.org/10.1080/09540121.2012.748171.

Halperin, D., T. Mugurungi, O. Hallett, T. B. Muchini, B. Campbell, B. Magure, and T. S. Gregson. 2011. "A Surprising Prevention Success: Why Did the HIV Epidemic Decline in Zimbabwe?" *PLoS Medicine* 8 (2): e1000414.

IEG (Independent Evaluation Group). 2005. "Committing to Results: Improving the Effectiveness of HIV/AIDS Assistance; An Evaluation of the World Bank's Assistance for HIV/AIDS Control." World Bank, Washington, DC.

ILO (International Labour Organization). 2010. "HIV and AIDS and the World of Work Recommendation No. 200." ILO, Geneva.

———. 2012. "National Floors of Social Protection Recommendation No. 202." ILO, Geneva.

Kaiser Family Foundation. 2013. *Financing the Response to HIV in Low- and Middle-Income Countries: International Assistance from Donor Governments in 2012*. Washington, DC: Kaiser Family Foundation. http://kff.org/global-health-policy/press-release/kaiserunaids-study-finds-no-real-change-in-donor-funding-for-hiv/.

Kakietek, J., T. Geberselassie, B. Manteuffel, K. Ogungbemi, A. Krivelyova, S. Bausch, R. Rodriguez-García, R. Bonnel, N. N'Jie, J. Fruh, and S. Gar. 2013. "It Takes a Village: Community-Based Organizations and the Availability and Utilization of HIV/AIDS–Related Services in Nigeria." *AIDS Care* 25 (S1): S78–87. http://dx.doi.org/10.1080/09540121.2012.740158.

Krivelyova, A., J. Kakietek, H. Connolly, R. Bonnel, B. Manteuffel, R. Rodriguez-García, N. N'Jie, A. Berruti, S. Gregson, and R. Agrawal. 2013. "Funding and Expenditure of a Sample of Community-Based Organizations in Kenya, Nigeria, and Zimbabwe." *AIDS Care* 25 (S1): S20–29. http://dx.doi.org/10.1080/09540121.2013.764390.

Low, C., C. Pop-Eleches, W. Rono, E. Plous, A. Kirk, S. Ndege, M. Goldstein, and H. Thirumurthy. 2013. "The Effects of Home-Based HIV Counseling and Testing on HIV/AIDS Stigma among Individuals and Community Leaders in Western Kenya: Evidence from a Cluster-Randomized Trial." *AIDS Care* 25 (S1): S97–107. http://dx.doi.org/10.1080/09540121.2012.748879.

Morra Imas, L., and R. Rist. 2009. *The Road to Results: Designing and Conducting Effective Development Evaluations*. Washington, DC: World Bank.

Riehman, K., J. Kakietek, B. A. Manteuffel, R. Rodriguez-García, R. Bonnel, N. N'Jie, L. Godoy-Garraza, A. Orago, P. Murithi, and J. Fruh. 2013. "Evaluating the Effects of Community-Based Organization Engagement on HIV and AIDS-Related Risk Behavior in Kenya." *AIDS Care* 25 (S1): S67–77. http://dx.doi.org/10.1080/09540121.2013.778383.

Rodriguez-García, R. 2013. "A Portfolio Approach to Evaluation: Critical Aspects and Lessons." *Evaluation Connections*, September 12–14. www.europeanevaluation.org.

Rodriguez-García, R., and R. Bonnel. 2012. "Increasing the Evidence Base on the Role of the Community in Response to HIV/AIDS." *Journal of Epidemiology and Community Health* 66 (S2): ii7–8.

Rodriguez-García, R., R. Bonnel, N. Njie, J. Olivier, F. B. Pascual, and Q. Wodon. 2011. "Analyzing Community Responses to HIV and AIDS: Operational

Framework and Typology." Policy Research Working Paper 5532, World Bank, Washington, DC.

Rodriguez-García, R., R. Bonnel, D. Wilson, and N. N'Jie. 2013. *Investing in Communities Achieves Results: Findings from an Evaluation of Community Responses to HIV and AIDS*. Washington, DC: World Bank.

Rodriguez-García, R., D. Wilson, N. York, C. Low, N. Njie, and R. Bonnel. 2013. "Evaluation of the Community Response to HIV and AIDS: Learning from a Portfolio Approach." *AIDS Care* 25 (S1): S7–19.

Rogers, P. 2008. "Using Programme Theory to Evaluate Complicated and Complex Aspects of Interventions." *Evaluation* 14 (1): 29–48.

Saggurti, N., R. M. Mishra, L. Proddutoor, S. Tucker, D. Kovvali, P. Parimi, and T. Wheeler. 2013. "Community Collectivization and Its Association with Consistent Condom Use and STI Treatment Seeking Behaviors among Female Sex Workers and High-Risk Men Who Have Sex with Men/Transgenders in Andhra Pradesh, India." *AIDS Care* 25 (S1): S55–66. http://dx.doi.org/10.1080/09540121.2012.749334.

Schwartlander, B., J. Stover, T. Hallett, R. Atun, C. Avila, E. Gouws, M. Bartos, P. D. Ghys, M. Opuni, D. Barr, R. Alsallaq, L. Bollinger, M. de Freitas, G. Garnett, C. Holmes, K. Legins, Y. Pillay, E. Stanciole, C. McClure, G. Hirnschall, M. Laga, and N. Padian. 2011. "Towards an Improved Investment Approach for an Effective Response to HIV/AIDS." *The Lancet* 377 (9782): 2031–41.

Semini, I., G. Batona, C. Lafrance, L. Kessou, E. Gbedji, H. Anani, and M. Alary. 2013. "Implementing for Results: Program Analysis of the HIV/STI Interventions for Sex Workers in Benin." *AIDS Care* 25 (S1): S30–39. http://dx.doi.org/10.1080/09540121.2013.784392.

Simms, B. 2013. "World Bank: Harnessing Civil Society Expertise in Undertaking and Disseminating Research Findings." *AIDS Care* 25 (S1): S1–3. http://dx.doi.org/10.1080/09540121.2012.733334.

Tashakkori, A., and C. Teddlie, eds. 2010. *SAGE Handbook of Mixed Methods in Social and Behavioral Research*, 2d ed. New York: SAGE Publications.

Taylor, N. 2010. "The Different Forms of Structures Involved in the Community Response for Vulnerable Children, and What Are They Best Placed to Do." *Vulnerable Children and Youth Studies* 5 (S1): S7–18. http://www.tandfonline.com/doi/full/10.1080/17450121003606509#.Uo1KbTwo7cs.

UNAIDS (United Nations HIV/AIDS Program). 2006. "The Essential Role of Civil Society." In *Report on the Global AIDS Epidemic: A UNAIDS 10th Anniversary Special Edition*, 202–22. Geneva: UNAIDS.

———. 2010. "Treatment 2.0 Fact Sheet." UNAIDS, Geneva. http://data.unaids.org/Pub/outlook/2010/20100713_fs_outlook_treatment_en.pdf.

———. 2011a. "AIDS at 30: Nations at a Crossroads." UNAIDS, Geneva.

———. 2011b. "People Living with HIV: Stigma Index Asia Pacific Regional Analysis (Bangladesh, Cambodia, China, Fiji, Myanmar, Pakistan, Philippines, Sri Lanka, and Thailand)." UNAIDS, Geneva.

———. 2012. "Together We Will End AIDS." UNAIDS, Geneva.

United Nations. 2000. "UN Millennium Declaration." http://www.un.org/en/development/devagenda/millennium.shtml.

Weiss, C. 1995. "Nothing as Practical as Good Theory: Exploring Theory-Based Evaluation for Comprehensive Community Initiatives for Children and Families." In *New Approaches to Evaluating Community Initiatives*. Denver: Aspen Institute. http://www.theoryofchange.org/what-is-theory-of-change/toc-background/toc-origins/#4.

World Bank. 2013. "World Bank Group Strategy." World Bank, Washington, DC.

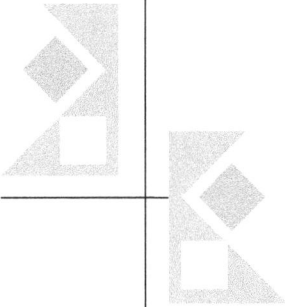

PART THREE: ASSESSMENT AND DESIGN OF PUBLIC MANAGEMENT SYSTEMS THAT REDUCE POVERTY AND INEQUALITY

CHAPTER 9

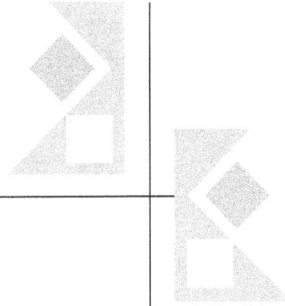

Evaluating How National Development Plans Can Contribute to Poverty and Inequality Reduction: The Cases of Cambodia and Costa Rica

Ana Maria Fernandez, Roberto Garcia-Lopez, Thavrak Tuon, and Frederic P. Martin

Introduction

Evaluations of public interventions to combat poverty and inequality generally evaluate projects and programs. More rarely, they address national development plans (NDPs). However, most developing countries

Ana Maria Fernandez and Frederic P. Martin are with the Institute for Development in Economics and Administration. Roberto Garcia-Lopez is with the Latin-America and the Caribbean Community of Practices on Managing for Development Results. Thavrak Tuon is with the Ministry of Planning, Royal Government of Cambodia.

and some intermediate and industrial countries have been organizing all of their economic and social policies within the framework of an NDP.[1] This document expresses the desired stage of development for a country, which often includes poverty and inequality reduction. This vision is then converted into strategic objectives with indicators of impact and final outcome as well as targets, which translate into programs and projects that are then implemented. As a road map for the period of a government mandate, an NDP is a planning instrument that helps to align the interventions of all actors (governmental, nongovernmental, and private) toward a common vision for the country's development in the medium run.

This chapter addresses how to assess the contribution of a national development plan to a country's economic and social development, including poverty and inequality reduction, through proper elaboration, budgeting, implementation, and monitoring and evaluation (M&E). This process has proved to be a challenge for at least four reasons.

First, by definition, an NDP covers all sectors of a given country, which means that it is huge in scope. These multiple sectors (economic, social, infrastructure) have quite different program objectives, institutional set-ups, and technical systems to deliver public services. The plan deals with a diversity of regions, milieus (urban, rural), and populations. It addresses a variety of cross-cutting issues, which are not easily delineated and measured, given the number of stakeholders and possible angles of analysis. It is supposed to integrate actions from all major stakeholders, including the national government, of course, but also subnational governments, the private sector, civil society, and development partners. The challenge becomes how to use a participatory approach involving all major stakeholders in elaborating an NDP, but to do so in a few months, to synthesize micro viewpoints into a macro perspective, and to make the plan a useful document for orienting all policies and programs of a new government. This macro perspective also makes it even more complicated to deal with the attribution issue during evaluation: in the absence of a counterfactual, how do we know that the NDP made a difference?

Second, the time dimension complicates evaluation. A typical NDP has a medium-term perspective (for example, four years in Costa Rica and five years in Cambodia). However, it needs to integrate long-term trends (20–30 years ahead), while also addressing shorter medium-term action plans, fiscal and expenditure frameworks, and yearly work plans and budgets. Even more than is the case for a program or a project, final outcomes and impacts will be felt long after the final evaluation takes place, which is typically at the end of the period covered by the NDP.

Third, actions and programs indicated in the NDP are not necessarily clearly identified with immediate outcomes linking outputs with final outcomes. Thus costing the NDP might face analytical challenges, issues related to the availability and reliability of data, as well as a huge amount of work.

Fourth, the dialogue and priorities between politicians and technocrats often make it difficult to harmonize the measure of objectives and goals, especially for poverty and inequality.

This chapter presents two case studies of the process of elaborating, implementing, monitoring, and evaluating an NDP: one in Cambodia[2] and one in Costa Rica.[3] These countries have different histories and face different situations. Costa Rica is an upper-middle-income country,[4] while Cambodia is a low-income country.[5] Despite their differences, they share some common features, starting with their dependence on a main source of income: ecotourism in Costa Rica, known as a "green destination,"[6] and cultural tourism in Cambodia, known as a "spiritual destination."[7]

In addition, both countries have a record of planning. The elaboration of an NDP in Cambodia (adoption of each document by law) and Costa Rica (Law no. 5525) is mandatory. Since 2006,[8] Cambodia has named its document the National Strategic Development Plan (NSDP), which is valid for a period of five years, the current one for 2014–18. The primary responsibility for preparing, monitoring, and evaluating the NSDP is assigned to the Ministry of Planning. In Costa Rica, the document is called the National Development Plan, which is valid for a period of four years; the analysis in this chapter is for the 2011–14 NDP. In 2013 Costa Rica celebrated 50 years of planning. Like in Cambodia, in Costa Rica the Ministry of National Planning and Economic Policy (MIDEPLAN)[9] has the leading role in formulating, supervising, monitoring, and evaluating the NDP.

Overall, even if there are some singularities depending on each country's context, the contents of both NDPs are organized in a similar way: (a) diagnosis, (b) key policy priorities and actions, (c) costs and resources, (d) charts with indicators and targets, and (e) M&E orientations. Both documents also share some limits. In particular, they (a) do not take a cross-cutting approach among sectors; (b) do not take a regional approach to service delivery; (c) include various planning levels without a hierarchical logic, sometimes mixing outcomes with outputs and not identifying immediate outcomes; (d) have limited target validation processes; and (e) are unable to link programs to the budget on a multiannual basis.

The next two sections of this chapter present case studies of NDP evaluations. The first one evaluates the process of NDP elaboration and implementation in Costa Rica, while the second one evaluates the NSDP M&E system in Cambodia. The case studies illustrate complementary approaches that can be used depending on the evaluation's objectives, time, and budget limits. They are not models to follow necessarily, since each methodology has to be tailored to the specific objectives of the evaluation, time and budget constraints, as well as the characteristics of the country and its NDP. Following these case studies, the chapter outlines lessons learned for future evaluations of an NDP and its contribution to poverty and inequality reduction.

Case Study of Costa Rica

Evaluation Objectives

The evaluation sought to accomplish the following:

1. Determine the extent to which the NDP achieves the objective of prioritizing the agencies' actions toward the national development targets
2. Determine the extent to which the NDP is binding for the public sector
3. Define whether the document could be evaluated according to its content
4. Assess the level of validation for priorities and targets among public and private actors.

Evaluation Process and Methods

The evaluation took place over a six-month period, applying a combination of qualitative and quantitative methods: document review, interviews and focus groups, direct observation, and a survey. The use of multiple lines of inquiry provided a level of rigor to the evaluation by offering an opportunity for triangulation. Findings from a particular method that deviated from those obtained by other methods were analyzed, giving special attention to reasons for the deviation.

The methodology was based on a five-step approach, in which the result of each step contributed to the next in order to build simultaneously on the collection of data and validation of findings, trying to incorporate the perspective of multiple actors (figure 9.1).

The first step was to conduct a desk review to obtain background information and analyze secondary data.

The second was to conduct 33 in-depth interviews using a semistructured questionnaire with civil servants from MIDEPLAN, the Ministry of Finance, priority line ministries, the presidency, the National Accounting Office, Congress, and civil society representatives.

Figure 9.1 Five-Step Approach Followed for the NDP Evaluation in Costa Rica

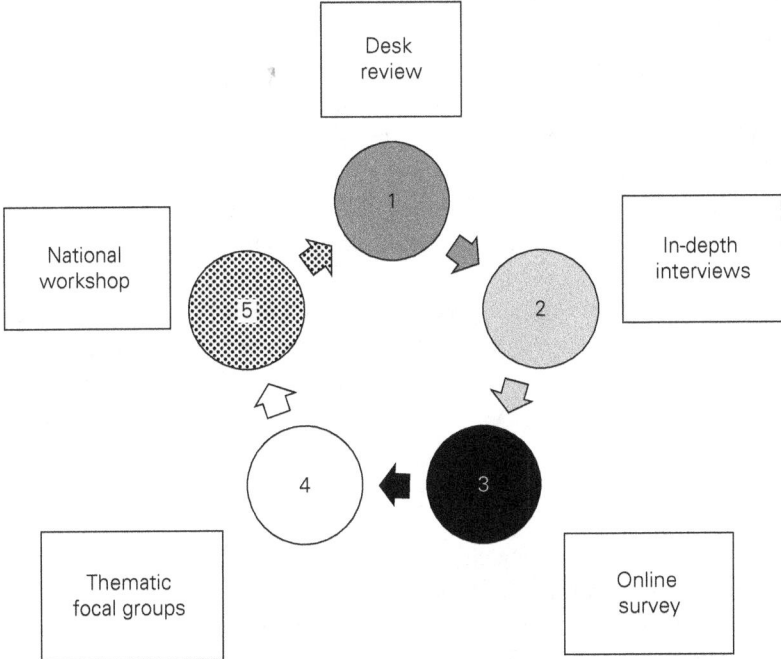

Source: Ministry of Planning 2013.
Note: NDP = national development plan.

After these interviews were processed, the third step was to conduct a civil servant survey, using a semi-open questionnaire (including 25 questions) administered online for seven days. The questions were graded on an ordinal scale so that the respondent could assess whether a given issue was considered to be a major challenge, a challenge, or not a significant challenge. Respondents to the anonymous online survey were 128 civil servants[10] out of a sample of 198 selected in the sampling agencies in which in-depth interviews had been conducted.

The fourth step was to conduct three focus groups in the three main thematic areas considered as cross-cutting issues for sustainable development in the country and as domains of unsatisfactory performance in the previous NDP: environment, regions and municipalities, and civil society and private sector initiatives. The focus group participants included a mix of academics, sector experts, and private sector and nongovernmental organization representatives, along with professional civil servants. The questionnaire for each focus group was designed based on the results of the online survey, so that the focus group participants were able, among others, to prioritize the major challenges identified by the civil servants surveyed and to add issues that the public sector did not consider priorities.

Finally, a workshop was organized with all participants in the evaluation to present, discuss, and validate preliminary findings, include issues that were not initially stated, and propose solutions to improve the next round of NDP formulation and implementation. The participants were divided into six groups corresponding to key results areas, and each group provided up to five solutions for each challenge. The results of this workshop were used as input for the methodology that was recommended for the next NDP.

After the national workshop, evaluators designed a comparison matrix of prioritized challenges grouped by theme according to different sources of information: online survey, focus group, national workshop, and evaluators (table 9.1).

Evaluation Effectiveness and Challenges

One of the main methodological challenges was to consult as many actors as possible in a short amount of time. According to participants, the five-step methodology enabled them to consider the view of multiple actors, to compare information from different sources, and to identify major challenges. They appreciated being included in the discussion of the findings and sharing cross-cutting ideas, saying that this ability is usually limited by insufficient coordination and communication between leading agencies and line agencies as well as between public sector actors and actors external to the public system.

Table 9.1 Criteria to Grade Challenges among Data Sources in Evaluation of the NDP in Costa Rica

Grade criteria	Implication for the NDP elaboration process
Graded as a major challenge by the four sources	Requires immediate modification
Graded as a major challenge by two to three sources	Continue with minor modifications
Graded as a major challenge by between zero and one national source, with the evaluators considering this challenge not to be a major challenge according to international good practices	Continue without modifications
Graded as not a major challenge by any national source, but considered a major challenge by evaluators according to international good practices	Indicates a possible area of modification that was not discussed thoroughly during the evaluation process

Source: Ministry of Planning 2013.

Note: NDP = national development plan.

Application of the methodology confronted the following challenges:

1. Absence of a common understanding of the underlying theory of change in public interventions
2. Tendency to operate with a micro perspective and a "silo" mentality, which made it difficult to conduct a systemic analysis
3. Perception that the evaluation process was a threat rather than a learning opportunity
4. Organizational inertia and resistance to change

The evaluation team addressed those challenges by (1) providing a brief introduction of concepts at the beginning of all group activities; (2) basing discussions on the responses of various actors and checking the consistency of responses among them; (3) using sensitization and group discussion management techniques and presenting findings to all actors in a neutral, constructive, and action-oriented way; and (4) supporting the dissemination plan for the findings after the evaluation was finalized.

Case Study of Cambodia

Evaluation Objectives

The evaluation sought to accomplish the following:

1. Conduct a rapid and participatory assessment of the current national M&E system for the NSDP[11]
2. Identify and prioritize bottlenecks for improving the M&E of the NSDP implementation and results
3. Identify characteristics of the desired M&E system of the NSDP and propose orientation guidelines for the system

Evaluation Process and Methods

The methodology used for the evaluation followed the assessment for results (A4R) process, supported by a Web-based software.[12] The process started with a review of relevant documentation. Then the evaluation team conducted in-depth interviews with 10 ministries and agencies and facilitated a two-day workshop with 42 key national actors. This workshop enabled the evaluation to (a) take stock of the existing initiatives in M&E that are relevant for NSDP implementation (supply side); (b) identify strengths, weaknesses, and challenges to meeting the information needs for decision making and accountability (demand side); and (c) seek concrete ways to improve both the demand for and supply of M&E information to monitor and assess NSDP implementation.

The A4R software supported the assessment in various ways:

- By making it easy to upgrade the indicators and subindicators of performance for diagnosing the M&E system; the subindicators were validated, and some were customized to reflect the specificities of Cambodia's situation
- By keeping a record of the assessment process to compare preassessment (done by an expert based on revised documentation and in-depth interviews), workshop assessment, and postassessment (after more documentation and revision with the Ministry of Planning and the United Nations Children's Fund, UNICEF)
- By collecting evaluation data online, which enabled the assessment to reflect immediate results and to facilitate the plenary discussions for the participatory diagnostic, to identify and analyze bottlenecks, and to formulate an action plan

A4R considers six technical and institutional dimensions in the assessment of an M&E system (table 9.2). The exact number and label of performance subindicators were adjusted prior to the workshop after finalizing the in-depth interviews and in close collaboration with the Ministry of Planning and UNICEF.

During the workshop, the evaluation team introduced the basic concepts to be used for assessing the six dimensions and for guiding the discussion of the challenges encountered in each dimension. Workshop participants assessed each dimension through several performance indicators, which included several subindicators, as presented in table 9.2. The six groups of

Table 9.2 Dimensions of the M&E System and Performance Indicators and Subindicators in A4R for Cambodia

Dimension	Name	Indicators	Subindicators
1	Preconditions for results-based M&E	4	16
2	Institutional framework for M&E	4	9
3	Plan and budget for M&E	4	10
4	Routine monitoring	5	17
5	Evaluation cycle	4	4
6	M&E information systems	3	3
Total		24	59

Source: Ministry of Planning 2015.

Note: A4R = assessment for results; M&E = monitoring and evaluation.

workshop participants gave a grade to each subindicator, using a four-level ordinal scale from 0 to 3. Each grade corresponded to specific assessable characteristics, which were indicated in A4R and followed international standards for M&E systems. The participants were asked to provide explicit justification of the grade as well as supporting documents.

The bottleneck analysis was conducted after the diagnostic to identify the main challenges. A nominal group technique was used to identify and prioritize the bottlenecks. Every participant had a chance to present three main bottlenecks. Some of those bottlenecks were regrouped when common areas were identified. Afterward, each participant selected five priority bottlenecks and assigned a grade on a scale from 5 to 1, where 5 is the most important bottleneck. The A4R software facilitated the scoring for ranking the bottlenecks.

Then the evaluation team proposed key characteristics of the M&E system and elements of guidelines for NSDP implementation based on the diagnostic and bottleneck analysis, and these were discussed by participants. Finally, participants were divided into three thematic areas based on bottleneck analysis and asked to come up with elements of a medium-term action plan, including (a) institutional arrangements, (b) capacity building, and (c) information systems.

Following the workshop, consultants revised the assessment of the participants, making sure that the grade given corresponded to the justification provided and, when necessary, complemented the information based on a review of relevant documentation conducted before the mission.

Evaluation Effectiveness and Challenges

The preliminary results were presented at the end of the workshop, and the full results were presented in a report a month later. This process was greatly appreciated, allowing the rapid presentation of results and creating momentum among national actors to move forward with the system and to coordinate their initiatives based on their roles and responsibilities.

Application of the methodology entailed three challenges: (1) the unequal level of knowledge of M&E concepts among participants, (2) the tendency to assess the M&E system with regard to a particular sector—for example, some ministries were conducting pilot initiatives that were not yet common to the bulk of ministries, and (3) the tendency to interpret some subindicators in the local context. The evaluation team addressed those challenges by, respectively, (1) providing basic knowledge about M&E concepts, (2) correcting some grades after the workshop to reflect the situation in the whole of government, and (3) clarifying and disaggregating some subindicators of performance.

Lessons Learned from the Two Case Studies

The Cambodia and Costa Rica case studies provide several lessons for future evaluations of the elaboration, implementation, and M&E of an NDP and its contribution to poverty reduction.

Assessing the Global, yet Functional, Positioning of the NDP within the Results-Based Management Cycle

A common limitation of NDPs is a failure to translate a good diagnostic and a desirable vision into a set of public interventions that will most likely achieve the set targets. The strategic planning process will be of very limited value if it is not positioned as part of a results-based management cycle that articulates the planning phase with the programming and budgeting phase and with the M&E and reporting phase, as depicted in figure 9.2.

This results-based management cycle involves three levels of decision making: (1) strategic (deciding on priorities and services to deliver), (2) programmatic (organizing service delivery), and (3) operational (delivering services). These levels correspond to the three rows in figure 9.2.

Talking about implementation of an NDP is misleading. What is being implemented are measures (changes in the law, new institutional arrangements), programs, and projects. Often, the missing link in planning between the strategic (NDP) and the operational (work plan) levels is the sector

Figure 9.2 Positioning the NDP in the Results-Based Management Cycle

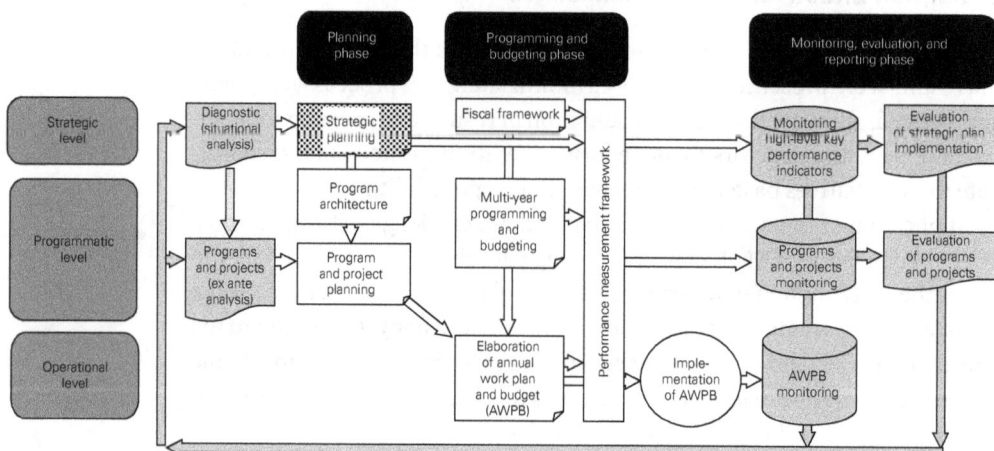

Source: IDEA 2014a.

Note: NDP = national development plan.

program level. Poor articulation between strategic and operational planning levels may explain why the NDP targets have not been achieved.

There is also much confusion about the definition of a program. At the programmatic level, a sector program is best defined as a coordinated set of (a) institutional subprograms, including routine activities[13] and specific projects[14] related to public service delivery and (b) investment projects, which enhance the quantity and quality of institutional subprograms to deliver public services. The design and articulation of sector programs benefit from the existence of a program architecture, which indicates how each institution in the sector is organized in terms of institutional subprograms and investment projects.

The objectives of programs (immediate outcomes and outputs) at the sector level must contribute to the achievement of high-level objectives (impacts and final outcomes) at the strategic level. The objectives (outputs) of an institutional subprogram or investment project should contribute to the achievement of objectives at the sector level (immediate outcomes and outputs in the sector). Typically, this analysis is conducted with a cause and effect relation methodology, such as the use of logic models or logical frameworks.

Apart from assessing the vertical articulation between strategic, programmatic, and operational levels, the evaluator should assess how the NDP addresses the following issues:

1. *Horizontal articulation between the NDP and sector strategic plans.* To what extent are those plans articulated in terms of time horizons, objectives, indicators, targets, strategies, and programs and to what extent do line ministries go beyond a silo mentality and consider cross-cutting issues?
2. *Articulation of a plan and budget.* A plan and a budget are both essential. To what extent does the NDP start from a realistic macro fiscal framework and estimate the costs of programs?
3. *Articulation of time horizons.* To what extent does the NDP analyze long-term trends and look at their medium-term implications and to what extent does the NDP lead to consistent medium-term action and yearly work plans?
4. *Inclusion of the space dimension.* Too often, the NDP is an intellectual exercise prepared by technocrats with good intentions, but limited knowledge and appreciation of local realities. However, public programs and projects are implemented at the local level in regions with different geographic, socioeconomic, and cultural characteristics. To what extent does the NDP integrate the territorial dimension and disaggregate

its objectives and strategies? To what extent are the strategic plans of subnational governments, if they exist, articulated with the NDP? And to what extent are responsibilities between the different levels of government and the executing agency of a program clearly identified?

Assessing the Comprehensive, yet Structured, Nature of the NDP Technical Process

The strategic planning process can be disaggregated into four phases, as illustrated in figure 9.3: diagnosing the issues to be addressed, setting strategic objectives, defining strategies and means to reach those objectives, and outlining the M&E system to measure the implementation and results of the strategic plan.

More specifically, the evaluation should determine whether the NDP has addressed all objectives of the strategic planning process, which are to:

1. Guide a diagnostic of the current situation, explicitly considering cross-cutting issues
2. Support the identification and prioritization of objectives at the higher level corresponding to a vision for the future
3. Identify the strategies that will contribute to the achievement of those objectives

Figure 9.3   Phases of the Strategic Planning Technical Process

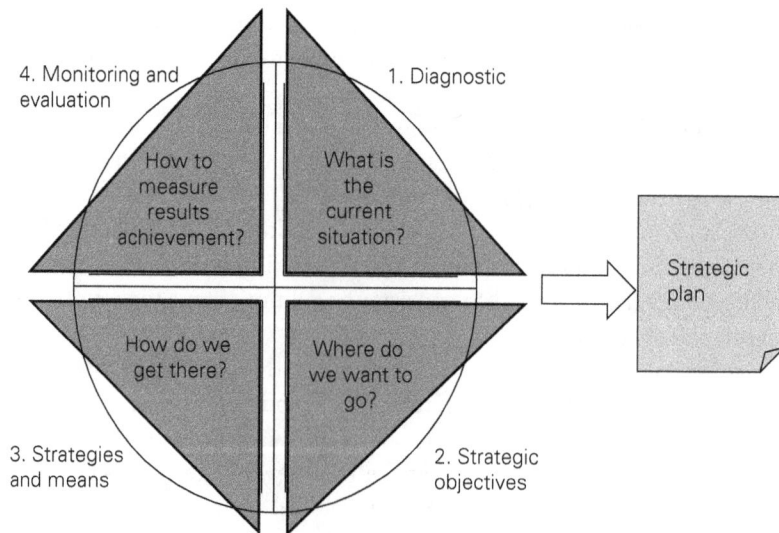

Source: IDEA 2014b.

4. Articulate the most important programs and projects corresponding to the strategies selected to achieve the objectives
5. Outline key institutional arrangements and technical systems that will enable government to implement and monitor implementation of the strategic plan
6. Provide for an indicative costing of implementation of the strategic plan
7. Facilitate the elaboration of a performance measurement framework at the strategic level, including consistent high-level and program-level targets
8. Consider various risk factors and different scenarios

Assessing the Inclusive, yet Coordinated, Nature of the NDP Institutional Process

More than just a technical process, the NDP process should provide an opportunity to discuss and express collective preferences. The evaluation should assess the degree of participation of all major actors, including central ministries, line ministries, and agencies, Parliament, subnational governments and assemblies, private sector representative institutions, civil society and other nongovernmental organizations, as well as international organizations and donors. Participation should take place not only during the diagnostic and formulation phases of the NDP, but also during implementation and M&E. Because of time and budget limits and uneven interest and capacity of stakeholders, participation is never total. This is especially the case for the poor, who face a high opportunity cost of participating in such exercises and are marginalized by definition. Sometimes, the NDP process pays lip service to participation and the representativeness of the speakers. However, as imperfect as they might be, the existence and functionality of discussion and consultation mechanisms at key moments of the NDP process should be assessed.

The second key issue for the NDP institutional process pertains to coordination. The Ministry of Planning is the official leader of the NDP process; however, it often lacks the monetary power of the Ministry of Finance, the executive power of the presidency or prime minister's office, and the field presence of big line ministries, all powerful actors who have their own initiatives that are not necessarily consistent with the NDP. International organizations and donors too often have their own agenda and are more accountable to their head office than to the government. If, in addition, the technical capacities of the Ministry of Planning are limited, the chances of a functional NDP process are also limited. Coordination mechanisms often exist on paper, but they are not always consistent or functional. The solution might include establishing win-win partnerships across stakeholders, clarifying roles and responsibilities, improving communication, providing incentives to promote consistency among public actions, and building the capacity of individuals and institutions. The evaluation should go beyond formal arrangements and consider actual practices and their underlying causes.

The third key issue is that the Ministry of Planning generally struggles to include "everyone" and solve "everything" with the NDP. The Ministry of Planning receives too much information from line ministries, which may fall into the trap of a silo mentality and consider only their sector as a priority. The Ministry of Planning has to conduct an "arbitrage" and choose between those priorities. Criteria such as relevance for national priorities set by the executive branch, consideration of cross-cutting issues, and focus on less advantaged regions could be considered in the arbitrage process. Finally, the NDP does not have to meet all of the strategic planning needs in the country. Rather it should provide overall consistency of public action and focus on national priorities.

Assessing the Relevance of the NDP for Addressing not only Poverty, but also Inequality and Vulnerability

The NDP is about economic and social development of the country, and therefore its target group is the whole population, not just the poor. However, most countries would consider poverty reduction as one of the objectives. Too often, though, poverty reduction is treated as a social issue to be addressed by targeted social protection programs. Although such programs are part of the solution, poverty needs to be addressed in economic and cultural dimensions as well. Poverty reduction programs should be carefully designed, among others, to maximize coverage of target groups, minimize leakage to nonpoor groups, address fundamental causes of poverty rather than just symptoms, encourage the poor to break away from the poverty trap and avoid the dependence on social programs, and consider the evolving nature of poverty and its dynamics. This requires the design of global cross-sector programs and local adaptation by subnational government offices and community workers who can best appreciate the specific situation of the poor in their region.

Beyond poverty reduction, the NDP should consider issues of inequality and vulnerability, which are gaining importance as a result of relative successes in poverty reduction over the last decades and the growing magnitude of inequality and vulnerability. The evaluation should consider the extent to which the NDP disaggregates the analysis of past performance, sets national objectives, and identifies programs that consider different groups in society, disaggregating, among others, by region, milieu (rural, urban), gender, age group (children and senior citizens, in particular), socio-economic group, and sociocultural and ethnic group. This is a challenge for a traditionally macro-level document. However, ignoring those differences within society jeopardizes the achievement of national goals, as the variance pushes down the national averages (human development indicators in the United States compared to those in more equal societies like northern European countries). Beyond the moral obligation to disadvantaged groups, those large differences also threaten social peace (in Latin America) and the social fabric and national unity (in several African countries).

The cross-cutting nature of the NDP provides interesting insights not easily considered in more traditional sectoral silo approaches. One good example is the "three-ones strategy" that many countries and international organizations have used with success in the fight against human immunodeficiency virus (HIV) and acquired immune deficiency syndrome (AIDS): one plan, one institutional coordinating mechanism, and one M&E system. In addition, most of the analysis and projections made in past NDPs have assumed a largely deterministic environment. Those days are over. Future NDPs should identify major risk factors, estimate their potential impacts using scenario analysis, and include multidimensional actions and programs that deal with preparedness for, response to, and recovery from the occurrence of risk events. Finally, the new generation of NDPs should address poverty, inequality, and vulnerability in an articulated way since the poor are the most disadvantaged group in society and the most vulnerable to falling into deeper poverty. Moreover, growing inequality and vulnerability translate into more poverty.

Conclusion

Many countries use a national development plan to provide a road map of public interventions over the medium run. Evaluating the process of formulation, implementation, and M&E of the NDP and its contribution to poverty reduction and inequality involves some challenges. This chapter has provided two methodologies as possible guidelines for such an evaluation: an evaluation of the NDP process of elaboration and implementation in Costa Rica and a rapid and participatory assessment of the NDP M&E system in Cambodia.

Those case studies illustrated the need for evaluators to (1) assess the global, yet functional, positioning of the NDP within the results-based management cycle to link planning with programming, budgeting, M&E, and reporting, while articulating strategic, programmatic, and operational goals; (2) assess the comprehensive, yet structured, nature of the NDP technical process to capture the complexity and diversity of development issues like poverty and inequality, while leading to measurable progress on specific outcome targets; (3) assess the inclusive, yet coordinated, nature of the NDP institutional process for relevance and effectiveness of public action; (4) assess the relevance of NDP for addressing poverty challenges, but also inequality and vulnerability; (5) assess the participatory process of main actors outside the public planning system to generate consensus on the main objectives and goals of the NDP; and (6) assess realistic main goals and objectives.

NDP evaluations are even more complex than project or program evaluations. They require a combination of macro, meso, and micro approaches, a grasp of technical and institutional issues, a knowledge of a variety of sectors, and an ability to deal with cross-cutting issues in addition to more traditional competencies. This provides food for thought for evaluator training programs!

Notes

1. The name varies from one country to the next and from one international organization to the next; for example, national development plan, national strategic plan, poverty reduction strategy paper, growth and poverty reduction strategy, and others. Both communist countries such as China and Vietnam and capitalist countries such as Colombia and Malaysia have national development plans, some being more coercive and others more indicative.
2. Cambodia became a protectorate of France in 1863. It obtained its independence in 1953. The last 30 years of the 20th century were a troubled period, with the U.S. bombing of Cambodia from 1969 until 1973, a military coup in 1970, and worst of all, the Khmer Rouge regime, which carried out genocide of an estimated 2 million Cambodians from 1975 to 1979. Only since 1997 has the country experienced political stability. See http://en.wikipedia.org/wiki/Cambodia.
3. Costa Rica has generally enjoyed greater peace and more consistent political stability than many other Latin American nations. A Spanish colony, Costa Rica obtained its independence in 1821 and experienced only short periods of trouble (military dictatorship during 1917–19, a short civil war in 1948). There was a new constitution in 1949, and since then democratic governments have been the rule. See http://en.wikipedia.org/wiki/Costa_Rican_Civil_War.
4. For Costa Rica, gross domestic product growth (2013) of 3.5 percent, gross national income per capita of US$9,550 (current), 1.4 percent of the population living on less than US$1.25 a day, and a Gini index of 48.6.

5. For Cambodia, gross domestic product growth (2013) of 7.4 percent, gross national income per capita of US$950 (current), 10.1 percent of the population living on less than US$1.25 a day, and a Gini index of 31.8.

6. For example, United Nations Educational, Scientific, and Cultural Organization (UNESCO) World Heritage sites of Talamanca Range–La Amistad Reserves and La Amistad International Park, Cocos Island National Park, Area de Conservación Guanacaste, and Precolumbian Chiefdom Settlements with Stone Spheres of the Diquís.

7. For example, UNESCO World Heritage sites of Angkor Wat and Temple of Preah Vihear and other Hindu and Buddhist temples in the Angkor Archaeological Park, such as Angkor Thom and Bayon as well as Banteay Srei.

8. Cambodia has had plans in the past; however, its troubled history related to the American-Vietnam war and the Khmer Rouge period put this process on the sidelines for several years.

9. In Spanish, the Ministerio de Planificación Nacional y Política Económica.

10. Civil servants who had direct responsibilities for NDP formulation, sector plans, annual work plans and budgets, and M&E of NDP implementation.

11. The term "rapid and participatory assessment" might sound like an oxymoron. However, the process and methods used make it possible to solve the apparent conflict.

12. Developed by the IDEA Solutions branch of the Institute for Development in Economics and Administration, Canada. See http://ideasolutionsonline.com /A4R.

13. For example, operation of primary health care centers.

14. For example, an immunization campaign.

References

IDEA (Institute for Development in Economics and Administration). 2014a. *Assessing for Results Manual*. Quebec: IDEA Solutions Branch.

——. 2014b. *A Guide for Strategic Planning*. Quebec: IDEA.

Ministry of Planning. 2013. MIDEPLAN. Government of Costa Rica. http://www .mideplan.go.cr/.

——. 2015. "Summary Assessment of the M&E System for NSDP Implementation." Ministry of Planning, Phnom Penh.

CHAPTER 10

Assessing the Performance of Poverty and Inequality Reduction Programs: The Cases of Malaysia and Sabah and Sarawak States

Frederic P. Martin, Marie-Helene Boily, and Sylvain Lariviere

Introduction

Malaysia's record of poverty reduction over the period 1970–2004 has been a great success story, as shown in figure 10.1.

For a long time, governments in Malaysia have made reducing poverty and inequality a top priority in their successive development plans. For

Frederic P. Martin and Sylvain Lariviere are with the Institute for Development in Economics and Administration (IDEA). Marie-Helene Boily is with the Auditor General's Office of the Province of Quebec, Canada. The authors would like to acknowledge significant contributions from Noriyah Ahmad and Sa'idah Haji Hashim (Economic Policy Unit of the Prime Minister's Department), Gaston Gohou (Institute for Development in Economics and Administration), and Chung Tsung-Ping (United Nations Development Programme).

Figure 10.1   Poverty in Malaysia, 1970–2004

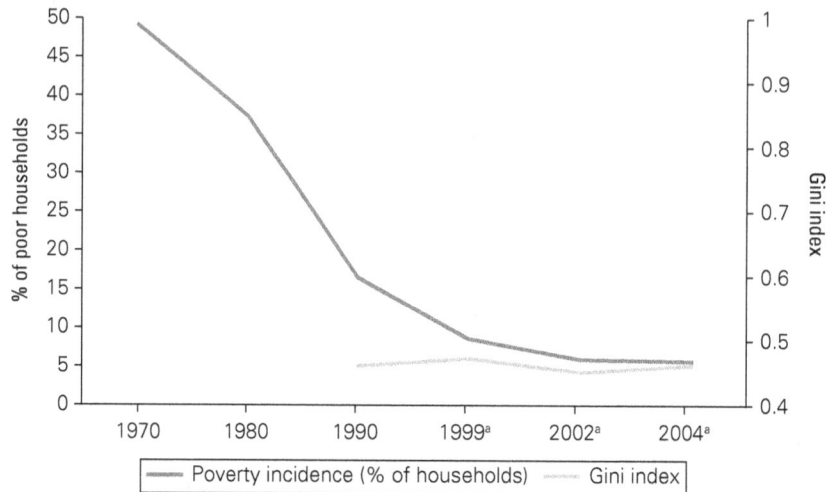

Source: Demery 2005.

a. Poverty incidence based on new poverty line.

instance, Prime Minister Abdullah made eradicating poverty one of the top priorities of the Ninth Malaysia Plan (2006–10). More specifically, the government set the following objectives: (1) halving poverty by 2010; (2) eliminating hard-core poverty by 2009, the time horizon for the Ninth Malaysia Plan; (3) raising the quality of life of the population; (4) developing human resources; and (5) raising human development values. Despite this impressive achievement (Economic Policy Unit 2004; Kinuthia 2010), pockets of high poverty remain in particular geographic areas and among certain population subgroups (Hatta and Ali 2013; Hill, Yean, and Zin 2011), as is often the case in middle-income countries (Weiss 2005).

Based on a study conducted in 2006–07 at the national level and in two states, Sabah and Sarawak, this chapter evaluates the performance of poverty and inequality reduction programs at national and subnational levels and provides a results-oriented approach for more relevant and efficient programs, which result in greater impacts. More specifically, it

1. Provides an overview of the poverty and inequality profile in Malaysia
2. Assesses the performance of public programs in reducing poverty and inequality, analyzing how the poor are defined, identified, and targeted and how poverty reduction programs address key dimensions and root causes of poverty
3. Proposes an operational approach for better planning, management, and monitoring and evaluation of those programs

The study used a variety of quantitative and qualitative methods to collect and analyze data: (a) a review of the relevant literature; (b) meetings with key ministries and other organizations involved in poverty reduction at the central level and with local authorities in two states chosen for their high level of poverty incidence, Sabah and Sarawak; (c) field visits to poverty reduction projects at the central and state levels; (d) analysis of secondary data from various household surveys; (e) the preparation of program or project reference sheets to be filled out by all ministries and organizations involved in significant poverty reduction programs at the central and state levels and the analysis of data provided on the sheets completed; and (f) working sessions with the main stakeholders—the Economic Policy Unit (EPU) of the Prime Minister's Department (PMD) and the United Nations Development Programme (UNDP)—to discuss preliminary results from the analysis and formulate policy and operational recommendations.

Overview of Poverty and Inequality Profile in Malaysia

Definition of Poverty

During the eighth plan period, the definition of poverty was reviewed to take into account social and economic changes since formulation of the poverty line in 1977 (Economic Policy Unit 2006, 2010). Malaysia's poverty line income (PLI) is made up of the food PLI and nonfood PLI. The PLI is defined separately for each household in the Household Income Survey based on its size, demographic composition, and location. Poor households are identified as households whose monthly incomes are less than their PLI. Hard-core poor households are identified as households whose monthly household incomes are less than the food PLI.

The food PLI is based on the cost of a food consumption basket that meets an individual's caloric requirements. The food PLI for Malaysia (overall) was RM 415 per month in 2004. The nonfood PLI was based on the actual expenditure of the bottom 20 percent expenditure group derived from the Household Expenditure Survey. The PLI in 2004 was RM 691 per month for Malaysia (overall), RM 687 for urban areas, and RM 698 for rural areas.

To facilitate the identification of poor and hard-core poor households, the establishment of a national poverty database, integrating both the rural and urban poverty registry and using a common definition of poor and hard-core poor households, was planned in the context of the Ninth Malaysia Plan.

At the time of this study, poverty data came only from income surveys, since no consumption expenditure surveys or qualitative studies on well-being had been conducted in the country.

Poverty and Inequality Profile in Urban and Rural Areas

Poverty is predominantly a rural phenomenon in Malaysia (figure 10.2). According to the 2002 Household Income Survey and using the new poverty line, rural poverty incidence was around 13.5 percent, while urban poverty incidence stood at around 2.3 percent. Further, rural poverty accounts for around three-quarters of total poverty.

While urban poverty incidence is quite low, the absolute number of urban dwellers in poverty is not insignificant. Further, there is reason to believe that in the course of urbanization "new" forms of poverty have begun to appear or to assume greater importance. These forms are associated with unskilled migrants from rural areas, low-wage foreign workers, and open unemployment.

Characteristics of the urban poor were analyzed in Kuala Lumpur and Petaling Jaya as part of the UNDP's Poverty Mapping of the Urban Poor Project. Two salient characteristics of the urban poor emerge from the household survey data collected as part of this study. First, around 20 percent of the poor are unemployed, and another 25 percent are

Figure 10.2   Poverty Incidence in Malaysia, 1970–2004

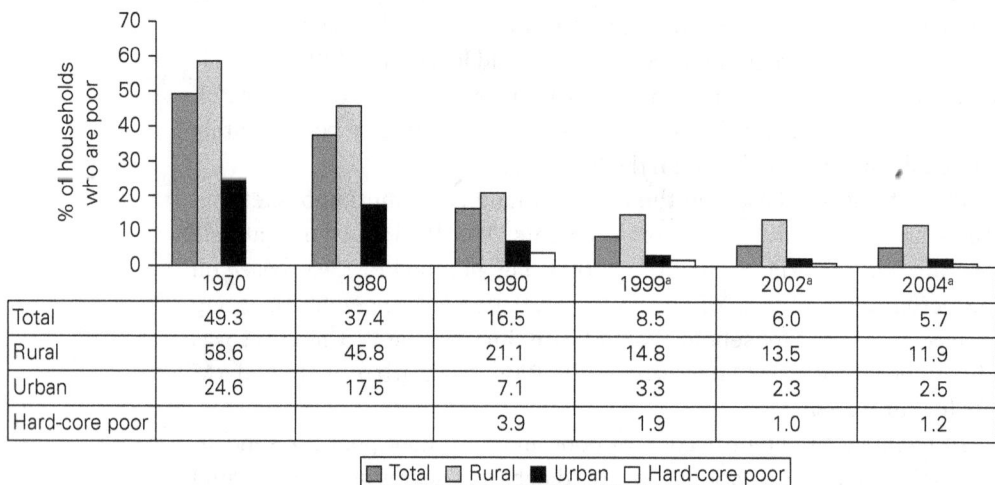

	1970	1980	1990	1999[a]	2002[a]	2004[a]
Total	49.3	37.4	16.5	8.5	6.0	5.7
Rural	58.6	45.8	21.1	14.8	13.5	11.9
Urban	24.6	17.5	7.1	3.3	2.3	2.5
Hard-core poor			3.9	1.9	1.0	1.2

Total ☐ Rural ☐ Urban ■ Hard-core poor

Source: Demery 2005.

a. Poverty incidence based on new poverty line.

pensioners in Kuala Lumpur. In Petaling Jaya, the unemployed make up a third of the poor. While more detailed information is required, open unemployment appears to be a significant component of urban poverty. Second, the coverage of social assistance benefits for the poor and hard-core poor is quite low.[1] Coverage rates for the various public schemes range from 30 percent (Baitulmal) to 0. It is worrying that only a third of the hard-core poor appear to benefit from the public transfer schemes under review.

Poverty and Inequality Profile by State

There is an important spatial dimension of poverty, as shown in table 10.1. According to the 2002 Household Income Survey and using the new poverty line, five states have high levels of poverty and hard-core poverty and contribute a large share of total poverty: Kedah, Kelantan, Terengganu, Sabah, and Sarawak. While more information is required on the characteristics of poverty within states, these data suggest the potential relevance of either geographic targeting of poverty programs and poverty-based public investment or resource allocation at the state level.

Table 10.1 Poverty Incidence by State, 2002

State	Poverty incidence (%)	Share of total poverty
Kelantan	17.8	16.1
Sabah	16.0	15.6
Terengganu	14.9	8.6
Sarawak	11.3	14.1
Kedah	9.7	12.9
Pahang	9.4	7.5
Perlis	8.9	1.1
Perak	6.2	10.9
Negeri Sembilan	2.6	1.7
Johor	2.5	5.4
Melaka	1.8	0.8
Negeri Pulau Pinang	1.2	1.3
Selangor	1.1	3.2
Kuala Lumpur	0.5	0.7
Total	5.1	100.0

Source: Demery 2005.

Poverty and Inequality Profile by Ethnic Group

Table 10.2 presents summary data on poverty incidence of ethnic minority populations in Peninsular Malaysia (Orang Asli), Sabah, and Sarawak.[2] Poverty incidence is extremely high, ranging from around 40 percent in Sarawak to 50 percent in Sabah and Orang Asli. Sabah accounts for around 55 percent of total ethnic hard-core poverty, followed by Orang Asli and Sarawak at around 36 and 8 percent, respectively. If accurate,[3] these data are quite striking, especially in light of past attempts to tackle ethnic minority poverty in Malaysia. They suggest the need for specially targeted programs to address the specific needs of particular subgroups.

Poverty and Inequality Profile in the State of Sabah

Table 10.3 presents data on various characteristics of poor and hard-core poor ethnic minority groups. Four points are particularly relevant for targeting purposes. First, with regard to occupational structure, the vast majority of the poor among ethnic minority households are economically active, but engaged in low-productivity activities. Households whose heads are agricultural or fishery workers make up close to 70 percent of total ethnic poverty (at the household level) and have very high poverty (65 percent) and hard-core poverty rates (21 percent). Second, those with no occupation have very high poverty (61 percent) and hard-core poverty (26 percent) rates and contribute a significant share of total ethnic poverty (15 percent) and hard-core poverty (20 percent). Third, the highest levels of ethnic minority poverty (64 percent) and second highest levels of hard-core poverty (28 percent) are found in households headed by persons 65 and above. This suggests the need for appropriate transfer mechanisms to supplement incomes of persons who are not economically active. Fourth, poverty rates

Table 10.2   Poverty Incidence of Ethnic Minority Populations in Malaysia, 2002
percent

Group	Poverty		Hard-core poverty	
	Incidence	Share of total ethnic poverty	Incidence	Share of total ethnic poverty
Orang Asli	51	35	16	36
Sabah	50	53	16	55
Sarawak	39	13	8	8
Total		100		100

Source: Economic Policy Unit Statistics Department database.

Table 10.3   Characteristics of Poor and Hard-Core Poor among Ethnic Minority Groups in Sabah, Malaysia, 2002
percent

Characteristics	Poverty		Hard-core poverty	
	Incidence	Household share of total ethnic poverty	Incidence	Household share of total ethnic poverty
Occupational structure				
Agricultural or fishery workers	65	68	21	69
No occupation	61	15	26	20
Total	51	100	17	100
Age structure				
65+	64	n.a.	28	n.a.
Total	51	n.a.	17	n.a.
Gender				
Female household head	62	18	27	24
Male household head	49	82	15	77
Total	51	100	17	100

Source: Economic Policy Unit Statistics Department database.

Note: n.a. = not applicable.

are considerably higher in female-headed than in male-headed ethnic minority households, at around 62 and 49 percent, respectively. Because female-headed households account for only 15 percent of all households, their contribution is around 18 percent to total ethnic minority poverty and around 24 percent to hard-core poverty.

Poverty and Inequality Profile in the State of Sarawak

As shown in table 10.4, many of the same characteristics of poor ethnic minority populations found in Sabah are present in Sarawak as well. First, an extremely high percentage of total ethnic minority poverty is composed of households whose heads are agricultural or fishery workers. They make up between 80 and 86 percent of total ethnic poverty (at the household level) and have very high poverty rates (51 percent). Second, the highest incidence of poverty (56 percent) and hard-core poverty (26 percent) is found among households whose head has no occupation. This category constitutes between 9 and 19 percent of total ethnic poverty.

Table 10.4 Characteristics of Poor and Hard-Core Poor among Ethnic Minority Groups in Sarawak, Malaysia, 2002

percent

Characteristics	Poverty		Hard-core poverty	
	Incidence	Household share of total ethnic poverty	Incidence	Household share of total ethnic poverty
Occupational structure				
Agricultural or fishery workers	51	86	10	80
No occupation	56	9	26	19
Total	39	100	8	100
Age structure				
65+	52	n.a.	17	n.a.
Total	39	n.a.	8	n.a.
Gender				
Female household head	46	20	15	30
Male household head	38	80	7	70
Total	39	100	8	100

Source: Economic Policy Unit Statistics Department database.

Note: n.a. = not applicable.

Third, the highest poverty and hard-core poverty rates are found in households whose head is 65 or above, which again points to the relevance of targeted transfers. Fourth, among ethnic minorities, female-headed households have higher poverty incidence than male-headed households, at 46 and 38 percent, respectively. Because they are relatively few in number, however, female-headed households constitute around 20 percent of total ethnic minority poverty and around 30 percent of hard-core poverty.

Performance of Poverty and Inequality Reduction Programs

All programs that give priority to reducing poverty and inequality were considered. Programs that have no specific focus with regard to target population or reduction of poverty and inequity were excluded. All selected program managers filled out a program or subprogram reference sheet to measure performance in terms of poverty and inequality reduction.

Performance was measured in two ways: (1) how the poor were defined, identified, and targeted in the program and (2) how programs addressed key dimensions and root causes of poverty. Overall, 18 program reference sheets were received for a total of 63 subprograms or projects.[4]

Some inconsistencies were noted in the identification of the poor by ministries and agencies. Most programs target the poor (38 percent), the low-income population (31 percent), and the hard-core poor (21 percent). Programs do not adequately target the most vulnerable groups identified in the poverty and inequality reduction profile analysis—that is, the rural population, the poorest states, poor and hard-core poor, women, and ethnic groups. Programs target mainly urban areas (84 percent against 40 percent for rural areas). Only two programs specifically target women. Most programs do not specifically target ethnic minority groups. It is therefore no surprise that programs aimed at individuals reach only 5 percent of the poor population, while programs aimed at households reach five times the number of poor households—that is, a combination of low coverage and high leakage.

Programs aim mainly to reduce absolute monetary poverty. The main types of programs relate to training and capacity building and the construction of residential units (urban areas) and social infrastructure, education, and income generation activities (rural areas). Programs are more diversified in urban than in rural areas.

There are both similarities and a few significant differences between programs conducted in the states. All divisions of Sabah and Sarawak are targeted by poverty reduction programs, and agricultural projects are the most frequently implemented. Most programs are not directed specifically toward the poor (23 percent in Sabah; 11 percent in Sarawak) and hard-core poor (11 percent in Sabah; 22 percent in Sarawak). Except for the Bumiputera, most programs do not target specific ethnic groups. The only major difference relates to the targeting of rural areas. Only 10 percent of the poverty reduction programs in Sabah explicitly target rural areas, while more than half of poverty reduction programs in Sarawak target rural areas.

The main challenges identified are how to tackle existing pockets of poverty, address inequality in living conditions, and develop mechanisms to cope with vulnerability. Significant progress has been made at the macro level in terms of linking planning and budgeting for results at the Ministry of Finance. However, issues remain in linking sector strategic objectives and targets to program outputs and costs. Finally, several subprogram managers could not provide data on (1) the number of targeted persons, households, and communities; (2) output targets; or (3) unit cost of providing outputs. This inability in itself indicates weaknesses in the planning, budgeting, and monitoring processes at national and, even more, state levels.

Recommendations to Improve Poverty Reduction and Inequality Programs in Malaysia

Recommendations were made first with regard to specific pillars of results-based management. Malaysia has made a lot of progress in the implementation of results-based management over the last 20 years. The Economic Policy Unit of the Prime Minister's Department and the Ministry of Finance have spearheaded several initiatives to reinforce results-based planning, budgeting, and monitoring and evaluation. Despite significant success, much remains to be done, especially at the subnational level.

With regard to the strategic planning process, improving the targeting of public programs for better coverage and reduced leakage is a must. This implies, among others, (1) including specific targets for reducing poverty in rural and urban areas and the poorest states and (2) setting targets for reducing income inequality, improving access to public services, and integrating the socioeconomic development process in favor of minority ethnic groups. Involving more minority ethnic groups in the identification of poverty reduction strategies would help to devise more relevant strategies for tailoring programs to the specificities of different target groups. Apart from better targeting, another major recommendation is to use a more global and integrated approach, looking beyond monetary poverty to capture (a) other dimensions of well-being, (b) inequality, which is a key cause of social instability and national disunity, and (c) vulnerability, which is becoming pervasive in open and small economies.

With regard to operational planning and budgeting, the elaboration of a medium-term fiscal framework and its companion sectoral medium-term expenditure framework helps to translate strategic plans into operational plans and contributes to greater consistency between poverty reduction targets and financial resources. However, the consistency between budget allocations and targets can be further improved by elaborating a more solid theory of change at the program level and devising better unit cost matrixes for outputs.

With regard to the monitoring and evaluation process, revising the definition of poverty to consider not only income data, but also expenditure data and nonmonetary dimensions of well-being would provide a more relevant and complete picture of poverty and inequality. Orienting existing monitoring and evaluation systems toward results would also contribute to better program design and impacts.

Beyond those recommendations, it is essential to integrate the various pillars of the results-based management cycle in two ways. First, it is important to articulate strategic planning at various levels (national, sector, subnational levels), on the one hand, and operational planning and budgeting at the program level, on the other hand. This can be done by revising program architectures and multiyear programming and budgeting frameworks and improving horizontal coordination across ministries and

Figure 10.3 Linking the Strategic Planning to Operational Planning and Budgeting

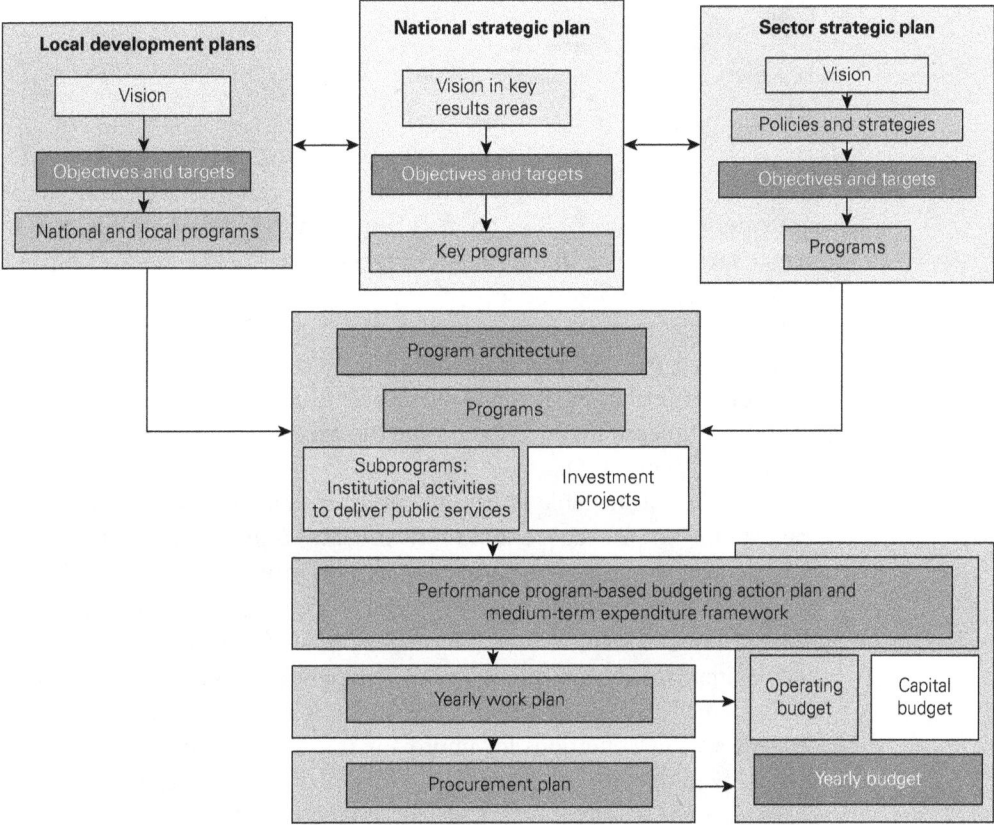

Figure 10.4 Articulation between Development Performance Measurement Frameworks and Monitoring and Evaluation Systems

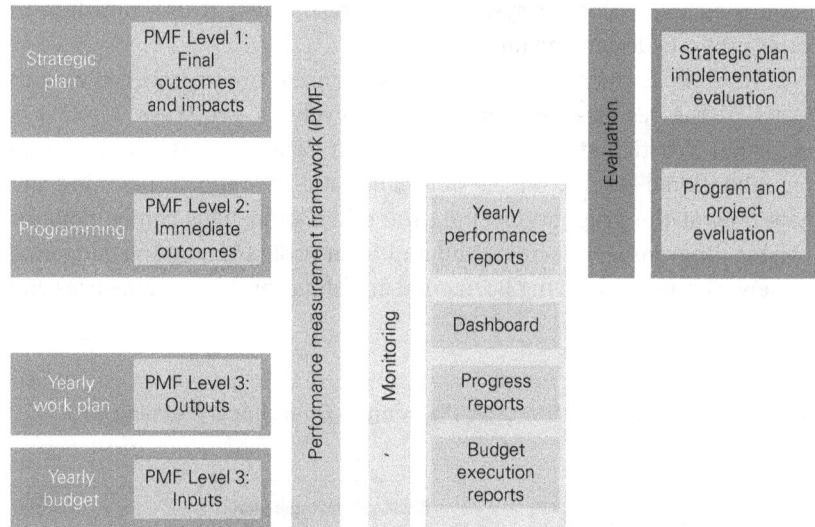

Note: PMF = performance measurement framework.

agencies and vertical coordination between central- and state-level strategies (figure 10.3). Second, it is important to formulate the performance measurement frameworks at various levels of the monitoring and evaluation system (figure 10.4).

In practical terms, the central government should support state governments with a package of capacity-building services. This package should touch on the various pillars of results-based management, concentrating on the weakest pillars that will determine the capacity of the whole management cycle (figure 10.5).

To achieve sustainable improvement of national and state government capacities, the package should (a) provide training in results-based management to a critical mass of public sector managers and professionals at national and, even more, state levels, (b) provide technical support to help them to design and implement relevant and practical management systems, and (c) improve the articulation of existing information systems and data quality. Finally, strong leadership and the design of a change management strategy are key conditions for improving the performance of poverty and inequality reduction programs. The record of recent governments of Malaysia at the national and state levels provides ample justification for this conclusion.

Figure 10.5 Integrated Approach to Building Capacities of Central and State Governments in Managing Poverty and Inequality Reduction Programs

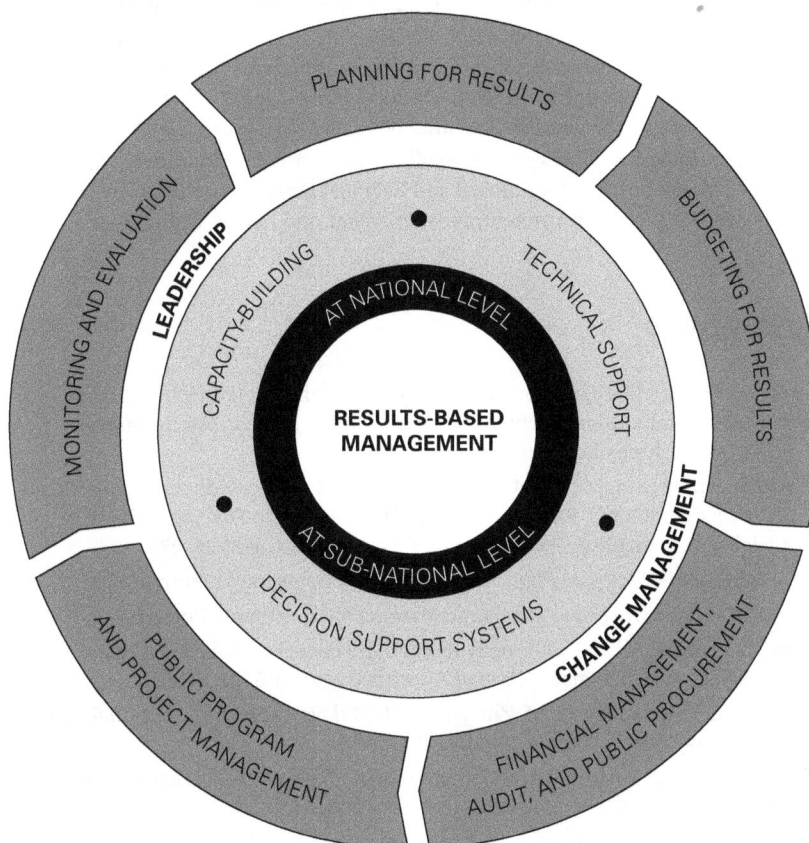

Notes

1. In places such as Baitulmal, Jabatan Kebajikan Malaysia, Perumahan Rakyat Miskin Tegar, Majlis Agama Negeri, and Agensi Inovasi Malaysia, among others.

2. All data originate from special Minority Surveys undertaken in 1999 (Peninsular Malaysia) and 2002 (Sabah and Sarawak). There are three caveats to bear in mind when reviewing these data. First, the poverty measures presented *appear* to be based on the government's official 1977 method for estimating the poverty line and making interpersonal comparisons of wealth. A major shortcoming of the approach is that household income is not deflated per capita or per adult equivalent. As a result, poverty levels are overstated in smaller households and understated in larger ones. This poses problems when making comparisons among population subgroups (ethnic populations) whose average household

size is different. Second, confidence intervals are not presented for the estimates of population proportions. Third, tests of statistical significance were not performed for differences in characteristics between population groups.

3. According to the regular Household Income Survey 2002 and using the new poverty line, poverty incidence in the "other Bumiputera" (that is, non-Malay) category stood at 18.6 percent (Demery 2005, table 13, p. 29). However, as discussed earlier, the data sets and methodologies used are different.

4. Ministry of Health, Ministry of Agriculture and Agro-Based Industry, Amanah Ihktiar Malaysia, Ministry of Rural and Regional Development, Ministry of Housing and Local Government, Jabatan Wakaf, and Majlis Agama Negeri.

References

Demery, L. 2005. "The New Poverty Line." EPU (Economic Policy Unit of the Prime Minister's Department) and UNDP (United Nations Development Programme), Kuala Lumpur.

Economic Policy Unit. 2004. "Malaysia: 30 Years of Poverty Reduction, Growth, and Racial Harmony." Paper presented at the Scaling up Poverty Reduction: A Global Learning Process and Conference, Shanghai, May 25–27.

———. 2006. *Ninth Malaysia Plan*. Prime Minister's Department, Putrajaya.

———. 2010. *Tenth Malaysia Plan*. Prime Minister's Department, Putrajaya.

Hatta, Z. A., and I. Ali. 2013. "Poverty Reduction Policies in Malaysia: Trends, Strategies, and Challenges." *Asian Culture and History* 5 (2): 48–56.

Hill, H., T. S. Yean, and R. H. M. Zin, eds. 2011. *Malaysia's Development Challenges: Graduating from the Middle*. London: Routledge.

Kinuthia, B. 2010. "Poverty Reduction in Malaysia." Africa Studies Centre, Leiden University, Leiden.

Weiss, J. 2005. *Poverty Targeting in Asia: Experiences from India, Indonesia, the Philippines, People's Republic of China, and Thailand*. Tokyo: ADB Institute.

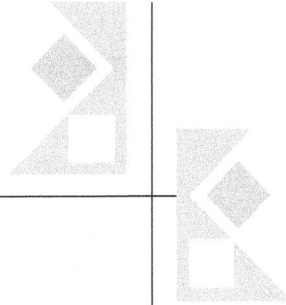

CHAPTER 11

Why Developing Monitoring and Evaluation Capacity Is Critical to Understanding and Addressing Issues of Poverty and Inequality

Robert Lahey

Introduction

Poverty has many dimensions and manifests itself in different ways, in addition to the obvious one of "too little income" for subsistence. The United Nations defines human poverty as the *deprivation* of three basic dimensions of human development: (a) a decent standard of living (in effect, a lack of access to overall economic provisioning), (b) knowledge (exclusion from the world of reading and communication), and (c) a long and healthy life (vulnerability to death at a relatively early age).[1] The reasons for poverty are

---

Robert Lahey is with REL Solutions, Inc.

generally many and multidimensional, reflecting social, economic, cultural, geographic, historical, and even political factors.

For many countries, there is strong political commitment to achieving the goals of poverty alleviation and a more equitable distribution of income. This may be reflected in a large number of programs or significant funding of social safety nets. However, it is not uncommon to hear of particular problems in understanding how or how well the various government interventions are performing, even in countries where poverty is deemed a policy priority. Questions arise about program design, implementation, delivery, and uptake by the intended recipients. Programs and policies meant to combat poverty may not be coordinated. Moreover, even if the programs are well designed, there is often uncertainty about their impact, largely because policies and programs are not properly evaluated to ensure that they are relevant, effective, efficient, and properly targeted. With limited or no impact analysis, it is virtually impossible to direct resources to where they are likely to be most effective and to make spending on social safety nets efficient.

These shortcomings stem in large part from a combination of inadequate data, limited monitoring and evaluation (M&E) capacity, and an institutionalized process that does not automatically provide public sector officials with evaluative information to support accountability and good governance.

This chapter makes the link between poverty reduction strategies and the new paradigm for the development of national evaluation (or M&E) capacity that has been emerging in recent years. If issues of poverty and inequality are deemed to be a priority of a country, then building capacity for M&E also needs to be recognized as a key part of the solution. Using the example of Botswana, the chapter identifies where and how countries need to invest in M&E capacity building if they are serious about alleviating poverty and addressing inequality.

Measuring and Monitoring Progress on Poverty Reduction and Inequality: The Experience of Botswana

Botswana is a middle-income country that has made poverty reduction and income distribution key priorities by establishing specific targets within its national vision, Vision 2016 (Botswana Vision Council 1996). Vision 2016 aims to build up the capabilities of poor people through education and better social services, so that they are able to escape from poverty and share in the country's prosperity. It identifies four objectives that deal with poverty and inequality:

- Reduce the percentage of people in income poverty by half, to 23 percent at most, by 2006, the first 10 years of the Vision 2016 period
- Eradicate absolute poverty, so that no part of the country will have people living with incomes below the appropriate poverty line
- Create a social safety net for persons who find themselves in poverty for any reason
- Make income distribution more equitable

While poverty levels in Botswana are relatively high (some 20.6 percent for headcount poverty in 2009–10, according to the World Bank's World Development Indicators), they are not excessive by the standards of comparable middle-income countries. Additionally, poverty levels are much lower than in some low-income countries in the region. Understanding the nature of poverty in the country, the progress being made toward the targets set, and the effectiveness of the various policy and program initiatives of the government is more difficult.

To measure and monitor progress, Botswana created the Vision Council, a tripartite organization representing the views of the public and private sectors as well as civil society. The council has been working with the national statistical agency (Statistics Botswana) and other agencies to develop the statistical database and capability to track performance on an ongoing basis. Although progress has been made in tracking and understanding poverty and inequality, the country still relies to a large extent on macro indicators of poverty, of the type shown in table 11.1.

More recently, the Gini coefficient has been added as an indicator of inequality. However, the data yield contradictory results in interpreting the trend: improving when examining consumption data, but worsening when examining income data.

Understanding poverty and poverty trends requires examining information at a more disaggregated level. Poverty rates in Botswana vary considerably across the country; the national average (20.7 percent using 2010 data) masks wide regional variations. In 2009–10, the urban poverty rate was 14 percent, while the rural poverty rate was 26 percent. Poverty rates in some districts are well over 40 percent. Nevertheless, the districts with high poverty rates tend to be sparsely populated, so the regions with the highest number of people in poverty are typically not those with the highest poverty rates. Analysis of poverty trends at this disaggregated level is confounded by contradictions in the data.

Table 11.1   Measuring, Monitoring, and Reporting on Poverty and Inequality in Botswana

Indicator	Trend	Overview
Population living in poverty (proportion of people living below the poverty line)	Improving	The share of Batswana living below the income poverty line decreased from 47% in 1993 to 37% in 2000, to some 30% in 2003, and to 28% in 2005.
Prevalence of underweight children (under five years of age)	Improving	The proportion of children under age five who are underweight for their age has been dropping steadily since 1996, when the figure was 17%. Since then, the prevalence of underweight children has dropped each year, to 13% in 2000, 7% in 2003, and 5% in 2006.
Access to safe drinking water	Improving	The proportion of the population with sustainable access to safe drinking water increased from 77% in 1996 to nearly 96% in 2004. This is higher than the target set by the Millennium Development Goals (MDGs). More than 80% of the people in all districts had access to safe water sources. This is significantly higher than the figure for Sub-Saharan Africa, which is 55%.
Access to adequate sanitation	Improving	Access to adequate on-site sanitation has improved over time. Comparing data from 2001 to 2006, households equipped with flush toilets or ventilated improved pit latrines (the Botswana sanitation standard) has increased from 39 to 52%. This varies substantially between urban and rural areas, where 2006 data show adequate sanitation in 77% of households in cities and towns, 63% in urban villages, and only 32% in rural areas.
Change in human welfare (human development index)	No trend	Botswana's human development index increased from 0.57 in 1980 to 0.67 in 1990, but has remained relatively constant since then at near 0.65 through 2005. Clearly, improvements in access to education and adult literacy in Botswana, along with a general improvement in standards of living, have not been enough to compensate for declining life expectancy at birth (that is, a lower probability of living a long and healthy life). In 2006 Botswana ranked 126 out of 179 countries with a human development index of 0.66. The country is ranked 13 in Africa.

Source: Botswana Vision Council 2009.

In general, identification and analysis of poverty trends are hampered by three types of data weaknesses: infrequent surveys, delays in publication of survey reports and data sets, and poor-quality analysis and uncertain methodologies in official publications. The inability to understand the effectiveness of government interventions also hampers strategies to alleviate poverty and inequality.

Table 11.2 Key Policies and Programs to Fight Poverty and Inequality in Botswana

Type of program	Program
Social safety net programs	Destitute Persons Program, Orphan Care Program, Old-Age Pension, World War I Veterans Program, Community Home-Based Care, Primary School Feeding, Vulnerable Groups Feeding Program, Ipelegeng
Economic support programs	Backyard gardening and alternative packages, Remote Area Development Program, Livestock Management and Infrastructure Development, Integrated Support Program for Arable Agricultural Development
Other programs (supporting economic growth, diversification, and employment creation)	Citizen Entrepreneurial Development Agency, Local Enterprise Authority, Internship Program, Youth Development Fund, National Masterplan for Arable Agriculture and Dairy Development, Economic Diversification Drive

Botswana has a wide array of programs aimed at eradicating poverty, and there is little doubt that there is strong political commitment to achieving this objective. Poverty alleviation programs can be categorized into two groups: social safety nets and economic diversification programs. The key programs are identified in table 11.2, which also identifies programs, policies, and institutions that are more generally supportive of economic growth, diversification, and employment creation.

Botswana clearly has an extensive network of social safety nets. They have been designed over the years to provide income or other support to a variety of categories of poor people and households. The total number of beneficiaries of these programs is large—around 550,000 or more than one-quarter of the population—but the true impact is difficult to assess because little is known about the extent of overlap—that is, receipt of multiple benefits. As a recent World Bank report notes, "The effectiveness of Botswana's key safety net programmes in terms of their coverage, targeting accuracy, and adequacy in raising beneficiaries' consumption or income has not been studied by Statistics Botswana or any other government agency" (World Bank 2012). In view of this knowledge gap, it is not possible to assess whether the Vision 2016 target with regard to safety nets is likely to be achieved.

In broad terms, it has been recognized that policies and programs are not properly evaluated to ensure that they are relevant, effective, efficient, and properly targeted. There is virtually no impact analysis, and concerns that programs and policies meant to combat poverty are not properly coordinated—and may even be contradictory—go unanswered.[2] In this situation, it is virtually impossible to direct resources to where they are likely to be most effective and to make spending on social safety nets efficient. In sum, such shortcomings stem from the country's inadequate capacity on three fronts: data, analysis, and M&E processes within the institutions of government decision making.

So what can and should be done differently? Botswana has recognized the importance of building a national country-owned M&E capacity. After some learning through unsuccessful attempts in the early 2000s, a new strategy has been developed that, if implemented, will provide an institutional basis for understanding the effectiveness not only of poverty programs and policies, but also of a wider range of social and economic programs and initiatives that could indirectly affect poverty or inequality.[3]

The latter is particularly important for a country like Botswana in which a wide range of other factors can have a bearing on whether goals associated with poverty alleviation and equality are achieved. This would include factors such as the global financial crisis or recession, which affected the market for diamonds, Botswana's major export; the subsequent fiscal restraint, which has constrained the amount of funds available for social safety net spending; the human immunodeficiency virus (HIV) and acquired immune deficiency syndrome (AIDS), which have negatively affected households in so many ways (death, loss of breadwinners, prolonged illness, extra expenses, orphans, and more); the costs of HIV and AIDS programs, which have reduced the funds available for other purposes; and the realities of a landlocked country, which result in higher production costs and a small domestic market, both of which negatively affect economic growth and employment creation and adversely affect poverty and equality reduction.

Devising a solution to problems of poverty and inequality for a country like Botswana needs to recognize poverty and inequality as multidimensional issues; to operate within a macro framework reflective of economic, social, and cultural factors in the context of the country's development; to rely on a credible database that is sufficiently rich in detail about the population, the state of the economy, and society in general; and to have a sufficiently sound capacity and ability to measure, monitor, and evaluate how well the country's poverty eradication programs and policies are performing so as to ensure a cost-effective approach to the various government initiatives.

The comprehensive M&E strategy developed for Botswana parallels what the international community has referred to as "the new paradigm for monitoring and evaluation"—a national, country-owned M&E system, developed in such a way as to respect current M&E capacity gaps in the country, but with a goal of building M&E and data capacity to achieve a sustainable and effective M&E system over a specified period of time.

What Is Implied by the New Paradigm for Monitoring and Evaluation?

The experience of Botswana illustrates the connectivity between (a) the ability to understand the issues surrounding poverty and inequality and devise appropriate solutions and (b) the capacity to carry out systematic M&E and evaluative research in a way that is credible, effective, and sustainable. For many countries, too little priority is given to M&E capacity development or key challenges are ignored when integrating M&E within a country's institutions. This is where the efforts of the new paradigm for M&E need to align with special efforts to tackle poverty and inequality.

The new paradigm regarding development of national evaluation (or M&E) capacity is centered on national ownership and evaluation capacity that is linked to the national vision of the country, accountability, and good governance. Menon (2010) describes the paradigm as follows:

> National ownership would require that development partners join in the evaluation project of the country; that this project is intrinsically linked to national vision and national accountability of citizens; that it be an integral part of strong democratic governance processes; that the evaluation method and process is complex and sensitive enough to capture a range of influences on public policy; that the results of the process are meaningful and can effect change in public action.

Put another way, the new paradigm would demand much more than historical calls for "harmonization and alignment" of M&E efforts in a country: "A new evaluation architecture . . . [needs] to be erected so as to give a privileged role to country-based evaluations with developing countries in the driver's seat" (Picciotto 2007). These are high expectations that would ultimately see, as is the case for Botswana, a national M&E system that

- Uses the two tools of monitoring and evaluation to measure the performance of a country's projects, programs, and policies;
- Is country-owned in that it is aligned with the national development goals of the country;
- Is national in scope;
- Is used effectively in public sector management; and
- Is sustainable.

Figure 11.1   Assumptions and Risks Underlying a Well-Functioning M&E System

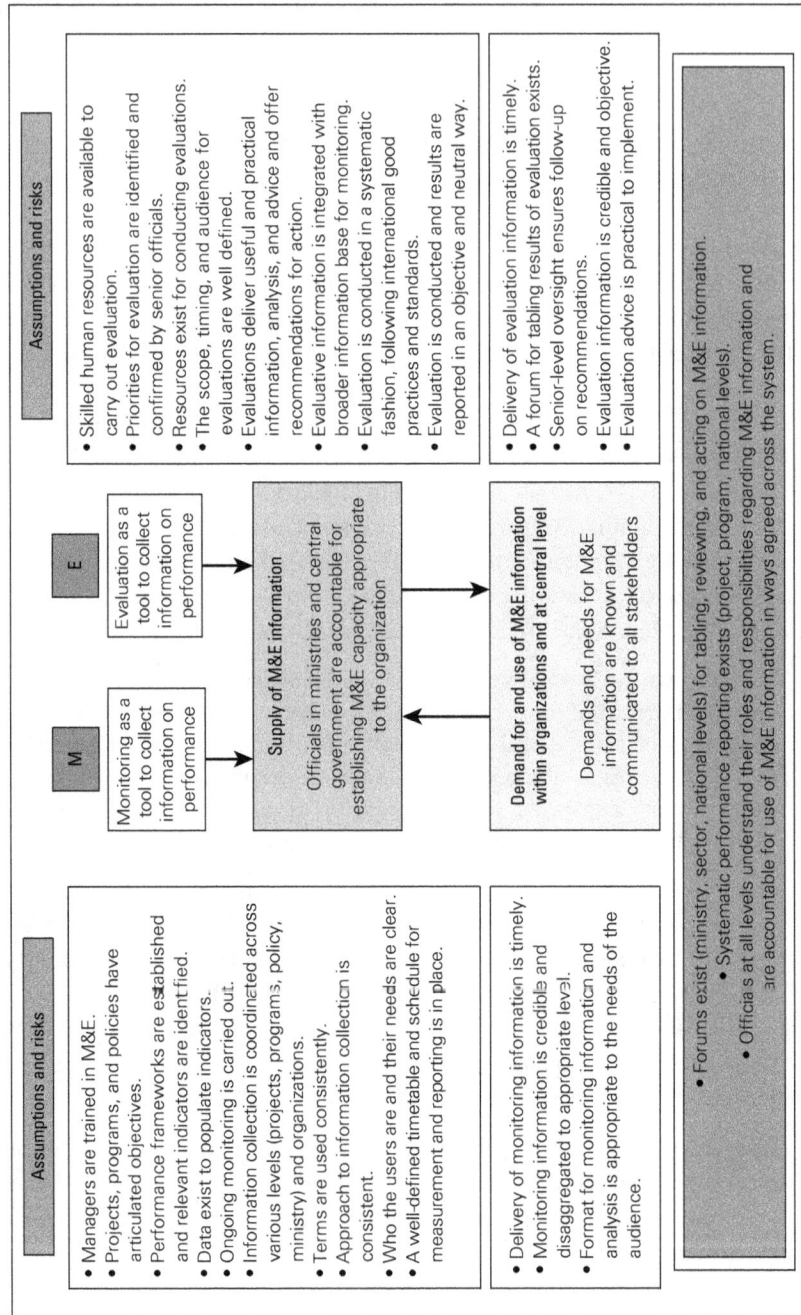

Assumptions and risks

- Managers are trained in M&E.
- Projects, programs, and policies have articulated objectives.
- Performance frameworks are established and relevant indicators are identified.
- Data exist to populate indicators.
- Ongoing monitoring is carried out.
- Information collection is coordinated across various levels (projects, programs, policy, ministry) and organizations.
- Terms are used consistently.
- Approach to information collection is consistent.
- Who the users are and their needs are clear.
- A well-defined timetable and schedule for measurement and reporting is in place.

- Delivery of monitoring information is timely.
- Monitoring information is credible and disaggregated to appropriate level.
- Format for monitoring information and analysis is appropriate to the needs of the audience.

| M | | E |

Monitoring as a tool to collect information on performance

Evaluation as a tool to collect information on performance

Supply of M&E information

Officials in ministries and central government are accountable for establishing M&E capacity appropriate to the organization

Demand for and use of M&E information within organizations and at central level

Demands and needs for M&E information are known and communicated to all stakeholders

Assumptions and risks

- Skilled human resources are available to carry out evaluation.
- Priorities for evaluation are identified and confirmed by senior officials.
- Resources exist for conducting evaluations.
- The scope, timing, and audience for evaluations are well defined.
- Evaluations deliver useful and practical information, analysis, and advice and offer recommendations for action.
- Evaluative information is integrated with broader information base for monitoring.
- Evaluation is conducted in a systematic fashion, following international good practices and standards.
- Evaluation is conducted and results are reported in an objective and neutral way.

- Delivery of evaluation information is timely.
- A forum for tabling results of evaluation exists.
- Senior-level oversight ensures follow-up on recommendations.
- Evaluation information is credible and objective.
- Evaluation advice is practical to implement.

- Forums exist (ministry, sector, national levels) for tabling, reviewing, and acting on M&E information.
- Systematic performance reporting exists (project, program, national levels).
- Officials at all levels understand their roles and responsibilities regarding M&E information and are accountable for use of M&E information in ways agreed across the system.

Figure 11.1 elaborates on what this might mean for configuring a national M&E system and critical areas for its development. It paints a picture that represents lofty expectations for an M&E system in *any* country, but more so in a country with little or no M&E capacity at the outset. It underscores the importance of recognizing that M&E capacity development is long term and iterative and that expectations need to be managed, particularly those of senior officials. Figure 11.1 highlights some of the main assumptions associated with the operation of an M&E system. Failure to meet these expectations poses risks to the effectiveness and long-term sustainability of the system.

A national M&E system has two key stakeholder groups: those who *supply* M&E information and those who *demand* or *use* M&E information. On the supply side, the use of the two tools to measure and analyze performance—monitoring and evaluation—rests on distinct sets of officials in the system having the capability and expertise as well as the specified role to carry out these functions. On the demand side, the effectiveness of the national M&E system to support good governance rests in part on senior officials understanding the role of M&E as a mechanism to improve accountability, to build knowledge for project and program improvement, and to inform planning, policy and program development, and budgeting decisions.

Implicit in a well-functioning M&E system are the enablers that help to ensure that the M&E system will function in practice. Such enablers include the existence of available data that are credible and senior-level commitment to invest in the M&E system and to allow it to operate in full public view. The following institutional arrangements are important for ensuring an enabling environment for M&E in a country:

- A national statistical agency to ensure that data and data development are not overlooked in the context of M&E system development
- A systematic planning function within government institutions to ensure that M&E information eventually becomes an integral part of the policy, planning, and budgeting cycle in government operations
- Oversight agencies (such as a national audit office) and indeed Parliament to provide independent feedback to support credible, objective, and transparent measurement and reporting of effectiveness
- M&E partners and networks, including professional evaluation associations, to develop a national M&E system in a cost-effective fashion
- Civil society engagement, while generally a challenge, to make government accountable to the public. This can be supported by an informed media and access to information legislation.

Steps to Building Capacity to Monitor and Evaluate across All Sectors

Recognizing and Addressing Capacity Gaps

A systematic approach to developing a national M&E system ought to start with a systematic approach to identifying key capacity gaps that may be inhibiting the ability to generate or use M&E information within the country. Different frameworks have been developed for carrying out such a diagnostic, but the mechanism recommended here has been developed and used in several countries for identifying M&E capacity gaps (Lahey 2012, 2013a, 2013b). Based on a model of a national M&E system resting on four building blocks, it assesses critical success factors—some 28 in all—that are important to the development of an effective and sustainable M&E system. These factors are described in annex 11A.

This model is intended as a guide rather than a one-size-fits-all prescriptive approach to national M&E development or determination of M&E needs. It recognizes that the broad requirements for an effective M&E system go well beyond simply technical issues. Put another way, the successful institutionalization of an M&E system means much more than simply producing good-quality M&E information.

Table 11.3 illustrates the typical challenges that countries with limited M&E experience often face. This is not specific to any particular country, but it illustrates the nature of typical M&E capacity gaps and provides potential responses that could be built into the strategy for developing a national M&E system.

Table 11.3 Typical Challenges and Realities to Consider in Developing a Country-Owned National M&E System

Challenge	Possible response
Gaining a common understanding of M&E: What is M&E? How can and will M&E be used? What are reasonable expectations regarding how far and how fast an M&E system can be developed?	• Increase understanding of M&E through training and orientation for both senior and operational levels • Build consensus through a participatory process to build understanding • Create senior champions for M&E at the political level and a strong central agency

(continued)

Poverty, Inequality, and Evaluation

Table 11.3   (continued)

Challenge	Possible response
Sorting out the institutional arrangements for a national M&E system: gaining a common vision of what a national M&E system looks like; identification of a central M&E champion—structure and mandate of the central M&E unit; clarity and coordination of roles and responsibilities for each of the central players; role of ministries in the M&E system—institutional and resource implications; clarity regarding how and by whom—centrally and within ministries—M&E information will be used; clarity regarding where and how civil society and the private sector fits into the national M&E system	• Increase understanding of M&E and institutional implications through training and orientation • Develop a plan for an appropriate institutional structure • Build consensus on roles and responsibilities of central players through the developmental and implementation phases • Determine resourcing and mandates of M&E institutional structures • Pilot and phase in the M&E system to allow time to assess how well the system is functioning and identify opportunities for adjustments
Lack of systematic measurement of results at all levels: lack of policies, guidelines, and standards; lack of infrastructure to support results-oriented monitoring (performance frameworks and indicators); data issues	• Increase knowledge through training of both technical and nontechnical officials • Clarify the need for clarity around accountabilities for measuring performance • Develop performance frameworks for major programs, sectors, and nationally • Develop results-oriented indicators • Develop appropriate performance measurement strategies at the level of ministry and nationally • Address data issues
Lack of evaluation of programs and policies: lack of policy, guidelines, and standards; little or no resourcing of evaluation	• Increase knowledge through training, focusing initially on *managing* evaluations and eventually on *leading* evaluations • Introduce at a manageable pace of one or two evaluations of priority areas a year • Establish a senior committee to ensure that evaluation is used to support decision making, demonstrating the utility of evaluation
Lack of skilled and experienced human resources in M&E	• Develop a comprehensive multiyear strategy for M&E training and development • Network with potential M&E partners—national, regional, and international—to establish cost-effective approaches to M&E human resource training and development

(continued)

Table 11.3 (continued)

Challenge	Possible response
Data issues: lack of data to populate indicators; inconsistency across data sets; too little subnational data	• As needed, support capacity building of the national statistics agency to improve data issues, linking development of a national M&E system to a broader national data development strategy • Conduct periodic surveys or special studies in areas where there is too little credible data or information
Communications strategy for M&E	• Have high-level officials endorse and place high priority on development of a national M&E system early in the process • Address the lack of clarity or ambiguity regarding M&E roles and responsibilities for the key central players early in the process • As a multiyear initiative, provide periodic updates to ensure that early enthusiasm is not lost due to M&E fatigue • Communicate lessons from early pilots so that others can benefit

Note: M&E = monitoring and evaluation.

Developing Key Components of Infrastructure

There generally has been too little focus on the components of M&E infrastructure and the institutional arrangements needed to support a national M&E system. While there are no simple answers to identifying what a good M&E system looks like, the experience of both developed and developing countries points to some key components of an effective and sustainable M&E system (Lahey 2012).[4] These components can be framed around six elements:

1. *The policies, guidelines, and guidance for M&E that set the expectations about what should be measured, monitored, and reported and how frequently, among others.* These represent the broad rules and expected standards for M&E. A central agency (for example, the Ministry of Finance or Planning) could be the lead agency here, with support as needed from international experts.

2. *A clear articulation of goals, objectives, and expected key results for each level of public sector involvement where performance is intended to be measured*—that is, at the national, sector or ministry, and program levels. These can be established through the development of a *performance framework* at each of those levels, which would then serve

Figure 11.2   A National Integrated M&E Framework: Measuring Performance at Three Levels (I, III, and IV)

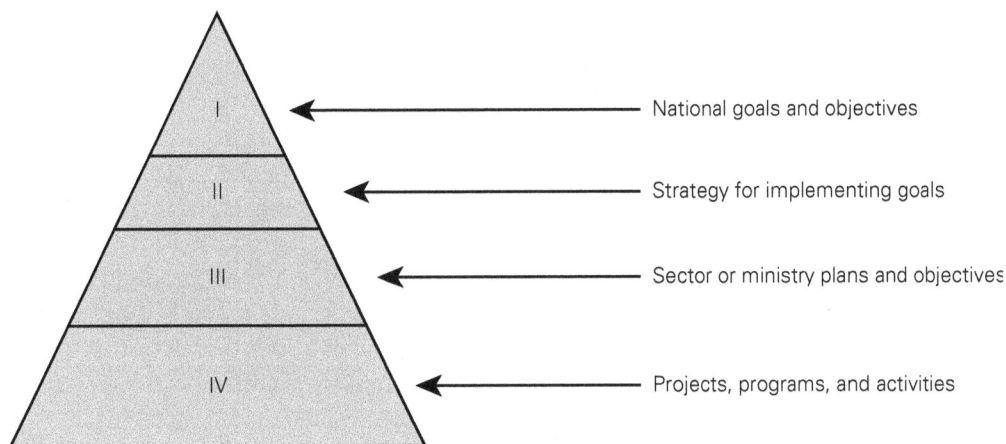

as the basis for identifying *key performance indicators* (KPIs). Ideally, the three levels of performance are recognized from the outset, and both expectations and measurement strategies are aligned. Further, a national integrated M&E framework could show the logical links between national goals and objectives, sector strategies, ministry action plans, and the contribution of individual programs and projects, as illustrated in figure 11.2.

3. *A performance measurement strategy that identifies how indicators can be populated with data in the most cost-effective way—that is, using performance monitoring, evaluation, and special studies, as appropriate.* Implicit in this is a data development strategy that would help to identify data sources and the need for new data. The national statistical agency would have an important role in this strategy.

4. *Institutional arrangements to develop and implement the M&E system.* Over the years, different countries have had different configurations, but in general it is recommended that the country have a central M&E unit to guide development and determine central needs of an M&E system and M&E capability within major ministries to address performance at the program, policy, and ministry or sector levels (Lahey 2010, 2012).

5. *A training strategy that would provide M&E training to different groups according to their needs.* This strategy would include technical training to M&E officers, analysts, and those tasked with developing data systems and M&E orientation to managers, senior officials, and other key stakeholders.

6. *Tasking of key officials to monitor the progress of M&E development and provide oversight of the quality of M&E being generated.* Both the central agency and the national audit office could play a role here.

Table 11.4 elaborates on each of these key components and identifies possible lead players in their development.

Several aspects of M&E infrastructure are important.

Most developing (and many developed) countries do not have a national M&E system as structured or as comprehensive as the one suggested here. Even countries deemed by the Organisation for Economic Co-operation and Development (OECD) to be leaders in M&E, such as Australia, Canada, and the United States, continue to work at developing their M&E systems.

The three levels of performance that could be identified within a national integrated M&E framework, shown as levels I, III, and IV in table 11.5, represent different levels of aggregation of indicators and the data needed to populate them. They also represent different levels of information serving the needs of different users of M&E information.

Table 11.4 Key Components of Infrastructure for a National M&E System

Component	Possible lead
1. Policies, guidelines, and guidance on M&E practices and standards	
Policy guidance on performance measurement, monitoring, and reporting	Central agency
A performance reporting strategy and guidelines	Central agency
A government-wide evaluation policy and standards	Central agency
2. Performance frameworks and key performance indicators (KPIs)	
National-level framework and KPIs	Central agency
Sector- and ministry-level framework, program activity architecture, and KPIs	Ministry
Frameworks and KPIs for key government programs	Ministry
3. Performance measurement strategy and data development plan	
National-level performance measurement and reporting	Central agency
Sector- or ministry-level performance measurement and reporting	Ministry
Program- and project-level performance measurement and reporting	Ministry
Data development strategy and plan	Central agency, national statistical agency, ministry

(continued)

Table 11.4   (continued)

Component	Possible lead
4. Institutional arrangements to support M&E development and use	
Central M&E unit in central agency	Central agency
M&E unit in each major ministry (phased in)	Ministry
Trained and experienced evaluators	Central agency, ministry
Analytical and performance reporting capability in each major ministry	Ministry
Data warehousing (storage and retrieval capability)	Ministry, national statistical agency
Senior committee to identify priority areas for possible evaluation	Central agency
Feedback mechanisms for input of civil society and private sector	Central agency, civil society, private sector
5. Training strategy and plan	
Training strategy for both providers and users of M&E information	Central agency
Training plan implemented in a timely way	Central agency, ministry
A national M&E professional network with international links	Central agency, ministry
6. Communications, oversight, and quality control	
Communications strategy to inform on the expectations, timeframe, and progress on M&E implementation	Central agency
Senior committees to monitor implementation of each pilot and the overall M&E system	Central agency, ministry
Ongoing quality control and oversight to monitor M&E system	Central agency, national audit office

Note: M&E = monitoring and evaluation.

Developing a national M&E system needs to take account of the country context and compare current capacity with the potential goals for the national M&E system. Of course the M&E infrastructure that is appropriate for one country may not be as workable in another country for reasons associated with the enabling environment.

For some countries, the M&E system may be mature and many of these elements may be in place. In some others, M&E components may be in place, but may not be well systematized or well articulated. For many countries, there is a significant capacity gap to achieving an effective and sustainable M&E system. In these cases, the M&E system should probably be implemented gradually, allowing the system to learn and adjust, though with an overarching goal of having an M&E system in place within a fixed period of time.

In countries with little or no current M&E capacity, a gradual or phased approach to M&E development and implementation is recommended. This would entail establishing a central M&E unit along with limited piloting—for example, establishing M&E units within two or three ministries. Following a period of learning and adjustment, the number of pilots could be expanded.

Sorting out Roles and Responsibilities of the Main Players

As noted, a wide range of key players are involved in a national M&E system—beginning with its development, implementation, and ongoing operation—to ensure that the system is effective and sustainable. Table 11.5

Table 11.5 Roles and Responsibilities of the Main Players in a National M&E System

National stakeholders	Possible roles and responsibilities
Senior government official (for example, Office of the President or Office of the Prime Minister)	• Serve as a champion for the drive to results-based M&E in the public sector
Central agency (for example, the Ministry of Finance or Ministry of Planning)	• Champion and facilitate M&E development and implementation activities • Coordinate the appropriate rollout of M&E across ministries • Establish guidance and guidelines for performance measurement, monitoring, evaluation, and reporting (government policy center for M&E) • Establish a central M&E unit • Facilitate or manage high-level evaluations or special studies • Monitor progress of M&E implementation across the system • Play a role in oversight and quality control regarding all M&E performance measurement and reporting • Establish an M&E professional development strategy for the country • Work with other partners in M&E capacity-building initiatives: workshops, training, and so forth • Lead development of a national performance framework • Lead and coordinate preparation of a national performance report • Advise senior government officials on all M&E matters • Work with civil society and private sector to promote feedback mechanisms as input to M&E • Facilitate development of a national M&E professional association

(continued)

Table 11.5   (continued)

National stakeholders	Possible roles and responsibilities
Senior M&E committee	• Determine priorities for the conduct of high-level evaluation or special studies • Serve as a forum for review of findings and decisions regarding follow-up • Provide oversight over pace of national M&E system development
National statistical agency	• Provide expertise on data capture and development • Provide national survey capability • Store data centrally • Serve as a focal point for national data development strategy • Assist ministries with data development strategies
National audit office	• Play a potential oversight role of M&E system (audits of the quality of data, quality of results-based performance reporting)
Training institutions (for example, a national or regional university or a public sector training institute)	• Serve as a potential partner to help to build M&E understanding through formal training
Civil society	• Work with central agency and ministries to formalize ongoing or periodic feedback mechanisms
Private sector	• Work with central agency and ministries to formalize ongoing or periodic feedback mechanisms
Other nonpublic agencies	• Serve as potential partners with a central agency or individual ministries in M&E development (where specific pockets of M&E knowledge or expertise exist)

Note: M&E = monitoring and evaluation.

identifies the key national stakeholders and their potential roles and responsibilities for the M&E system. Clearly, these roles are going to be a function of how M&E is institutionalized in a particular country. In addition, as the system evolves from the early formative (development or implementation) phase to a fully operational phase, roles and responsibilities for some will likely alter.

The model described in table 11.5 is consistent with the discussion in the previous section in that both a central agency of government and individual ministries play key roles in the national M&E system. In this respect, some key factors are worth highlighting.

It is important to recognize that champions are needed to build a national M&E system at two levels—at the political level (for example, a minister of finance or planning) and at the operational level (for example, the central unit that may be leading the national M&E system development efforts).

The central agency will likely play a larger role, particularly in early stages of national M&E development, both in creating demand for M&E information and in ensuring that M&E is institutionalized across the full public sector. If a central M&E unit is created (say, within the Ministry of Planning or Finance), it could serve as the M&E focal point or policy center as well as potentially lead or facilitate the conduct of higher-level evaluations that deal with more strategic or broader issues of government policy.

Individual ministries represent the front line in terms of what will be needed and expected for measuring and reporting public sector results. In many countries, certain ministries (such as education or health) are generally better equipped for M&E: for example, they may have better data systems, a history of an M&E unit, and international or nongovernmental organization (NGO) support, among others. They often are good candidates to serve as pilots if a more comprehensive or systematic national M&E system is being contemplated.

A key capacity challenge that most national M&E systems face to varying degrees relates to data: the quality, credibility, and integrity of the data or information used to measure performance. For this reason, the national statistical agency—the data experts—ought to play a key role in supporting development of the national M&E system. Investment and a long-term strategy for data development are needed, but are often overlooked in planning and resourcing development of a national M&E system.

The other (and generally most recognized) capacity gap for national M&E systems is the short supply of M&E expertise needed to develop and operate an effective and sustainable national M&E system. This would include two levels of expertise: M&E analysts and more highly qualified evaluators. Building M&E skills and orienting officials to use M&E in decision making are generally not formalized within the curricula of teaching institutions, putting the onus on other agencies to support or deliver training. Additionally, long-term training of officials can become cost-prohibitive if reliance is primarily on international trainers. Over time, a comprehensive strategy needs to be developed for training and development of the skills needed to supply and use M&E information.

Civil society and the private sector generally do not play a lead role in M&E development and frequently play a minor role in implementation of a national M&E system. That said, an effective national M&E system ought to have capabilities for ongoing and systematic gathering of information from citizens of the country. Moreover, the media and media associations can be important elements in the public reporting and dissemination of M&E information to civil society. For this to happen, political will is needed to allow transparency and public disclosure of information.

Implications of the Model for M&E Capacity Development

In the context of national M&E capacity development, the model for a national M&E system described in this chapter suggests the following:

- A needs assessment must go far beyond addressing the technical capacity to supply M&E information. In other words, a good evaluation or performance report on its own is not enough.
- Focus is needed on building M&E infrastructure and integrating M&E into appropriate institutional arrangements within the public sector of the country in question.
- M&E needs to move from being a special initiative to being part of the mainstream functioning of the public sector. In many countries, this likely implies some form of public sector reform.
- The functioning of the system—where and how M&E information gets used, by whom, and for what purpose—likely needs more attention than it generally gets. While there is often broad agreement on the concepts of M&E and results-based management, too little attention is generally paid to addressing issues of implementation or critical issues like poverty and inequality.
- Capacity-building efforts to develop a national evaluation (or M&E) system need to be far broader than the traditional training initiatives, which, though still important, are insufficient in the context of the new paradigm.
- Training needs to be built around a more comprehensive strategy that is closely aligned with M&E implementation and recognizes the training and development needs of a broad set of players.
- Regardless of what is driving the need for an M&E system—whether it is donor requirements, political or public sector reforms, citizen demand, or legislative requirements—different motivating forces and likely a different set of champions will be promoting M&E development. This speaks to a need to ensure that politicians and senior officials are aware of the importance and the role of M&E and results-based management for good public sector management, implying another nontechnical (and high-level) audience for training on the basics of M&E.

- It is likely prudent not to seek the information technology solution too early in the process of M&E system development, allowing flexibility to try, adapt, change, and improve as needed.

These are practical considerations that officials spearheading M&E development need to recognize and factor into system development. They represent capacity gaps that are present in most developing countries at the outset of embarking on development of a national M&E system.

Some Concluding Remarks

This chapter has made the connection between the challenges of dealing with poverty alleviation and inequality and the challenges of developing effective and sustainable national monitoring and evaluation systems. It suggests that aligning efforts to address the first with efforts to address the second will be mutually beneficial.

Countries often have difficulty grappling with the issues of poverty and inequality, even when they are government priorities. This difficulty is due, in part, to the tendency to give too little priority to what some may deem as the more technical, administrative, or bureaucratic aspects of governing—that is, systematic collection of data, monitoring of indicators, and evaluation of performance. In many developing countries, in spite of the growing interest and discussion of results-based management and managing for results, the system is often poorly equipped to measure and analyze results. Even in countries that speak of their M&E system, data deficiencies may limit monitoring to the *implementation of programs* and perhaps the *production of outputs*. Moreover, the evaluation may be all but absent, with little or no evaluation to inform decision makers on how well their various programs are meeting objectives, reaching target audiences, achieving cost-effectiveness, and so on. In this environment, officials are at a disadvantage in their attempts to understand the multidimensional problems of poverty and inequality and to decide how best to deal with them.

This chapter has spoken of what the international community has referred to as the new paradigm for M&E and how it has raised the bar, as well as the expectations, for country-owned national M&E systems. The declaration by the United Nations of 2015 as the Year of Evaluation will raise the bar even higher. This needs to be recognized as an opportunity not only for evaluators and M&E specialists to make inroads in development of a national M&E system, but also for officials who specialize in poverty eradication to work together toward a goal where all will benefit.

What this may mean is that they will have to work across traditional boundaries, both organizational or institutional and professional. This is also likely true for international partners who are supporting a country's poverty reduction programs and efforts aimed at reducing inequality, building capacity of the national statistical agency and data development in general, and developing monitoring and evaluation capacity. To address issues of poverty alleviation and inequality, there is a need to invest not only in development of poverty reduction programs, but also in development of a national M&E system and provision of technical and analytical support for a national data development plan. None of these efforts is cost-less and, in a world where most countries are still being affected by the global economic recession, there is a need to recognize the economies of coordinated efforts. This chapter suggests that a participatory and inclusive approach to development of a national M&E system would be a good way to move forward.

Such an approach quite likely means that countries and the international community (United Nations agencies, donors, and other international bodies) need to be seeking new approaches to supporting M&E development. For example, such an approach may require a more multipronged and comprehensive approach to training and orienting officials to M&E.

In addition to investment in training, now more than ever, there is a greater need to focus on what the institutional structure, roles, and responsibilities of a national M&E system could look like and how best to integrate M&E into the mainstream of public sector operations so that it eventually becomes part of the normal course of doing business.

Annex 11A Critical Success Factors for Developing a National M&E System: A Mechanism for Identifying M&E Needs

To aid those involved with the development and implementation of a national M&E system, this annex provides a mechanism for identifying M&E capacity gaps concerning national M&E capability. It has been derived from the model of a national M&E system resting on the four building blocks referenced in this chapter and is based implicitly on the infrastructure and institutional arrangements for a national M&E system discussed in the text.

For each building block, several critical success factors have been identified. Associated with each factor is a set of key considerations for success, presented in the form of questions. As noted, this is intended as a guide rather than a one-size-fits-all prescription for development of a national M&E system or determination of M&E needs. It recognizes the importance of taking a broad and comprehensive approach to developing a national M&E system that is effective and sustainable.

The rest of this annex presents the building blocks and critical success factors for developing a national M&E system.

Building Block 1: Vision and Leadership

Appreciation for the importance and role of M&E

- Are political and senior officials aware of the importance of M&E and results-based management to good governance and management practices?
- Is there an understanding of how M&E information can assist public sector managers, decision makers, and the country in moving to achieve national goals?

Central and strategic leadership

- Is leadership supportive? Leading the way?
- Is there central leadership on change management initiatives?
- Has leadership formally identified development of a national M&E system as a priority of government?

M&E champions

- Are there M&E champions at political, senior, and operational levels?

Communications strategy

- Has a communications strategy and plan been devised to support the development and rollout of the national M&E system? Does it recognize the need for ongoing communication with different audiences?

Building Block 2: Enabling Environment

Demonstrated Commitment
A formal plan and resources for M&E development and implementation

- Is there a formal plan, with committed resources and a timeline to launch development of an M&E system?
- Have resources been identified for sustaining the M&E system over the long term—that is, beyond its initial development stage?

Commitment to public sector improvement

- Is there a commitment to results orientation in the public sector and good governance?
- Is there an agenda of public sector reform initiatives that is being acted upon?

Opportunity to challenge the status quo

- Are there a willingness and an ability to challenge the status quo and current culture within organizations?

Support for values and ethics underlying an M&E system

- Does leadership allow transparency via access to information, open discussion, and communication?
- Is speaking truth to power considered appropriate within the public sector? Within the nation?
- Is evidence-based decision making encouraged?
- Does public sector management encourage and foster initiatives aimed at improving accountability?

Supporting Institutional Arrangements
National statistical agency

- Is there a national statistical agency to facilitate a national data development strategy and assist ministries and agencies in data capture?
- Are sufficient resources being invested in national and subnational data gathering?
- Is there skilled statistical and survey expertise?

Systematic planning function in government

- Are there strategic and operational planning units within ministries?
- Is M&E information used in any fashion in the policy, planning, and budgeting cycle?

Oversight to support an effective M&E system

- Does the national audit office play any role in monitoring the M&E system? In the use of performance information across government? In the performance of government?
- Does Parliament use or seek information to assess the performance of government?

Professional evaluation association

- Is there an active professional network to support training and development, information exchanges, and national, regional, and international networking or mentoring on M&E methods and practice?

M&E partners and networks

- Are M&E partners and potential M&E networks available to increase national M&E capacity in a cost-effective manner?

Civil society engagement

- Is civil society informed and engaged, providing input to government consultation on project, program, and policy decisions and direction?
- Is there a formal access to information law that increases transparency and accessibility of M&E information to the media and civil society for their participation in the national system?
- Is government accountable to the general public?
- Are civil society, the private sector, and the media adequately informed about M&E concepts and the role M&E can play in good governance?

Building Block 3: Capacity to Supply M&E Information

Central M&E policy center

- Is there a central policy center to provide policy direction, oversight, and assistance for the systemwide development and use of M&E?

M&E policies, guidelines, and practice standards

- Are there rules to clarify expectations regarding M&E practice and conduct?
- Is there clarity regarding roles, responsibilities, and accountabilities for monitoring and evaluating performance?

Institutional structure to support the systematic collection of M&E information

- Is there an institutional structure that can provide credible results-based M&E information on a timely basis?
- Are M&E units in the public sector resourced to carry out or facilitate results-based performance monitoring?
- Do government organizations carry out systematic effectiveness evaluation of projects, programs, and policies on a regular basis?

Performance frameworks and indicators

- For major government programs, are the intended objectives, outputs, and outcomes clear?
- Have performance frameworks and results-based indicators been developed for major programs, ministries, or sectors and the national level?

Availability of skilled personnel for performance monitoring

- Are there sufficient numbers of trained personnel with technical capacity and competencies for monitoring performance, including gathering, analyzing, and reporting on the performance of policies and programs?
- Is there a resourced capacity for ongoing training, development, and skills upgrading of M&E experts?

Availability of skilled personnel for evaluation

- Are there skilled personnel with technical capacity and competencies to conduct or manage evaluations?

Credible and relevant data

- Is there quality, reliable, timely, and comprehensive data that are easily accessible and relevant to results-oriented M&E?
- Are there credible information-gathering and -storage systems?

Routine performance monitoring

- Is there routine monitoring of the performance of projects, programs, and policies within ministries, sectors, and nationally?

Evaluation and research

- Is there systematic evaluation of projects, programs, and policies to assess their delivery, effectiveness, and continued rationale?

Building Block 4: Capacity to Demand and Use M&E Information

Drivers and uses of M&E information

- Is there clarity around what is driving the M&E initiative?
- Is there clarity around where and how M&E information will be used at the project, program, ministry or sector, and national levels. Is it linked to planning, management, budgeting, policy or program development, or reporting?

Policies, guidelines, and other requirements instructing on use of M&E information

- Do formal guidelines or policies exist that inform and instruct officials on where and how M&E information is to be used, presented, and reported in the public sector—for example, in the context of planning, project or program management, policy or program development, decision making, budgeting, and performance reporting?
- Are there adequate incentives (rewards or sanctions) within organizations and centrally to ensure that managers use results-based M&E information—for example, reporting credible information in a timely fashion?

Accountability for use of M&E information

- Does any oversight body monitor how and how well M&E information is being used in government?
- Have roles and responsibilities regarding use been firmly established? For example, have clear responsibilities and accountabilities been established within organizations and centrally for performance reporting and implementation of evaluation recommendations?
- Are government managers and senior officials held accountable for ensuring that the M&E system is a functioning part of the public sector?
- Is results-based performance factored into personnel appraisals?

Institutional capacity to use M&E information

- Is there adequate capacity within government institutions to incorporate and use M&E information as part of the normal process of business?
- Does a process exist, within organizations or centrally, to identify priority areas in need of evaluation?
- Are there forums, within organizations or centrally, that serve as formal vehicles and mechanisms for reporting and sharing M&E information and evaluation results?
- Does M&E information get linked with discussions and decisions—within organizations and centrally—related to program development, policy, planning, or budgeting?

Awareness and understanding of M&E by nontechnical officials

- Is there a program of training and orientation of nontechnical personnel (government program and senior managers as well as nongovernment officials) on M&E concepts and potential use(s) of M&E information?

Notes

1. See UNDP (various years) and technical notes related to the human development index.
2. Such concerns were raised in 2012 in both the keynote policy paper and the macroeconomic outline for the mid-term review of Botswana's current national development plan (Botswana Vision Council 2013).
3. I worked with the World Bank and Botswana's National Strategy Office on developing a comprehensive strategy and five-year action plan for developing and implementing a national M&E system for Botswana.
4. Factors affecting the configuration of an M&E system include, among others, government demand for M&E information, the uses to which M&E information will be put, the availability and quality of data and information, the existing evaluation and analytical capacity within the country, and the amount that government is prepared to spend on M&E. See Mackay (2010).

References

Botswana Vision Council. 1996. "Vision 2016: Towards Prosperity for All." Vision 2016 Council, Gaborone.

———. 2009. *Botswana Performance Report*. Vision 2016 Council, Gaborone.

———. 2013. "Botswana's Performance 2012: A Progress Report on Vision 2016." Unpublished report, Botswana Vision Council, Gaborone, February.

Lahey, R. 2010. *The Canadian M&E System: Lessons Learned from 30 Years of Development*. Evaluation Capacity Development Series 23. Washington, DC: World Bank, November.

———. 2012. "Guidance for National Evaluation Capacity Development: A Report for the United Nations Evaluation Group (UNEG) Task Force on National Evaluation Capacity Development." International Labour Office, Geneva.

———. 2013a. "An Assessment of the Market for CESAG CLEAR Monitoring and Evaluation (M&E) Services in Francophone Africa." Paper prepared for the World Bank CLEAR Secretariat, World Bank, Washington, DC.

———. 2013b. "National Performance Reporting as a Driver for National M&E Development." In *Development Evaluation in Times of Turbulence: Dealing with Crises That Endanger Our Future*, edited by R. C. Rist, M.-H. Boily, and F. R. Martin. Washington, DC: World Bank, IDEAS.

Mackay, K. 2010. "Conceptual Framework for Monitoring and Evaluation." PREM Note 1, Special Series on the Nuts and Bolts of M&E Systems, World Bank, Washington, DC.

Menon, S. 2010. "A Perspective from the United Nations on National Ownership and Capacity in Evaluation." In *From Policies to Results: Developing Capacities for Country Monitoring and Evaluation Systems*, edited by M. Segone. Geneva: UNICEF.

Picciotto, R. 2007. "The New Environment for Development Evaluation." *American Journal of Evaluation* 28 (4): 509–21.

UNDP (United Nations Development Programme). Various years. *Human Development Report*. New York: UNDP.

World Bank. 2012. *Botswana: Challenges to the Safety Net, Preparing for the Next Crisis*. Washington, DC: World Bank, July.

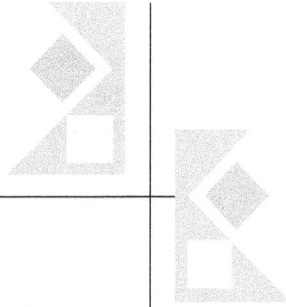

CHAPTER 12

Managing to Reduce Inequality: Does the Changing Aidscape and the Need to Reduce Inequality Require a New Approach to Managing Aid?

Tom Ling

Introduction: The Current Approach to Managing Aid Is Confused

At the heart of this chapter is an important and difficult question: How should aid agencies manage themselves to be most effective? A supplementary question asks whether the answer will be different in the light of a changing aid environment, in particular, if we are to reduce inequalities. Before addressing these questions about the future, it is useful to examine today's confused approach to managing aid.

Tom Ling is with the Rand Corporation.

Confusion exists when two or more mutually contradictory arguments or beliefs are held to be true. The heart of the confusion considered here is that the development sector simultaneously seeks to act in two ways that are in tension. First is the rise of a results-based approach to management—focusing rewards and behaviors on measurable improvements in key indicators achieved during the life of a project or program. Second is an equally strong emphasis on the need to achieve system change and transform underlying constraints—focusing program activities on complex behavioral change and long-term structural shifts, which the program could only have indirect influence over, with few opportunities to measure significant change in the lifetime of the program. Practitioners and managers do not and cannot resolve this confusion and so operate one and then the other approach or say one thing while doing something else.

To understand how this situation has arisen, we need to look briefly at the historical origins of these two trends. The aidscape has never been a unified entity; rather, it combines a variety of initiatives from a wide range of aid agencies and funders coupled with a small number of international agreements intended to align overall behaviors and goals. Since the 1990s, these international agreements have articulated principles of strengthening beneficiary participation and ownership, harmonizing and aligning action focused on global goals, and strengthening results-based behaviors among international nongovernmental agencies (NGOs).

Acting on these principles requires the generation of evidence to demonstrate results. Monitoring and evaluation (M&E) and related operations research have been rhetorically (at least) elevated as key ways to entrench both accountability and learning. In recent years, the quality of the best evaluations and research has been greatly improved not only by the adoption of more rigorous experimental and quasi-experimental techniques but also by a growing maturity in the use of qualitative approaches. However, while the quality ceiling for the best has been raised, the floor has remained depressingly low, with too many evaluations being either unused or unusable. A useful step forward in this respect is to recognize that some (perhaps many) programs may not be evaluable either because they lack underlying coherence and stability or because the data to evaluate them simply are not available (Davies 2013).

Improved M&E is part of an overall effort to establish global standards and principles. The agreements articulating these principles and providing the various blueprints for this aid architecture include the International Monetary Fund's Poverty Reduction Strategy Papers, the Paris Declaration (OECD 2005), the Accra Agenda for Action (OECD 2008), and the Busan Partnership Agreement (OECD 2011).

The Paris Declaration (OECD 2005) identifies five core principles:

1. Ownership of development priorities by recipient countries
2. Alignment of donor funding behind these priorities
3. Coordination between donors to avoid duplication
4. Focus on the results of aid, which should be measured and used as a management tool
5. Transparency and accountability between donor and recipient countries

If these agreements defined core global aid principles, the Millennium Development Goals (MDGs) of 2000 shaped more substantively what aid should deliver. The 0.7 percent target identified the level of resources that should be dedicated to aid, and, in general, aid budgets increased significantly from the 1990s to the 2010s. However, these high-level designs produced not a single unified system but a complex ecosystem (Rogerson 2010) that cannot be planned or driven but can be shaped to some extent through leadership and mobilizing from below. This mobilization is more similar to a social movement than to a planned economy. But it is also a space where institutions compete for legitimacy, leadership, and a space in which to operate. This chapter looks at this ecosystem—a deliberately vast arena—and its conclusions will be appropriately careful. But it is a space we need to consider directly if we are to act responsibly and demonstrate stewardship of the resources that international NGOs have been given.

So if this loosely aligned competitive interdependence describes the aid architecture, how should aid agencies manage their resources and deliver their goals? To a significant and understandable extent, the increasing aid budgets also led donor countries to take an active interest in how resources should be accounted for and outcomes measured. One aspect of this relates to one form or another of results-based management (RBM), which has its roots in the work of Peter Drucker in the 1950s. RBM was popularized and given focus in Drucker's book, *Managing for Results* (Drucker 1964). The idea of "management by objectives" became increasingly important in public management in the 1960s and 1970s, and it features in the Paris Declaration (2005), where managing for results, results-based management, and results-oriented reporting and assessment frameworks are given prominence. The approach was intended not only to apply to the management of aid agencies but also to encourage accountability among governments and partner agencies. The focus on results and their implications for partner agencies was also evident in the arguments found in the "new public management" of the 1970s and 1980s (Ling 2000) and, more recently, in the Anglophone world, with the reemergent emphasis on "value for money" (Ling and Eager 2013).

These ideas were developed and nurtured outside of aid agencies but were introduced to the sector primarily by funders of various sorts.

Alongside RBM, and reinforcing its core features, is the logical framework approach (LFA). As an approach to managing aid, LFA first arose in 1969, when the U.S. Agency for International Development asked consultants to produce a model for managing development aid projects. Both RBM and LFA share a conceptual model involving inputs, processes, outputs, outcomes, and impacts. Both require decision makers to focus attention on the causal links between operational activities and the results achieved. This requirement is very visible in how both funders and aid agencies describe their approach and outline their programs and intended outcomes. Despite this, by 2000, the OECD's Development Assistance Committee could still argue (with little disagreement) that aid management remained oriented toward budgeting, activity, and control (Binnedjikt 2000).

Since 2000 we have seen continuing efforts to develop and strengthen an approach that builds, in theory, on the focus on results underpinned by the LFA. However, this effort has, in practice, been partial at best. There are two plausible explanations for this limited effectiveness. The first explanation is that RBM and LFA could be made to work well, but have never been implemented as intended. The second is that RBM and LFA have support, in principle, but are hard to work in practice. I look briefly at each explanation in the following paragraphs.

Anecdotal evidence is that RBM and LFA have rarely been implemented as intended. Log frames might be completed at the proposal development stage of a program and not revisited until the final evaluation. Project managers (often in a context of very difficult operating environments with limited operational platforms and high staff turnover) might do very well simply to manage budgets and ensure that tasks are completed on time. Ongoing monitoring to support adaptation and flexibility to maximize results is rare. In this environment, the capacity to integrate thinking around causal chains with active program management is often absent. Worse still, as a review of efforts to focus interagency cooperation on results management shows, "The inter-agency dialogue revealed wild differences in results perspectives, terminology, typologies, and the general meaning of results management and associated objectives and indicators" (Vahamaki, Schmidt, and Molander 2011, 14).

The second argument is that RBM and LFA have not been implemented as intended because they are not fit for the development task. The strongest expression of this view comes from the argument that, in complex environments, RBM will not incentivize the pursuit of optimal outcomes and LFA will blind organizations to the "real world" developments that are driving results on the ground and instead focus attention on things that matter less to the intended delivery (Ling 2003, 2012). According to this approach, learning, adaptability, participation, and scenario thinking all trump adherence to log frames and rigid pursuit of predetermined results. Implicit in this approach is the argument that aid agencies are too tightly coupled to the political and administrative apparatuses of Western governments and publics and therefore unable to adapt to the shifting realities of a complex and emergent environment. This argument suggests that RBM and LFA might, in some cases, inhibit successful delivery.

There are significant reasons to approach RBM and LFA critically. However, criticisms emphasizing the importance of engaging with complexity have not cohered into a compelling alternative that would not only ensure cost-effectiveness but also deliver accountability to both beneficiaries and donors. They have contributed to debates about how aid is managed but identified no convincing alternative. Consequently we see a sense of resignation that RBM and LFA are inevitable, but no great confidence in using them.

In the absence of a management paradigm that meets the various requirements of improving impact, achieving measurable results, strengthening accountability, and supporting learning and improvement, aid agencies have, in effect, struggled on. At best this has resulted in intelligent responsiveness and adaptability to context. At worst it has resulted in a half-learned management discourse packaged in the latest babbling from management gurus and business schools.

Finally, these confusions and tensions have recently become more intense as a result of changes in aid. Various disruptors are reshaping traditional aid. Kharas and Rogerson (2012) offer the following list:

- New philanthropy and impact investment (for social progress)
- Trade-aid blends and South-South transfers (for growth)
- Climate change financing (for shared space)

Add to this a well-rehearsed list of developments requiring aid agencies to change their more traditional ways of working. This includes addressing entrenched inequalities, adapting to rapid urbanization and peri-urbanization, responding to new forms of conflict and violence, applying mobile technologies, and engaging with new social and political movements around identity and religion. Duncan Green of Oxfam has nicely lampooned this message to aid agencies:[1]

- Everything is changing. Mobile phones! Rise of China!
- Everything is speeding up. Instant feedback! Fickle consumers! Shrinking product cycles!

- You, in contrast, are excruciatingly slow, bureaucratic, and out of touch. I spit on you and your log frames.
- Transform or die!

In the following section, I seek to avoid the breathless sense of immediate crisis lampooned by Green and instead work through the confusion to identify a more measured and potentially effective approach to the role of aid agencies and the management of activities designed to reduce inequality. The exploration of these confusions, tensions, and pressures has been necessary because the efforts to manage inequality are built on these.

Implications for International NGOs

Why Has Inequality Become Such an Important Goal for International NGOs?

The argument is now well known. Between the 1990s and the 2010s, we have seen reductions in extreme poverty, severe acute malnutrition, and children with no access to schools. Only progress on one MDG (maternal mortality) remains well behind the target. However, despite these overall improvements, the people excluded from these gains are found in increasingly predictable locations. They are individuals who belong to groups that are discriminated against and excluded within their own societies. This discrimination may be on grounds of religion, ethnicity, gender, or disability. The poor are also likely to be chronically poor—rather than dipping in and out of poverty—and their poverty is variously described as deep seated, embedded, or deep rooted. Poverty is about power, and the distribution of chronic poverty is about inequality.

It is clearly illusory to imagine that aid budgets—substantial as they are—are even remotely capable of removing this deep-seated inequality-related poverty on their own:

> Official development assistance (ODA) totaled $133.5 billion in 2011 with approximately 2.5 billion people living on less than $2 per day (OECD 2011). So, at current levels, if aid is regarded as directly delivering benefits/resources, aid could offer under $0.15 to each poor person each day. In the context of rising global food prices as population pressure increases, this would barely make an impact on the majority of people's lives. Therefore, for aid to be effective, it has to stimulate wider change, and there is a need to leverage current levels of aid to produce greater outcomes. There has been an increasing recognition in recent years that this is not likely to happen through traditional direct delivery of "charity" (Pronk 2001; Rogerson 2011). Instead, donors have begun, discursively

at least, to incorporate objectives of systemic change into a great number of their programmes in an increasing range of sectors. (Taylor 2013, 14–15)

Consequently for the world's poorest to survive and thrive would require removing the inequalities that bind them. Without addressing systemic change, the benefits of economic growth will be sequestered by the already-rich, and jobless growth will mean that unemployed people—and often unemployed youth—will live in extreme poverty alongside a high-income elite. Programs may be improved by using mobile technology, improving cash transfers, achieving higher agricultural yields, or improving cold supply chains to deliver vaccines. But without transforming the binding constraints that reinforce the deep-seated causes of chronic poverty, substantial progress is unlikely. In turn, reducing inequalities in income, wealth, and social and cultural power requires achieving change in the systems or underlying causes of impoverishment.

What Resources Are Available for International NGOs to Reduce Inequality and How Might These Be Managed?

International NGOs can seek to reduce inequalities in various interlocking ways. None of these necessarily implies discontinuing more traditional approaches, but they do involve adding new ways of working. They are all designed to address underlying drivers of inequality.

The first is to focus on the transformation of systems and not only on the delivery of goods and services. Engaging with systemic change would involve, first, understanding the system boundaries, actors, relationships, and information flows and, second, identifying the entry points through which international NGOs can influence or shape the way they operate. The third step involves managing these activities to deliver systemic change. At this point the limits of a narrowly defined results-based management and logical framework approach become apparent. Systems flex and adapt, and entry points shift. However, in the absence of a clear alternative to RBM and LFA, what is perhaps needed is an adaptation involving greater participation, step-back moments, renegotiated aims, and so forth.

A similar issue arises if aid agencies focus on changing underlying behaviors. Insights from behavioral economics, from understanding how norms shape social action, and from understanding the roots of altruism and cooperation could all inform approaches to changing behavior. This would include understanding how behavior is nested within social norms and the values that bond us one to another. Potentially, behavior change can be harnessed to strengthen the impacts of traditional programs (for example, by nudging specific behavior changes, such as concordance with drug regimens), to identify more radical ways to achieve traditional development goals (such as transforming norms relating to the age of marriage), and to change harmful behaviors more commonly not included as traditional development goals (alcohol abuse or road traffic accidents, for example). The first two imply essentially an extension of traditional management practices. The third, in contrast, cannot be defined by rigid adherence to an LFA or RBM. Metaphorically, we might see managing this sort of change as a conversation rather than a lecture. In a conversation we cannot stick to the predetermined script.

Third, aid agencies will struggle to find the organizational reach to address the needs of the poorest. Consequently, they will form partnerships with multiple agencies of varying sorts. These partnerships may include those established with large corporates—for example, to transform supply chains and stimulate research into treatments most needed by the poor. But they might equally involve partnerships with local faith-based organizations, for example. As multiple agencies collaborate, the log frame can be a crucial means to establish clarity of purpose; but agreeing can become more difficult, as each agency brings its own preferred outcomes and ways of working.

Addressing the Binding Constraints: Structural, Underlying, and Proximal

It is often commented that international NGOs—and the aidscape more widely—are on a journey. However, just as the aidscape is often both confusing and in tension, there is also no single way forward. The successful pursuit of different kinds of achievements will need different kinds of management. The routes to protecting human rights and to helping people in the poorest communities and harshest environments are varied.

Addressing immediate needs for goods and services requires the targeted, economic, efficient, and effective delivery of timely and appropriate quality goods and services. Where international NGOs are involved in the direct delivery of these goods and services, there should be a focus on value for money and measurable impact on the ground. Where partnerships are involved, they should be concerned with, among other things, developing capacity, strengthening supply chains, and enhancing legitimacy. Management should rightly use a straightforward application of RBM and LFA. Payment by results, for example, might be negotiated meaningfully within this framework. For evaluators, in more stable environments randomized control trials or stepped wedge methodologies might be used to measure and demonstrate success.

However, in both development and humanitarian contexts, international NGOs are exploring not only how to improve the efficiency and effectiveness of delivery but also how to transform local responsiveness to emergencies. For example, Save the Children is developing a Humanitarian Leadership Academy whose purpose is to "work with the humanitarian sector and new partners from the technology industry, private sector, and universities to help communities become more resilient in the face of disaster and give them the training and skills to respond to crises in their own countries."[2] The success of the academy will be measured by how successfully it grows away from its incubation home at Save the Children and evolves to deliver a public good for the whole sector and transform local capacities. In the end, the measure of success will include getting boots on the ground in emergencies, but they will not be the boots of staff from international NGOs, shipped in from more developed countries. They will be the boots of local, self-sustaining, and skilled networks.

International NGOs are also increasingly aiming to address harmful behaviors. The *World Development Report 2015*, for example, "is based on three main ideas: bounds on rationality, which limit individuals' ability to process information and lead them to rely on rules of thumb; social interdependence, which leads people to care about other people as well as the social norms of their communities; and culture, which provides mental models that influence what individuals pay attention to, perceive, and understand (or misunderstand)" (World Bank 2015).[3] Drawing not only on behavioral economics but also on ethnography, understanding norms, and exploring the roots of altruism and cooperation, the report promises to open up a range of possibilities and new ways of doing good. The programs to be managed may finish up looking more like participating in a social movement than delivering goods and services.

Finally, lasting reductions in poverty will require structural change. This focuses on how beneficiaries' lives are shaped by social, political, and economic relationships and institutions. These differences in access to resources are observable in social stratification, organizational relationships, political economy, and social norms. These are the products of possibly hundreds of years of history, and they will not be changed by the more efficient delivery of goods and services. Success is more likely to be measured in terms of the development of new financial models, measures and standards in a sector, new or transformed leadership, or new rights and powers ensuring that benefits to the poorest can be preserved and entrenched. Partnerships to achieve this will be less about strengthening capacities and supply chains and more about engaging with structural power and social stratification.

Table 12.1   Addressing the Binding Constraints: Structural, Underlying, and Proximal

Constraint	Definition	Example	Management focus and evidence of success	Skills to develop and relationships to foster	Who to partner with in achieving change
Structural	How beneficiaries' lives are shaped by social, political, and economic relationships and institutions. These are observable in social stratification, organizational relationships, political economy, and social norms.	*Context*: historic, religious, and ethnic practices *Problem*: entrenched inequalities and harmful practices *Opportunities*: strong bonding and social capital	Whole system with new financial models, measures, and standards; new or transformed leadership; new rights and powers ensuring that benefits to the poor can be entrenched	*Understand structural power and social stratification*: see whole picture; learn from those in the system how to be effective; work with systematic patterns and different perspectives; work through (and not just around) politics; build local relationships to achieve legitimacy	*Transformative partnerships*: national and local governments; national and local social and political movements; local NGOs; United Nations agencies; World Bank; global social movements; other international NGOs
Underlying	The present but not always immediately observable mechanisms that indirectly shape the behaviors, opportunities, and outcomes facing beneficiaries	*Context*: parenting practices passed from one generation to the next *Problem*: violence against street children *Opportunities*: access points for social improvement	Real-time feedback on transforming target causal pathways (for example, gender norms); observable changes in behavior; new networks established	*Understand diversity, conflict, and community*: identify existing networks and who is included and excluded; influence norms; use behavioral economics to nudge; recognize but, when necessary, challenge existing power relations	*Sustainable improvement partnerships*: local delivery partners; other aid agencies; corporate partnerships; local NGOs; national political movements; national media
Proximal	The immediate factors directly shaping impacts on the ground and the experiences of intended beneficiaries	*Context*: attitudes toward attending clinics *Problem*: habitual nonattendance at school *Opportunities*: information or incentives regarding behavioral change	Results-based management, logical framework approach; value for money	*Shape availability of goods and services and enhance choice*: deliver more economically, efficiently, and effectively; reduce inequities of access; use incentives smartly; partner to deliver	*Sensitive partnerships*: local implementation partners; corporate partnerships; community leaders

Note: NGO = nongovernmental organization.

Programs may begin to have more in common with political movements than with the delivery of goods and services.

These different approaches to reducing the binding constraints on the poorest are summarized in table 12.1.

Conclusion: Managing beyond RBM and LFA

On the face of things, there is much confusion about how to manage further improvements in delivering aid. Donor agencies and governments have a legitimate need for accountability, and the public expects to see demonstrable results. These expectations are reinforced by the aims of the evidence-based policy movement and the view that measurable results are key to incentivizing effective delivery. All of this creates a gravitational pull toward RBM and LFA.

However, there is an equally strong gravitational pull toward changing systems and engaging with complexity. This includes engaging with complexity both as a fully developed theory and as a metaphor suggesting the existence of inevitable feedback loops and unanticipated outcomes. Accordingly, systems thinking offers the opportunity for long-term, sustainable change and, in principle, allows for a transference of power. This has established an alternative mind-set (but not, it seems, an alternative approach to management).

Between these two forces is a vacuum. The former offers an approach to managing delivery, which broadly includes the following steps:

1. Define the problem
2. Measure its extent
3. Analyze the cause
4. Identify how to improve
5. Implement, measure, and control
6. Demonstrate results and learn lessons

The latter offers an approach that Draper (n.d., 3) describes as follows:

1. Experience the need for change
2. Diagnose the system
3. Create pioneering practices
4. Enable the tipping point
5. Sustain the transition
6. Set the rules of the new mainstream

Both of these are attractive, but each has its limitations. The former risks excessive linearity in a nonlinear world. But the latter risks unaccountable actions and a worrying absence of legitimacy around who does, or should, set the rules of the new mainstream.

Filling this vacuum in any detail is well beyond the scope of this chapter. However, it is possible to identify a set of high-level protocols for good management in either case.

First, *recognize that different groups and individuals define problems differently*. Likewise they might have differing views of what success looks like and how they would trade off among a range of potential improvements and costs. Also recognize that the definition of problems, and their relative importance, changes with experience and that this should be factored into program design to achieve optimal outcomes. The more consensus there is on the nature of the problem and the definition of what success looks like, the easier it will be to adopt an RBM approach.

Second, *be more explicit and detailed about the causal pathways through which the approach is intended to create good and reduce harm*. LFA has often become, in practice, a substitute for careful causal analysis rather than a consequence of it. There is no reason why a causal analysis should not identify nonlinearity and key feedback loops and show how specific lessons and evidence would make these more effective in achieving change. However, it is not sufficient to talk in vague terms about how "lessons will be learned" and "adaptations made."

Third, *if learning is inherent to the envisaged causal pathway, ensure that people will be held to account for failing to learn in ways that have a clear line of sight to delivering benefits*. Ensure that there are regular step-back moments where the log frame can be reviewed and revised, if necessary, and that structured learning from evidence and experience are part of the management approach.

Fourth, *do not pretend that change will not be social and political*. The more the focus is on systemic or underlying causes and the less it is on goods and services, the more important this becomes. Working through rather than around politics becomes part of the process. This requires a license to operate that can only be won by demonstrating that systemic change is part of a transfer of power away from donor governments and multilateral agencies.

Notes

1. In his blog, "From Poverty to Power." See fp2p@oxfamblogs.org.
2. See http://www.humanitarianleadershipacademy.org/.
3. See http://econ.worldbank.org/WBSITE/EXTERNAL/EXTDEC /EXTRESEARCH/EXTWDRS/EXTNWDR2013/0,,contentMDK:23456590~pag ePK:8258258~piPK:8258412~theSitePK:8258025,00.html.

References

Binnedjikt, A. 2000. "Results-Based Management in the Development Co-operation Agencies: A Review of Experience." Development Assistance Committee Working Party on Aid Evaluation, OECD (Organisation for Economic Co-operation and Development), Paris.

Davies, R. 2013. "Planning Evaluability Assessments: A Synthesis of the Literature with Recommendations." DFID Working Paper 40, Department for International Development, London.

Draper, S. n.d. "Creating the Big Shift: System Innovation." Sustainability Forum for the Future, London.

Drucker, P. 1964. *Managing for Results*. Cambridge, MA: Harvard Business.

Kharas, H., and A. Rogerson. 2012. "Horizon 2025: Creative Destruction and the Aid Industry." Overseas Development Agency, London.

Ling, T. 2000. "Unpackaging Partnerships in Healthcare." In *New Welfare New Managerialism?* edited by J. Clarke, S. Gewirtz, and E. McLaughlin. New York: SAGE Publications.

———. 2003. "Ex ante Evaluation and the Changing Public Audit Function: The Case of Scenario Planning." *Evaluation* 9 (4): 437–52.

———. 2012. "Evaluating Complex and Unfolding Interventions in Real Time." *Evaluation* 18 (1): 75–87.

Ling, T., and R. Eager. 2013. "Delivering Value for Money Evaluations." Paper prepared for the U.K. Evaluation Society Annual Conference, University of London.

OECD (Organisation for Economic Co-operation and Development). 2005. "The Paris Declaration on Aid Effectiveness." Development Assistance Committee, Paris.

———. 2008. "Accra Agenda for Action." Development Assistance Committee, Paris.

———. 2011. "The Busan Partnership for Effective Development Co-operation." OECD/DAC, Paris.

Pronk, J. P. 2001. "Aid as a Catalyst." *Development and Change* 32 (4): 611–29.

Rogerson, A. 2010. "The Evolving Development Finance Architecture: A Shortlist of Problems and Opportunities for Action in Busan." Consultation paper for Seoul Workshop, OECD, Paris.

———. 2011. "What if Development Aid Were Truly 'Catalytic'?" ODI Background Note, Overseas Development Institute, London.

Taylor, B. 2013. "Evidence-Based Policy and Systemic Change: Conflicting Trends?" Springfield Working Paper 1, Springfield Centre, Durham.

Vahamaki, J., M. Schmidt, and J. Molander. 2011. "Review: Results-Based Management in Development Cooperation." Rijksbanken Jubileumsfond, Stockholm.

World Bank. 2015. *World Development Report 2015: Mind, Society, Behavior*. New York: Oxford University Press.

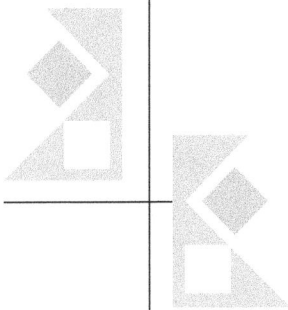

PART FOUR: IMPLICATIONS OF MOVING FROM POVERTY REDUCTION TO INEQUALITY REDUCTION FOR EVALUATION

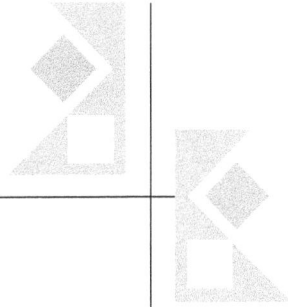

Bringing Inequality Back In from the Cold: Toward a Progressive Evaluation Model

Robert Picciotto

There are moments in history when people all over the world seem to rise up to say that something is wrong.

—Joseph Stiglitz

Introduction

The major theme of this chapter is that the unprecedented 2008 financial crisis, its root causes, and its aftermath call for a thorough reconsideration of evaluation models and practices. Public perceptions have changed, and there is no turning back. Equality, long neglected as an explicit objective of

Robert Picciotto is with King's College.

public policy, has made a comeback. As a result, evaluators everywhere have to engage more critically and independently with the antecedents and effects of inequality in society.

After sketching the global context and analyzing international trends in income and inequality, the chapter lays out five major challenges for the evaluation discipline: (a) fill the ethical deficit that underlies the neglect of inequality in evaluations, (b) engage with the policy research literature, (c) design new metrics, (d) address global policy issues, and (e) adopt a progressive evaluation model.

The Context

In rich and poor countries alike the problems of others have become our own. From the clamor of the Arab Spring to the labor unrest of African mining communities and the Occupy Wall Street protests, the social arrangements and political dynamics that allow a few individuals to accumulate enormous wealth while depriving large segments of the population of basic necessities have spawned widespread popular anger and resentment.

Differences in income and wealth attributable to effort, skill, or entrepreneurship are not resented. But public indignation spreads and social cohesion is undermined when distorted rules of the game, predatory behavior, or unethical practices are richly rewarded. The 2008 crisis brought to light that the current economic system breeds insecurity, inefficiency, and unjustified wealth disparities. The world's 1,210 billionaires have a combined fortune of US$4.5 trillion—more than half of the net worth of 3 billion adults.[1] The richest 0.5 percent hold well over a third of the world's wealth, while 68 percent share only 4 percent (Credit Suisse Research Institute 2010).

These glaring inequalities, combined with the collapse of the loosely regulated global financial system, have thoroughly shaken policy complacency among voters and policy makers, as well as academics. We could be living a time in history when fundamental societal change is about to occur. But the shape of things to come is still shrouded in uncertainty. No compelling political program capable of bringing together scattered interests, ideas, and energies has yet materialized. In the interim, uncertainty about economic prospects prevails. The long awaited global economic recovery remains elusive, and another financial upheaval cannot be ruled out.

On the one hand, the lingering crisis has created room for policy adjustment and social renewal. On the other, strong and enlightened political leadership is lacking so that there is no guarantee that coherent and timely public policy decisions will be made in a global system characterized by political fragmentation, economic interdependence, and multilateral institutions afflicted by severe democratic deficits. Now more than ever there is need for dispassionate, independent, and rigorous assessments of public policies and programs.

This opens up a window of opportunity for the international evaluation community. It is now widely recognized that principled policy making has all too often been hobbled by the disproportionate influence of powerful lobbies and vested interests. Even where democratic processes are assumed to be in place, the risk of faulty policy analysis remains. The potential consequences (that is, populist, incoherent, or unsustainable policies) constitute a clear and present danger to society. Enhanced public sector accountability is at a premium.

But is the evaluation discipline equipped to take on the diverse, unprecedented, and interconnected challenges of economic disparities, social exclusion, and governance weaknesses? Are evaluation models, practices, and priorities adapted to the new policy environment? How should evaluation evolve to meet the inequality challenge?

The Inequality Challenge

The current global economic predicament has shaken public opinion, but it should not cloud the remarkable achievements of the development enterprise since its post–World War II origins, when swords were turned into plowshares, the development idea took shape, and evaluation emerged as a distinctive discipline. Globally living standards have risen dramatically over the last decades. Whereas the United Kingdom took almost 60 years (1780–1838) to double output per person, Turkey did it in 20 years (1957–77), Brazil in 18 years (1961–79), and China and the Republic of Korea in 10 years (1977–87). Between 1966 and 1990, Thailand tripled and India doubled real per capita incomes (World Bank 1998).

This said, the development processes that have propelled emerging market economies toward the top of economic league tables have a dark side: inequality. On the one hand, economic growth in emerging market countries has been remarkable, but in the absence of adequate redistributive measures at international and country levels, the combination of footloose capital, constrained migration, trade protectionism, and restrictive intellectual property regimes has concentrated wealth as well as power in all regions of the world.

Is economic growth inevitably associated with greater inequality and concentration of wealth? What does the record show?

A Remarkable Economic Transformation

Thirteen developing countries have managed to grow for 25 years or more at an average annual rate of 7 percent or more using export-led strategies. At this rate, incomes double every decade. This extraordinary achievement would not have occurred without the increased interconnectedness of the global economy.

Despite a 35 percent increment in the global population, the share of the world population living in extreme poverty (on incomes of US$1.25 a day or less) has declined from 52 percent three decades ago to 22 percent in 2008. The decline is being sustained. The bottom line is that the world already has achieved the first Millennium Development Goal (MDG) target of halving the 1990 poverty rate by 2015. In fact, we are now midway through a century of high and accelerating growth in the developing world, which translates into economic convergence with the advanced countries (Olinto and Saavedra 2012).

Shrinking Inter-Country Inequality

The economic travails of the Western world triggered by the 2008 financial crisis are accelerating the global economic convergence. The center of gravity of the global economy has shifted toward Asia, and the North-South model of international relations that lumped together emerging middle-income economies with low-income and vulnerable least developed countries has become anachronistic (Dadush and Stancil 2010). China's gross domestic product (GDP) already exceeds Japan's, while Brazil will overtake France and the United Kingdom by the middle of this decade.

The development transformation of the past three decades means that international income inequality, a measure of *inter-country* income disparity, has dropped consistently since the early 1980s. Inter-country convergence is not simply due to the dynamic growth of emerging market countries. Europe has successfully reduced regional inequality as a result of its deliberate social cohesion policies focused on redistribution to the poorest members. For example in 1986, when Portugal became a member of the European Union (EU), its GDP per capita was 45 percent below the EU mean. Two decades later, its GDP per capita is only a third smaller than the EU average.[2]

For two decades the decline in inter-country inequality was attributable mostly to China, but since the turn of the century most developing countries, including those in Africa, have grown at a rapid pace so that per capita income convergence of the emerging market countries with the flagging economies of Europe, Japan, and the United States is now well under way almost across the board. This said, developing countries remain poorer than developed countries—by a long shot. The emerging market countries still have a long way to go to catch up with the industrial countries.

Growing Intra-Country Inequality

While *inter-country* inequality has been reduced, *intra-country* inequality tells a starkly different story: divergence, big time. Imagining that, in John Lennon's words, "there is no country"—that is, calculating global income inequality by capturing changes in income distribution within countries as well as among countries—wipes out the improvements observed at the international level. Specifically analysis of household surveys suggests that, despite the rapid catch-up observed at the level of nations, global income inequality measured one person at a time (rather than one nation at a time) has risen between the late 1980s and the middle of the last decade and has not changed much thereafter (Milanovic 2012a).

In other words, reduction in inequality among countries has been accompanied by a significant divergence in the economic fortunes of different income groups within countries so that internal divergence has more than cancelled out external convergence. The data show that global income inequality rose in the 1980s and the 1990s in all developing regions, while the record has been mixed since the turn of the millennium.

These aggregate results conceal considerable variations across regions. Between 1990 and 2005, inequality increased in 15 out of 22 advanced economies. It rose sharply in 20 out of 22 emerging European countries as a result of their transition from the plan to the market. In Latin America and the Caribbean, inequality increased in 11 out of 20 countries, but nearly all countries in the region have become more equal since the turn of the century. In Sub-Saharan Africa, inequality rose in 10 out of 26 countries, but overall inequality declined. In Asia and the Pacific, inequality increased in 13 out of 25 countries, and in the Middle East and North Africa it increased in 9 out of 12 countries.

Income disparities are more unequal in developing countries than in developed countries. The major reason lies in differences in the redistributive impact of fiscal policy between advanced and developing countries.

As a group, the latter are characterized by low levels of taxation, widespread tax exemptions and loopholes, poor tax compliance, low levels of public spending, reliance on regressive taxes, limited resort to targeted pension schemes and social safety nets, and distorted subsidy policies (Bastagli, Coady, and Gupta 2012).

Unfinished Business

In the aggregate, development has dramatically improved the lot of humanity. Impressive gains in social indicators have accompanied the rapid rise in average incomes. For the world as a whole, according to the World Health Organization, life expectancy at birth increased from less than 47 years in 1950–55 to 65 years in 1995–2000.[3] The MDG of halving the share of people with no access to clean water has been reached; the world has achieved parity in primary school education between girls and boys; under-five deaths fell from 12 million in 1990 to 7.6 million in 2010; malaria mortality rates have decreased by 25 percent since 2000; the 1990 death rate from tuberculosis is expected to be halved by 2015.

This said, according to the United Nations, inequality has detracted from these gains and has slowed advances in key areas (United Nations 2010). Achievements have been unequally distributed across regions and countries, and the ongoing economic crisis has slowed down progress. For example, progress in reducing hunger and malnourishment has been very limited so that almost a billion people still go to bed hungry every night; decreases in maternal mortality are off-track; the 2010 target of achieving universal access to treatment for human immunodeficiency virus (HIV) was missed; unemployment and underemployment rates remain high; and the slum population continues to grow. Out of 5 billion people in developing countries, 2.5 billion people are still living on less than US$2 a day and 1.3 billion are living in abject poverty (less than US$1.25 a day). Without a resumption of robust growth combined with a substantial reduction in income disparities not only across countries but also within countries, it will not be possible to eliminate poverty.

Development progress as well as social equity trends have been especially disappointing in countries lacking the resources, skills, and institutions to hook up to the mighty engine of the global economy. These small and disadvantaged countries, caught in a poverty trap, have been unable to trigger or sustain economic growth. Most are classified as least developed and figure prominently in the league tables of fragile and conflict-prone states.[4] Finding solutions to their predicament—that is, figuring out the policy sequences and providing the resources that would allow slow or no-growth economies to take off, while ensuring social and environmental sustainability—remains the most intractable development challenge.

Implications for Evaluation

The diversity of trends across regions and countries demonstrates that there is nothing inevitable about the frequent association between increased inequality and economic growth. It also suggests that no single "big idea" is likely to explain what is happening and what needs to be done (Cohen and Easterly 2009). Context and initial conditions matter, and this is why tailor-made evaluations are needed to guide policy formation in pursuit of equitable growth.

To fulfill this promise, however, as the rest of this chapter tries to establish, evaluators will have to (a) give far more weight to the ethical dimensions of their craft, (b) emphasize equity in their evaluations, (c) design new metrics to capture human well-being as the overarching goal of public policy, (d) focus on the global policy distortions that underlie inequality trends, and (e) adopt a progressive evaluation model in preference to the client-controlled, goal-based approaches that currently dominate the field.

Filling the Values Gap

Most social scientists take pride in their "value-free" pursuit of truth. By contrast, evaluators are explicitly tasked with assessing the merit, worth, *and* value of policies and programs (Scriven 2003/04). According to most evaluation textbooks, identification of the right values framework belongs at the front end of the evaluation process. Next, the identification of evaluation questions is guided by the concerns and values of stakeholders. Finally, findings are interpreted in light of relevant standards of value. In other words, the concept of value lies at the very core of evaluation practice.

A Paradoxical Neglect of Values

Inequality raises fundamental questions about civic virtues and moral values. Egregious disparities in the quality of livelihoods violate a basic sense of justice and fairness. The perpetuation of inequality through the blunt exercise of power undermines social harmony. According to Johan Galtung, severe inequality is akin to structural violence since it is avoidable, impairs fundamental human needs, and causes premature death or disability (Galtung 1969).

Yet evaluators have been notably reluctant to engage broadly and critically with the ethical issues that inequality entails. There are notable exceptions of course. Ernest House has long promoted evaluation in the public interest and identified "clientism" as a threat to the integrity of the evaluation process (House 1991). Michael Scriven has championed judicial and consumer models of independent evaluation (Scriven 2000). David Fetterman has advocated evaluation facilitation approaches designed to foster self-determination and level the policy playing field (Fetterman 1994). Finally, Jennifer Greene has boldly asserted that evaluation is advocacy interpreted as value commitment (Greene 1997).

But in the domain of day-to-day practice, evaluators have rarely engaged in a robust fashion with inequality issues or the ethical concerns that they raise. This is because more often than not they have been tasked with assessing policy and programs against predetermined goals shaped by prevailing interests. Without adequate protection from these interests, evaluators have been prone to downplay the values and goals of the poor and disadvantaged.

Furthermore and quite apart from the overt or covert and subtle capture of evaluation processes by the rich and the powerful, far too many evaluators have lacked the skills or the dispositions to involve the poor and disadvantaged in their work, as advocated by participatory evaluation advocates. Nor have they routinely elicited competing views about the policies or programs they are evaluating, as recommended by realist evaluators. Most of all, the insights of moral philosophers about equality, fairness, and justice have yet to be widely grasped within the evaluation community.

The Dilemmas of Moral Philosophy

The reconciliation of liberty with equality raises fundamental moral questions. Value judgments rooted in rival conceptions of justice are rarely made explicit in evaluations. Yet they are central to the assessment of public policies and programs.

Should the normative evaluative benchmarks reflect the stance of *utilitarian* philosophers such as Jeremy Bentham who advocate normative rules geared to the greatest good for the largest number? Should the perspective of *libertarians* such as Robert Nozick be adopted instead? They hold a minimalist view of government action and consider that the justice of wealth distribution depends not on outcomes but on how it came about (force or fraud versus prudence and hard work)? Alternatively should the *constructivist* concept of justice articulated by John Rawls and other contemporary philosophers be put to work?

In terms of shaping public policy, left-wing philosophers promote equality of outcomes ("to each according to his needs")[5], while mainstream philosophers advocate equality of opportunity. The latter approach tends to dominate, since it preserves incentives for socially responsible behavior—that is, it rewards hard work and thrift, and it penalizes idleness. Thus a growing consensus holds that suitable weight should be given to the equality of basic liberties and the opportunities for self-advancement irrespective of the advantages or disadvantages conferred by the "lottery of birth."

In order to level the playing field of the marketplace, John Roemer has proposed to distinguish between the influences on distributional outcomes caused by *circumstance*, on the one hand, and *effort*, on the other (Roemer 1998). Circumstances are attributes of the person's environment for which he or she cannot be held responsible. Efforts are the choice variables for which he or she can be held responsible. With these concepts wielded as policy tools, the benefits of economic activity may be distributed to reward effort rather than circumstance.

Especially relevant to evaluation practice are the insights of Amartya Sen, the Nobel laureate, who defines poverty as a deprivation of basic capabilities and proposes a comparative concept of justice that rejects the notion that any single set of principles can be conjured to design just institutions and a perfect society. He argues instead for a pragmatic evaluative approach that takes full account of contextual variables and focuses on developing the full range of human capabilities to exercise choice (Sen 2009).

Evaluation as a Democratic Process

Cutting across the ideological rivalries that underlie diverse concepts of justice are contrasting views about where to draw the lines between markets, government, and the civil society. For Michael Sandel, excessive reliance on markets is corrosive of democratic life (Sandel 2012). He and other moral philosophers conclude that achieving just outcomes in diverse social contexts can only be achieved through a judicious balance among rival interests mediated by the political system.

Just as Michael Sandel argues that only an open and robust public discourse can determine appropriate values for social goods and achieve a healthier public life, Amartya Sen advocates a process of open public reasoning in which diverse policies, strategies, and institutions are compared so that social choices are better informed. This is precisely the space that evaluation should occupy in the public square.

Engaging critically with the ethical dilemmas of public life, restoring the preeminence of values in the evaluative process, and supporting democratic debate through systematic collection and dispassionate interpretation of evidence are basic prerequisites for reinvigorating the role of evaluation in public affairs.

Putting Equity at the Center of the Evaluative Process

Laissez-faire policies are grounded in the belief that growing inequality is the unavoidable consequence of economic growth in its early phases—an undesirable side effect later corrected by the magic of the market. This influential proposition has long been favored by powerful interests. It is inspired by a seductive historical narrative about the industrial revolution that took place between about 1750 and 1850 in the United Kingdom, when technological innovation made investment in manufacturing profitable.

The story goes as follows. First, the mechanization of agriculture induced large-scale urbanization. Next, entrepreneurs and capitalist owners of manufacturing industries took risks and captured well-earned rewards generated by the increased productivity of the U.K. economy, economic specialization, and division of labor. By contrast, the mass of workers displaced from traditional rural occupations to labor in factories were offered a living wage determined by the dynamics of the free market.

Through innovation, thrift, and judicious risk taking, private entrepreneurs created considerable wealth, which inevitably induced growing income and wealth disparities. But as labor markets tightened and as presaged by neoclassical economic models, a threshold of average income was eventually reached, as competitive pressures raised the market value of labor. Trickle-down benefits materialized, and inequality decreased.

The Controversial Kuznets Curve

This plausible historical account has inspired the dynamics of Simon Kuznets's celebrated inverted U-shape curve that relates inequality with national income levels (Kuznets 1955). This ingenious construct has been used to justify trickle-down economic policies. But it has been refuted by a careful examination of the actual record.

While market forces did play the role described above, democratization and progressive legislation more than the magic of the market were key factors behind the reduction of inequality that laid the groundwork for the welfare society. Specifically free public education, stronger trade unions, and progressive taxation were introduced, along with social welfare programs.

As knowledge and skills were spread throughout the society, structural change took place, whereby human capital gradually replaced physical capital as the main engine of growth.

When this stage of more mature industrialization was reached, inequality was reduced further, providing an extra boost to economic growth. It is therefore social policy, in combination with Adam Smith's providential hidden hand, that underlies the economic prosperity of the industrial democracies.

Recent Policy Research Evidence

The contemporary empirical evidence regarding the economic trajectories of developing countries has also undermined the theory of change underlying the Kuznets curve. It is now widely acknowledged that there is no inevitable correlation between economic growth and inequality (Deininger and Squire 1998). In regression analyses, different choices of countries have yielded inequality-growth associations at sharp variance with the Kuznets model (Fields 2001). Initial conditions, demographic trends, and political and economic policy all appear to matter (Lempert 1987).

Initially lopsided patterns of land distribution are associated with undemocratic institutions and inferior economic performance. Similarly, heavy economic reliance on extractive industries seems to lead to concentration of wealth and official corruption. Conversely, the impressive economic and social performance of Asian economies has been explained by sensible land reforms (Japan, Korea, and Taiwan, China) combined with heavy human capital investments and the adoption of policies friendly to agriculture and growth of the export-oriented manufacturing sector (Stiglitz 1996).

The marginal propensity to save has often been proposed as a rationale for income disparities in sustaining growth. But it does not always hold, since the middle class typically displays a relatively high savings rate and fares poorly in highly unequal societies. High fixed costs of investment opportunities that would justify wealth disparities are not a significant consideration either, for example, in contexts where small and medium enterprises dominate.

Equally, incentive effects that would explain a negative association between income equality and growth (as illustrated by the example of the former Soviet Union) do not seem to matter much in democratic welfare states. On the other hand, credit market imperfections related to differential income levels and collateral availability do seem to have had a negative effect on the aggregate level and productivity of private investment.

The proposition that equality can go hand in hand with prosperity is supported by economic theory. Monopolies increase inequality and involve large social costs. Rent seeking and corruption feed inequality and reduce growth. If capable children are denied access to education, the returns to education investments are lowered. If discrimination in land and credit markets prevails, resources do not flow where returns are the highest. Inequalities are transmitted from one generation to the next.

Poorly designed privatization policies implemented within inappropriate regulatory frameworks have been associated with large increases in inequality while jeopardizing long-term growth prospects (Caselli 2006). Finally, extreme inequality appears to have induced illegal activities as well as political and social instability (Deininger and Olinto 1999). The devil is therefore in the policy details, and this offers vast scope for evaluation to identify what works, does not work, and why.

From Income Inequality to Social Equity

Income distribution is a critical dimension of inequality, but it is not the only one. The economic and social status of individuals varies according to personal characteristics associated with gender, age, health, and disability. It is also affected by environmental circumstances, access to social services, community relationships, and the extent of participation in political decisions. Institutions that favor the powerful and enforce rights selectively yield inequality as well as inefficiency. The damage they inflict is lasting and hinders the prospects of future generations.

Thus the deleterious economic impact of discriminatory racial and gender policies has received considerable attention in the theoretical and empirical policy research literature as well as in evaluation practice. The perverse impact of natural resource–based economic activity on inequality and governance has been probed. Similarly, the association of civil strife and armed conflict with chronic horizontal inequalities and youth unemployment has been unveiled by a burgeoning conflict prevention literature (Picciotto, Olonisakin, and Clarke 2007).

Severe malnutrition is symptomatic of inequitable policies. Early childhood cognitive development is stunted by inadequate nutrition. Nutritional supplements combined with mental stimulation offset this cruel disadvantage. Better teachers' incentives, improved teaching skills, and enhanced school infrastructure, among others, are required to improve school attendance. Inequitable access to social services is a major source of economic and social disparities. Conversely, health insurance and social protection programs reduce the risks to livelihoods faced by vulnerable groups. Improved justice systems help to level the playing field by upholding human rights.

Learning from Experience

To be sure, much remains to be learned so that, once again, the heterogeneity of factors that underlie inequality provides evaluators with ample scope for tailor-made evaluations informed by social science findings. For example, policy research evidence suggests that, while community-based and participatory development projects have been the instruments of choice selected by aid agencies to reduce poverty, such schemes have often been captured by local elites, especially in the most disadvantaged regions. They have rarely led to the creation of sustainable local institutions in undemocratic contexts. In fact, local participation may well increase the need for central oversight and accountability (Mansuri and Rao 2012).

Learning from outliers is a hallowed tradition in evaluation so that the case of Brazil, where inequality has been declining steadily over the past 15 years, deserves attention (Lopez-Calva 2012). Half of the total decline in poverty experienced in Brazil is due to reduced inequality. How did Brazil manage to swim against the tide of rising income disparities in other emerging market countries? By combining the taming of inflation and the generation of growth-induced employment opportunities with social policies, including educational investments, social security improvements, a raised minimum wage, and targeted cash transfer programs to poor Brazilian families that send their children to school and vaccinate them.

Pro-poor redistribution programs were made possible because tax revenue rose as a share of GDP and also because education programs geared to improve access by the poor helped to sustain economic growth. Direct cash payments to the extreme poor and increased spending on education and health also underlie the decline in inequality and poverty in other Latin American countries.

This said, much remains to be done in improving the targeting of cash transfers, improving the quality of education and health services, and making tax policy more redistributive throughout the continent (Lustig 2012).

Adopting New Metrics

The MDGs have displaced economic growth as the dominant objective of development. National income is no longer considered a satisfactory indicator of economic and social progress since it fails to (a) capture highly valuable services provided within the household, (b) account for environmental losses, and (c) reflect the inequities and social disruptions associated with unbridled economic growth.

It follows that the goals, principles, and practices that have long guided the choice of metrics and influenced economic policy can no longer be assumed to provide a sound basis for the future. It is the advent of quality growth (rather than economic growth per se) that constitutes the overarching economic, political, and ethical imperative of public policy. How to achieve it is no longer considered straightforward in the wake of the unprecedented financial crisis that has turned decades of economic orthodoxy on its head.

Experimenting and Surveying Life Satisfaction

Development theory that focuses on standard policy prescriptions is in crisis. Sobering facts have discredited the notion that individual economic agents act in isolation and that collective behavior can be assimilated to that of individuals or even countries (Kirman 2010). Distributional considerations are now acknowledged as critical for maximizing well-being in a society.

Recent social research findings have demonstrated that in a wide variety of cultural settings the standard utility maximization principle does not govern actual human behavior. There is now little doubt that fairness motivates economic agents. Rigorous experiments conclude that most people do not act so as to maximize their own utility at the expense of others.

This has been proved in a variety of games that would allow subjects to profit from inequality anonymously. Fairness considerations are shown to explain decision making better than selfish profit maximization. Other human experiments confirm that inequality aversion exists and is, in fact, quite large: subjects find it desirable to transfer resources from rich to poor persons even if this leads to a substantial reduction in aggregate rewards.

Surveys of life satisfaction have also generated relevant and robust results about the relationship between income and reported happiness within societies (Klasen 2008). While there is a positive relationship between income levels and reported well-being, the increments decline sharply as incomes rise beyond a threshold. This confirms that inequality

Poverty, Inequality, and Evaluation

reduces aggregate well-being and suggests that progressive taxation is in the public interest.

Furthermore, international happiness surveys have disclosed that inequality reduces perceived well-being significantly over and above its effect on individual income levels. Average income growth in a society does not seem to have a material impact on reported well-being. Relative incomes matter more than absolute incomes. Consequently, greater equality generates higher well-being both because of positional effects and as a result of what appears to be a general distaste for social inequality.

Regional comparisons illuminate the interface between inequality and human well-being:

- In Sub-Saharan Africa, well-being is only half as high and in Latin America it is just above one-third as high as suggested by per capita incomes. High inequality in these regions has meant lower well-being compared to more equal regions in East and South Asia.
- Well-being losses between 1988 and 1995 in transition countries of Eastern Europe and the former Soviet Union were caused by a combination of declining income and increasing inequality. Well-being losses were as a high as 50–80 percent in seven years, with inequality increases contributing to about half of the decline in overall well-being.
- In the United States, the annual growth in well-being was at least four times larger in the 1960s than in the 1990s. The 1960s were associated with falling inequality, while the (lower) economic growth during the Reagan-Bush era was accompanied by sharply rising inequality that offset most of the gains related to income growth.

Tracking Human Opportunities

One practical way of putting John Roemer's distinction between effort and circumstance to work is illustrated by the World Bank's design of a human opportunity index.[6] Rather than computing aggregate coverage rates to social services, the human opportunity index is sensitive to the variation in coverage among social groups. It measures the extent to which personal circumstances (birthplace, wealth, race, or gender) affect access to services such as schools, water, sanitation, and electricity.

The index is now used in Latin America and the Caribbean, Africa, and the Middle East. It demonstrates that new evaluation metrics can be fashioned to help to evaluate the equity dimension of country social policies, and it illustrates that new metrics can be fashioned to help to address the inequality challenge.

Table 13.1   Human Well-Being and Evaluation

Evaluation characteristics	Material well-being	Relational well-being	Perceptual well-being
Major discipline	Economics	Sociology	Psychology
Dominant evaluation approach	Cost-benefit analysis	Participatory evaluation	Empowerment evaluation
Investment focus	Physical capital	Social capital	Cultural capital
Main unit of account	Countries	Communities	Individuals
Main types of indicators	Socioeconomic	Resilience	Quality of life

Measuring Human Well-Being

Building on Amartya Sen's conception of development as the freedom to realize human capabilities (Sen 1999), the three-dimensional model proposed by Allister McGregor and Andy Sumner offers a timely analytical tool that captures the material, relational, and perceptual characteristics of human aspirations and social progress (McGregor and Sumner 2010).

For evaluators concerned with development, the matrix in table 13.1 points to the diverse and complementary evaluation disciplines, approaches, and concepts that will have to be marshalled to do justice to the holistic conception of development embedded in human well-being aspirations. Much work lies ahead to develop a full set of indicators adapted to the new policy paradigms associated with human well-being.

Examining the Global Policy Dimension

In addition to focusing on values and ethics, keeping abreast of the moral philosophy, economics, and policy research literature, and selecting new metrics adapted to the new human well-being objective of public policy, evaluators should take stock of the global policy dimension of the inequality challenge and address it in their evaluation work programs.

Addressing Economic Policy Imbalances

Current inequitable development patterns can be traced to the rising interconnectedness of a global system transformed by the information and communications revolution that is unmatched by global policy actions geared to equity concerns. Growing income inequality has been associated with a chronic reliance on debt-driven economic expansion in developed countries accompanied by macroeconomic imbalances between rich and poor nations.

Specifically, increased dependence on emerging market countries for the production of manufactured goods (combined with outsourcing of services) has kept workers' wages low in Organisation for Economic Co-operation and Development (OECD) countries. For example, the U.S. median wage has remained stagnant for 25 years, despite an almost doubling of GDP per capita. Rather than addressing the structural issues underlying increasing inequality, OECD policy makers have relied on monetary policy and unsustainable deficit financing (Vandermoortele 2009).

In turn, cheap credit and poor regulation have fed real estate bubbles and contributed to financial sector instability. They have also provided lucrative arbitrage opportunities for international financial agents and huge rewards for multinational corporations commanding the heights of the global economic system. Polarization has been buttressed by an extraordinary buildup of foreign exchange reserves in emerging market countries (ultimately funded by the private savings of their citizens). In turn, the bulging reserves have been invested in the sovereign bonds of OECD nations.

In other words, the rich countries of the world have been allowed to purchase the goods and services produced by poor countries on credit, as Asia and oil-exporting economies have bought up dollar-denominated assets to protect themselves from future global crises. This is what has enabled unsustainable deficits and rising private consumption in industrial countries. Many OECD countries have been purchasing developing countries' goods and services with developing countries' money.

This paradoxical arrangement has had the singular advantage of providing productive employment for developing countries' workers. But it has also reduced the returns to labor in rich countries and reduced the fiscal space available to governments in rich and poor countries alike. As a result, it has prevented citizens in rich and poor countries from enjoying the full fruits of their labor, and it has restricted the expansion of social programs.

The 2008 financial meltdown and the subsequent great recession have not reversed the inequality trend under way in OECD countries. Stock markets and corporate profits have recovered, and most chief executive officers have succeeded in protecting their high pay. Conversely, worker wages have stagnated, millions of workers have lost their jobs, and millions of families have been made homeless (Stiglitz 2012). In parallel, austerity measures have begun to undermine government programs and are threatening social safety nets. Middle-class savings are eroding, and unemployment remains stubbornly high, especially among the young. The social fabric is fraying. The risk of civil strife has grown.

The aggregate transfer of capital from rich to poor countries that had long been the economic rationale for development aid has been reversed and, except for the least developed, aid-dependent countries, the quality of other policy linkages between rich and poor countries has become far more critical to global development prospects than aid.

In a nutshell, global transfer mechanisms facilitated by the new information and communications technologies need critical assessment since they have allowed elites in rich and poor countries to capture the bulk of benefits arising from the new international division of labor. It is high time for evaluators of countrywide programs to cease treating these policy dynamics as exogenous (Picciotto 2005).

Tackling Problems without Passports

Hunger, disease, pollution, climate change, financial stability, regional conflict, international crime, and terrorism do not respect national borders. These "problems without passports" constitute serious obstacles to equitable and sustainable development: the problems cannot be tackled one country at a time or by one country alone. In this context, the case for multilateralism has been considerably strengthened: states must join together if they are to achieve the shared objectives of international peace and prosperity.

Effective solutions require multilateral cooperation. In the words of Kofi Annan, "Ours is a world in which no individual and no country exists in isolation. All of us live simultaneously in our own communities and in the world at large" (Annan 2002). Similarly, Richard N. Haas, president of the Council on Foreign Relations, a U.S. think tank, announced, "We are all multilateralists now (or at least need to be)" (Haas 2010). A wide variety of ad hoc global and regional collaborative programs involving international organizations, official donors, and private foundations has sprouted to fill gaps in multilateral governance. Many of them have escaped systematic evaluation.

Reforming Global Policy

Global inequities are massive. The average citizen of Luxembourg earns 62 times more than the average citizen of Nigeria in terms of purchasing power. Child mortality is 18 times higher in Mali than in the United States.

The average person has more than 13 years of schooling in OECD countries compared to less than 6 years in Sub-Saharan Africa (World Bank 2006).

Since developing countries have little voice in global governance, the rules of the game of the international marketplace are often costly to poor countries. It follows that evaluation of policies and programs at the national level needs to take explicit account of the systemic global factors that have shaped the allocation of benefits derived from economic growth.

A reorientation of evaluation toward global systemic policy dysfunctions is critically important since links other than aid have become major mechanisms of resource transfer that are dwarfing the "money" impact of aid and creating new and powerful connections between rich and poor countries (as well as among poor countries):

- Developing countries' exports (about US$5.8 trillion) are 45 times the level of official aid flows.[7]
- Remittances from migrants (US$283 billion) are 2.2 times the level of aid flows.
- Foreign direct investment (US$594 billion) is 4.6 times the level of aid flows.[8]
- Royalty and license fees paid by developing countries to developed countries (US$27 billion) are more than one-fourth of aid flows.
- The huge damage to developing countries caused by climate change, as a result of OECD countries' unsustainable environmental practices, is getting worse given rapid growth in emerging market countries (United Nations Framework Convention on Climate Change 2007).

Developing countries face punitive obstacles in selling agricultural products and labor-intensive manufactured products. Unskilled workers from poor countries are not allowed to migrate to rich countries. Patent protection hinders access to life-saving drugs and knowledge-based products.

MDG 8 sets out modest commitments aimed at strengthening official development assistance; developing an open, rules-based, predictable, non-discriminatory trading and financial system; managing the debt burden of developing countries; ensuring access to affordable essential medicines; and ensuring the availability of new technologies in cooperation with the private sector.

Progress toward these objectives has been limited. Official aid flows are currently declining. They would have to more than double in order to meet the United Nations target of 0.7 percent of donors' national income, and 20 developing countries remain at high risk of debt distress.

With respect to trade, the Doha Development Round remains gridlocked. The least developed countries face constant difficulties in gaining duty-free and quota-free market access in developed countries. Trade restrictions on agricultural products and labor-intensive manufactures continue to hinder their economic and employment prospects (United Nations 2011).

Here again, evaluation has been asymmetrical. It has concentrated resources and skills on the assessment of poor countries' efforts to reduce poverty, while neglecting to scrutinize the reciprocal obligations of individual rich countries in the global poverty reduction compact solemnly endorsed by all United Nations members in 2002.

Toward a Progressive Evaluation Model

Evaluation has always adapted to changes in the operating environment. As the social context evolves and policy paradigms shift, evaluation priorities are reassessed and new approaches are adopted to meet emerging needs. For example, over the past decade, the emphasis of international development evaluation was adjusted to reflect the aspirations of the Millennium Development Goals (Picciotto 2007) and the persistence of state fragility at the development periphery (OECD 2008). Greater rigor in assessments of development impacts has also been emphasized (Center for Global Development 2006).

Adapting to the Operating Environment

Since then, the world has been shaken by a global economic crisis that originated in the United States and still plagues Europe and the rest of the world. It has brought to light severe global economic imbalances as well as the growing economic and social disparities within countries that have accompanied the rapid growth of emerging market countries. Their accumulation of vast foreign exchange reserves and their shift in status from aid recipients to aid donors has transformed the development landscape.

By now, the dominance of the Western economic model has been shaken; adjustment problems similar to those endured by debt-burdened developing countries in the mid-1930s are now plaguing developed countries, and the locus of development evaluation is migrating to developing countries. Following the demise of the North-South model that characterized international relations in the second half of the twentieth century, full integration of development evaluation within the evaluation mainstream is within reach.

The internationalization of evaluation has proceeded apace. This is fortunate since the economic and social problems faced by poor and rich countries alike have become increasingly interconnected; the process of inter-country economic convergence seems irreversible, and the severe economic and social problems caused by growing intra-country inequality do not respect national borders.

Unless evaluators respond to the popular clamor for more equitable and sustainable policies geared to human well-being and social solidarity, the evaluation discipline will gradually lose its legitimacy.

Reforming Evaluation

Goal-oriented, client-controlled evaluations have contributed to the timidity of evaluation agendas. Delivering evaluation results matters, of course, but whose results and to which actors should they be attributed?

Methodological biases have given pride of place to experimental methods that cannot contribute meaningfully to assessment of the full-coverage policies that hold the key to social equity and public welfare. In the international development arena, evaluators have been mostly preoccupied with the use of aid funds by developing countries, while aid delivery mechanisms and non-aid policies shaped by donor countries have escaped similar scrutiny. More attention has been devoted to assessing developing countries' performance than to fulfilling donor countries' reciprocal partnership obligations.

Given that they are fee dependent, evaluators have been prone to frame their evaluations to meet the needs and concerns of program managers rather than those of citizens. They have found ample justification for their supine stance in the organizational management literature and in utilization-focused evaluation textbooks. Yet evading or downplaying the summative dimension of evaluation in order to make evaluation findings palatable does not serve to make authority responsible or responsive to the public interest.

The American Evaluation Association Guiding Principles have urged evaluators to meet legitimate clients' needs whenever it is feasible and appropriate to do so. But giving pride of place to the use of evaluation results by program managers and policy makers undermines evaluation independence. While the principles recognize evaluators' responsibilities for the general welfare, the topic is treated gingerly.

The principles have had an influence well beyond America's borders. They have focused on doing no harm rather than on "doing good"—that is, evaluators have been encouraged to take cognizance of clear threats to the public good rather than to privilege human well-being and social harmony proactively. The unintended consequence has been a neglect of the social dimensions of policies and programs.

Engaging in Progressive Evaluation

Bringing equality back from the cold implies an activist evaluation stance at variance with the client-controlled, goal-based, randomization-obsessed approaches that currently dominate the field. What, then, is to be done for evaluation to help to tackle the challenges of a troubled and inequitable world?

As highlighted above, evaluators will need to seek inspiration in the ethical imperatives and contemporary ideas of social justice. They will have to reach out to their social sciences colleagues in order to benefit from the far-reaching policy research findings about inequality. They will have to develop metrics fully consistent with the pursuit of equitable and sustainable growth. Last but not least, they will need to give higher priority to the global dimensions of policies and programs.

But in order to do so, important changes will have to be initiated and sustained within the evaluation establishment. First and foremost, the approaches that dominate evaluation practice should be supplanted by a progressive evaluation model that combines the vision of democratic, committed, morally engaged evaluation (Schwandt 1989) with an emphasis on results that serve the public interest.

Progressive evaluation would be based on values and geared to the public interest. It would put the spotlight on the distributional consequences of policies and programs and unveil the political mechanisms that underlie them. It would treat the global policies that underlie economic and social disparities as endogenous since they are shaped by governments and the institutions they control.

Through objective assessments of performance, it would challenge entrenched institutions to live up to their legitimate mandate.

Progressive evaluation would embody democratic values, amplify the voice of citizens, and resist capture by vested interests through rigor and professionalism. To transform this vision into practice, new evaluation coalitions promoted by evaluation societies and private foundations will have to be nurtured to take on vested interests by tapping the energy and idealism of the civil society and their allies in government and the private sector. Only then would evaluators be equipped with the ideas, the autonomy, and the resources they need to face up to the global inequality challenge.

Notes

1. "The World's Billionaires." *Forbes Magazine*, March 9, 2011.

2. The current crisis is a serious setback for Portugal and for other EU Southern Rim countries, and the convergence gains that are still being reaped risk are being eroded (Milanovic 2012b).

3. See http://www.scielosp.org/scielo.php?pid=S0042-96862005000300013&script=sci_arttext&tlng=es.

4. A country is classified as least developed if its per capita income is less than US$2.5 a day, if its human resources are limited, and if its economy and society are vulnerable to shocks; 48 countries currently meet these criteria. Only three least developed countries have graduated to developing country status since the late 1960s.

5. "From each according to his ability, to each according to his need (or needs)" is a slogan popularized by Karl Marx in his 1875 critique of the Gotha Program. See Walicki (1995).

6. See http://web.worldbank.org/WBSITE/EXTERNAL/COUNTRIES/LACEXT/0,,contentMDK:21915630~pagePK:146736~piPK:146830~theSitePK:258554,00.html.

7. This is the 2008 level according to the World Trade Organization. It dipped by 8 percent in 2009 but more than fully recovered in 2010, according to the International Monetary Fund. See http://www.imf.org/external/pubs/ft/weo/2011/01/index.htm and http://www.wto.org/english/thewto_e/coher_e/mdg_e/development_e.htm.

8. 2008 estimate (World Bank 2010).

References

Annan, K. A. 2002. "Problems without Passport." *Foreign Policy*, September 1.

Bastagli, F., D. Coady, and S. Gupta. 2012. "Enhancing the Redistributive Role of Fiscal Policy in Developing Countries." *Inequality in Focus* 1 (3): 4–8.

Caselli, M. 2006. "Does High Inequality in Developing Countries Lead to Slow Economic Growth?" *Undergraduate Economic Review* 2 (1): art. 2.

Center for Global Development. 2006. *When Will We Ever Learn? Improving Lives through Impact Evaluation*. Report of the Evaluation Gap Working Group. Washington, DC: Center for Global Development.

Cohen, J., and W. Easterly. 2009. *What Works in Development? Thinking Big and Thinking Small*. Washington, DC: Brookings Institution Press.

Credit Suisse Research Institute. 2010. *Global Wealth Report*. Zurich: Credit Suisse.

Dadush, U., and B. Stancil. 2010. "The World Order in 2050." Policy Outlook, Carnegie Endowment for International Peace, Washington, DC.

Deininger, K., and P. Olinto. 1999. "Asset Distribution, Inequality, and Growth." Policy Research Working Paper 2375, World Bank, Washington, DC.

Deininger, K., and L. Squire. 1998. "New Ways of Looking at Old Issues: Inequality and Growth." *Journal of Development Economics* 57 (2): 257–85.

Fetterman, D. 1994. "Empowerment Evaluation." *Evaluation Practice* 15 (1): 1–15.

Fields, G. 2001. *Distribution and Development: A New Look at the Developing World.* New York: Russell Sage Foundation; Cambridge, MA: MIT Press.

Galtung, J. 1969. "Violence, Peace, and Peace Research." *Journal of Peace Research* 6 (3): 167–91.

Greene, J. C. 1997. "Evaluation as Advocacy." *Evaluation Practice* 18 (1): 1–16.

Haas, R. N. 2010. "The Case for Messy Multilateralism." *Financial Times* [op-ed], January 5.

House, E. R. 1991. "Evaluation and Social Justice: Where Are We?" In *Evaluation and Education: At Quarter Century*, edited by M. McLaughlin and D. Phillips, 233–46. Chicago: University of Chicago Press.

Kirman, A. 2010. "The Economic Crisis Is a Crisis for Economic Theory." *CESifo Economic Studies* 56 (4): 498–535.

Klasen, S. 2008. "The Efficiency of Equity." *Review of Political Economy* 20 (2): 257–74.

Kuznets, S. 1955. "Economic Growth and Income Inequality." *American Economic Review* 45 (1): 1–28.

Lempert, D. 1987. "A Demographic-Economic Explanation of Political Stability: Mauritius as a Microcosm." *Eastern Africa Economic Review* 3 (1): 77–90.

Lopez-Calva, L. F. 2012. "Declining Income Inequality in Brazil: The Proud Outlier." *Inequality in Focus* 1 (1): 5–8.

Lustig, N. 2012. "Taxes, Transfers, and Income Distribution in Latin America." *Inequality in Focus* 1 (2): 1–5.

Mansuri, G., and V. Rao. 2012. "Community-Driven Development, Participation, and Inequality: What Does the Evidence Say?" *Inequality in Focus* 1 (3): 1–4.

McGregor, A., and A. Sumner. 2010. "Beyond Business as Usual: What Might 3-D Well-Being Contribute to MDG Momentum?" *IDS Bulletin* 41 (1): 104–12.

Milanovic, B. 2012a. "Global Inequality Recalculated and Updated: The Effect of New PPP Estimates on Global Inequality and 2005 Estimates." *Journal of Economic Inequality* 10 (1): 1–18.

———. 2012b. "Income Inequality in Europe and the U.S.: Regional vs. Social-Class Inequality." *Inequality in Focus* 1 (2): 5–8.

OECD (Organisation for Economic Co-operation and Development). 2008. "Evaluating Conflict Prevention and Peace Building Activities." Development Assistance Committee, OECD, Paris.

Olinto, P., and J. Saavedra. 2012. "An Overview of Global Inequality Trends." *Inequality in Focus* 1 (1): 1–5.

Picciotto, R. 2005. "The Evaluation of Policy Coherence for Development." *Evaluation* 11 (3): 311–30.

———. 2007. "The New Environment for Development Evaluation." *American Journal of Evaluation* 28 (4): 509–21.

Picciotto, R., F. Olonisakin, and M. Clarke. 2007. *Global Development and Human Security*. New Brunswick, NJ: Transaction Publishers.

Roemer, J. 1998. *Equality of Opportunity*. Cambridge, MA: Harvard University Press.

Sandel, M. 2012. "If I Ruled the World." *Prospect*, September 19.

Schwandt, T. A. 1989. "Recapturing Moral Discourse in Evaluation." *Educational Researcher* 18 (8): 11–16, 34.

Scriven, M. 2000. "Evaluation Ideologies, Evaluation Models." In *Evaluation in Education and Human Services: Viewpoints on Educational and Human Services Evaluation*, 2d ed., edited by D. L. Stufflebeam, G. F. Madaus, and T. Kellaghan, 249–78. New York: Springer.

———. 2003/04. "On the Differences between Evaluation and Social Science Research." *Evaluation Exchange* 9 (4): n.p.

Sen, A. K. 1999. *Development as Freedom*. Oxford: Oxford University Press.

———. 2009. *The Idea of Justice*. Cambridge, MA: Harvard University Press.

Stiglitz, J. E. 1996. "Some Lessons from the East Asian Miracle." *World Bank Research Observer* 11 (2): 151–77.

———. 2012. *The Price of Inequality*. New York: Penguin, Allen Lane.

United Nations. 2010. *The Millennium Development Goals Report*. New York: United Nations.

———. 2011. *Annual Report of the Secretary-General*. Sixty-sixth session, follow-up to the Millennium Summit, New York.

United Nations Framework Convention on Climate Change. 2007. *Impacts, Vulnerabilities, and Adaptation in Developing Countries*. Bonn: UNFCC Secretariat.

Vandermoortele, M. 2009. *Within-Country Inequality, Global Imbalances, and Financial Instability*. London: Overseas Development Institute.

Walicki, A. 1995. *Marxism and the Leap to the Kingdom of Freedom: The Rise and Fall of the Communist Utopia*. Stanford, CA: Stanford University Press.

World Bank. 1998. *Assessing Aid: What Works, What Doesn't, and Why*. New York: Oxford University Press.

———. 2006. *World Development Report 2006: Equity and Development*. New York: Oxford University Press.

———. 2010. *Global Development Finance 2010: External Debt of Developing Countries*. Washington, DC: World Bank.

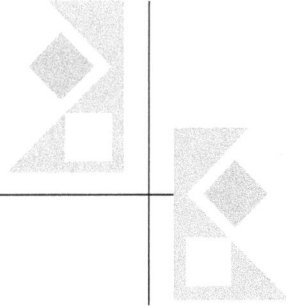

Conclusion

Ana Maria Fernandez and Frederic P. Martin

The theme of this book, *Poverty, Inequality, and Evaluation: Changing Perspectives*, is both challenging and sensitive. Poverty is about human suffering. Inequality is about different treatments of different groups or persons. Both are often at the heart of policy choices and reforms. Elections can be won or lost on this issue, and revolutions are often started by people who feel they have nothing to lose or are unfairly treated. What can the evaluation domain bring to this political hot potato? Reading through the chapters of this book leads to the conclusion that evaluation can make at least three contributions, which are presented below.

First Contribution: Clarifying the Underlying Analytical Framework

The starting point of any evaluation is having a good grasp of the concepts at stake: what do poverty, inequality, and related concepts such as inequity

Ana Maria Fernandez and Frederic P. Martin are with the Institute for Development in Economics and Administration. They wish to express their appreciation for comments from Paul Shaffer on an earlier draft.

and vulnerability mean, what are their causes, and what are their effects? *Poverty* is often defined as a level of well-being that is considered insufficient to lead a normal life in a given society and time in history. The definition of poverty is thus relative and multidimensional, reflecting a deprivation of well-being. In most developing countries, poverty is defined in a more absolute way to reflect the proportion of the population living below a poverty line—that is, unable to meet their basic needs, expressed usually in monetary terms. A poverty line is defined as a level of food and nonfood expenditures[1] that enables a representative person or household to meet basic caloric needs and some basic nonfood needs.[2] In most industrial countries, there are absolute poor as well, but their relatively small numbers and the monetization of the economy lead most analysts to use a relative notion of poverty, usually expressed as the percentage of the population below a certain threshold in the income distribution—for example, in Canada the low-income cutoff is set at 63 percent of average family income. In international comparisons, faced with the diversity of definitions of poverty used in different countries, standard norms are applied such as US$1 or US$2 a day per person, and corrections are made to capture differences in cost of living through purchasing power parity calculation methods. The Millennium Development Goals (MDGs) astutely went around the issue by using as the baseline the poverty situation in 1990 in any given country, as defined locally.

There is a huge literature on poverty analysis. Poverty has been a recurrent theme in the social sciences for centuries. However, it gained major attention in the development world toward the last part of the 20th century. Of note are (a) the seminal article of Foster, Greer, and Thorbecke (1984) in *Econometrica*, with poverty measures that consider not only the incidence of poverty, but also its depth and severity;[3] (b) the contributions of Ravallion (2008) on the evaluation of a variety of antipoverty programs; (c) the Living Standards Measurement Study survey program to obtain quality household data from which to derive a poverty profile; (d) the contribution of participatory rural appraisals to using qualitative methods to analyze perceptions of poverty (Chambers 1997) and to capture the voices of the poor (Narayan et al. 1999); and (e) the contribution of proponents of combined qualitative and quantitative methods, the so-called Q2 approach promoted by Ravi Kanbur and Paul Shaffer. Various poverty analysis manuals were published beginning in the 1980s, including the *Handbook on Poverty Statistics: Concepts, Methods, and Policy Use* (United Nations Statistics Division 2005) and the *Handbook on Poverty and Inequality* (Haughton and Khandker 2009).

Several authors went beyond the standard definitions of poverty focusing on income or consumer expenditures to include nonmaterial dimensions of well-being. Among the best known, are Sen's theory of capabilities (Sen 1995) and Bhutan's King Wangchuck's concept of gross national happiness. Some have argued for using a multidimensional index like the United Nations human development index that considers not only income, but also access to education, health, equity of rights, and opportunities across genders, while others have argued for using several one-dimensional indexes (Ravallion 2008).

With regard to development policy, poverty reduction became a major policy objective of the late twentieth century. Several countries pioneered the elaboration of poverty reduction strategies such as Mali in 1997 (MEPI 1997). The World Bank in the late 1990s switched its emphasis from structural adjustment policies to poverty reduction policies and made its support conditional on the elaboration of a Poverty Reduction Strategy Paper. The United Nations adopted poverty reduction as one of the eight MDGs to be achieved by 2015 and included poverty eradication as one goal of the future 17 Sustainable Development Goals to be achieved by 2030.

Great progress has indeed been achieved in reducing poverty at the global level. The United Nations 2014 MDG report indicates that extreme poverty has been reduced by half (UNDP 2014). In many developing countries, some of the poor have jumped over the poverty fence and joined an emerging middle class. This considerable progress should not hide the continued existence of significant poverty. There are about 1.2 billion poor in low- and middle-income countries, with pockets of hard-core poverty. The bulk of progress took place in Asia, with China biasing results at the global level. Several countries have not made any progress at all over the last 30 years, and some have actually lost ground in the face of a growing population and a stressed natural resource base. An honest assessment leads us to conclude that public policies and development aid have not been that efficient in addressing the complex web of social, economic, political, and cultural factors involved in poverty.

While still concerned with poverty reduction, the attention of governments and the world's development community is focusing more and more on the issue of *inequality*, which is not to be confused with equity.[4] This is partly the result of (a) the reduction in poverty, (b) the significant gap between countries in terms of living standards, and (c) the significant increase in inequality over the last 30 years in many industrial and developing countries alike. Milanovic (2011) points out that 9 percent of the world's population receives half of all income.

More than three-quarters of global inequality is due to differences across countries, not within countries. The evolution of the relative position of industrial and developing countries regarding poverty and inequality responds to a variety of country-specific factors, resulting in different patterns of poverty and inequality. There has been a relative stagnation of industrial countries and regions (Europe, especially its southern part, Japan, and North America). The middle class is struggling to maintain its purchasing power, new groups of poor holding low-paid, part-time, and unsecure jobs have emerged, while a minority has seen its wealth increase significantly. A study by the Organisation for Economic Co-operation and Development (Cingano 2014) shows that the ratio of the income of the richest decile to the income of the lowest decile went from 7 in 1980 to 9.5 in 2011–12, while the Gini coefficient went from 0.29 to 0.32. Piketty (2013) demonstrates the long trend analysis of growing inequality in select industrial countries based on a detailed analysis of time series. For the first time since the industrial revolution, the new generation is not assured of enjoying better opportunities and living conditions than the previous generation.

Some developing countries have become emerging countries or even newly industrial countries. China is, of course, the new world superpower, but several other countries such as Brazil, India, the Republic of Korea, and Malaysia are also becoming major economic powers, not to mention smaller states like the other tigers in Asia and elsewhere. This significant growth has translated in some cases into greater inequalities in income distribution, with a tiny minority of the population being super-rich and a majority experiencing a modest and fragile improvement in living conditions. In other countries and regions (China, India, Latin America), both poverty and inequality have been reduced, with the emergence of a significant middle class. A study by the International Monetary Fund concludes, "In advanced economies, the gap between the rich and poor is at its highest level in decades. Inequality trends have been more mixed in emerging markets and developing countries, with some countries experiencing declining inequality, but pervasive inequities in access to education, health care, and finance remain" (Dabla-Norris et al. 2015, 4).

Here again a vast literature on inequality comes in waves according to the popularity of the theme. In addition to the World Bank's *Handbook on Poverty and Inequality* (World Bank 2009) are the *Handbook on Income Inequality Measurement* (Silber 1999), the *Handbook on Income Distribution* (Atkinson and Bourguignon 2000, 2007), and, of course, the ongoing public debate about Piketty's book, *Capital in the Twenty-first Century*, published in 2013.

There are debates about the causes of those increasing inequalities. Among various contributions, Piketty focuses not only on income distribution, but also on wealth distribution. The higher return on capital than economic growth rates means that the real and growing gap is between the haves and the have-nots.

While the evidence for a greater return on capital than on labor seems strong, a finer analysis of specific kinds of capital and labor seems necessary if we are to understand the complex dynamics of the relative income levels of various groups in society. The financial sector has benefited from significant increases in income over the last 30 years, as exemplified by bonuses paid to its executives and dividends paid to its shareholders. The deregulation of financial markets launched in the Reagan-Thatcher era led to the increasing power of banks and other financial institutions such as pension funds and investment funds, the creation of financial derivatives characterized by high returns and high risk, lower safety measures, and more opacity in transactions. Returns in the financial sector have no common measure with returns in the real economy. Piketty shows that a big part of the increasing skew in the distribution among the top 1 percent is due to labor income (bonuses and golden parachutes for executives), not capital income. A second sector that has enjoyed a boom in many countries over the same period is the real estate sector, fueled by growing urbanization and a scarcity of premium land, leading to investment opportunities for legal and illegal money and real estate speculation. The mining and energy sector is the third growth sector, benefiting from the ever-growing demand of newly industrialized and emerging countries.[5] Beyond those three obvious sectors, some other sectors, subsectors, and firms have experienced changes in economic status, with significant positive or negative financial outcomes for the owners of capital and workers. The major underlying determinants are globalized product and factor markets, access to financial and human capital, and technological change. The value of companies like Nokia, RIM, Apple, and Samsung plays roller-coaster, enjoying or losing a temporary technological edge, with huge implications for shareholder values, job creation, and others.

The evolution of the labor market is also quite diverse. Well-educated youth, either in technical jobs or with university-level specialized competencies and management skills with international exposure, face extraordinary opportunities, while unskilled labor in industrial countries, who cannot compete with robots and cheaper unskilled labor in developing countries, are more and more out of a job, poor, and marginalized in society. In this race between education and technology, Goldin and Katz (2011) show that providing higher education has an equalizing effect on labor income by reducing skill premiums. In industrial countries, not to mention developing countries, the vast majority of private sector retirees do not have access to pension funds and see their purchasing power erode, while public sector retirees benefit from inflation-adjusted pensions. This differentiated analysis could go on and on beyond the simplistic opposition of capital versus labor revenues.

Those rapid changes in capital and labor markets should not hide the long-term changes in relative economic, financial, and therefore military and political power among major regions of the world and superpowers. As a result of long-term vision and significant and enduring individual and collective efforts to raise human, physical, and financial capital, Asia is the world's powerhouse, with China manufacturing more than half of what is produced around the world. Stuck in its national visions and sociological divisions, anesthetized by its social protection, Europe is slowly, but surely, relegated to secondary power roles. The United States has been losing ground in relative terms, in large part due to its political gridlock and short-term financial orientation, but it has been saved so far by its entrepreneurial spirit and technological inventiveness. In spite of significant progress, demonstrated by Lustig, Lopez-Calva, and Ortiz-Juarez (2012), Latin America has yet to overcome huge structural inequalities originating in its colonial history and culture. Africa and the Russian Federation are more than anything suppliers of raw materials for industrial countries, so their economic fate depends on the economic situation in major consumer markets.

A third concept related to poverty and inequality is *vulnerability*, which can be defined as the downward risk of falling into poverty in the future as a result of a shock such as illness, loss of employment or income source, natural catastrophe, ethnic strife, and religious and political conflict. Vulnerability has increased significantly in a context of greater dependence on markets and trade, wider and quicker market swings in a globalized economy, the palpable effects of climate change and increased weather-related calamities, and the growing insecurity around the world caused by political and religious conflicts. At the individual level, individuals and households can see their living conditions strongly affected by the increased frequency and strength of such shocks. At the collective level, crises like the 2009–10 financial markets crisis generated by the bankruptcy of Lehman Brothers in 2008 have led directly to a loss of wealth of large segments of the population through loss of share value, loss of employment, loss of houses too heavily mortgaged, and the use of taxpayer money to bail out major financial institutions.

Chapter 1 by Shaffer highlights differences between the concepts of poverty and inequality and discusses the implications for evaluation. Specifically, it argues that the "inequality turn" expands the dimensions of deprivation or "social bads" under consideration, changes the focus of causal analysis from households and individuals to social structures and relationships, and enlarges the range of policy instruments under review. The net effect is to expand the scope for evaluation, but also to increase its complexity and difficulty.

Second Contribution: Assessing the Impact of Policies, Programs, and Projects and Making Recommendations for Poverty and Inequality Reduction

Poverty reduction and inequality reduction are desirable goals, not only for moral reasons, but also to promote economic growth and social and political stability. Mora and Rist (2009) underline the importance of explicating a theory of change for every intervention. Evaluators have used a variety of qualitative and quantitative methods to measure this theory of change, ranging from the quick and dirty rapid results assessment approaches to complex and long impact evaluation studies promoted by the Poverty Research Lab at the Massachusetts Institute of Technology to analyze the impact of various poverty reduction programs, and all the intermediate approaches. Among others, Boily et al. (2000) demonstrate the relevance and efficiency of a sequential approach using the example of Canadian International Development Agency microfinance support programs in Mali. This sequential approach starts with qualitative methods for understanding the broad changes taking place and for identifying the key variables and relationships, moving to quantitative methods for measuring the links between key outputs (microfinance services) and immediate outcomes (knowledge, attitudes, and behavior of target groups), and finally returning to qualitative methods for understanding specific causal relationships of specific outputs for specific target groups (for example, the impact of combining microfinance services with education for hard-core poor rural women).

Chapter 2 by Agrawal and Rao indicates that evaluation can help to orient policy makers toward policies, programs, and projects that combat inequality:

- Highlighting inequalities through periodic reviews of information
- Evaluating the impact of general economic or social policies on different segments of society
- Conducting ex ante social impact evaluations of development programs or projects to assess if they are likely to reduce or enhance inequalities
- Conducting evaluations of completed projects and the flow of benefits to different sections of society
- Conducting evaluations of development projects specifically aimed at reducing inequalities

Two chapters of this book analyze how evaluation methods can help to design better economic development interventions. Chapter 3 by Ruben demonstrates the complexity of impact evaluation when applied to programs that support value chains for specific agricultural commodities. It advocates for moving beyond simple analysis that concludes modest net welfare effects since substitution effects dominate growth effects, while externalities for neighboring nonparticipants can be substantial. It suggests using a more integrated framework of analysis to generate insights into the welfare and distributional effects of value chain development programs through spatial reallocation of activities, economies of scale and scope, or quality upgrading of production systems.

Chapter 4 by Freeman and Yenice presents an honest assessment of the difficulties of a major agency financing the private sector to focus on pro-poor growth projects, translating strategic intentions into operational activities that deliver tangible benefits for the poor. One strategy is to focus on sectors and regions with relatively high employment of the poor. One interesting finding is that, particularly in middle-income countries, the largest concentrations of poor people may not be in the locations with the highest poverty rates. Overall, the evaluation of projects that have this pro-poor orientation shows that these projects also perform well financially. The authors conclude that a project can be both pro-growth and pro-poor and that more consideration of distributional impacts needs to be factored in during project elaboration and feasibility studies.

Chapters 5 to 8 provide case studies of the contribution of evaluation to the design of social development interventions. Chapter 5 by Doucette focuses on a community empowerment project in Jordan. The evaluation methods used included an analysis of the theory of change, the degree of participation, and the shared perspective of various community stakeholders and a variety of qualitative methods, including the use of case studies based on interviews, focus groups, and "most significant change" stories. Those evaluation methods enabled a better appreciation of the effectiveness and impact of the community empowerment approach used in the project, including commitment of the population, capacity building, reduction in inequalities across genders and tribes, and promotion of social mobility.

Chapter 6 by Nichols, Darnell, and Unterreiner presents a quick evaluation of the Koudmen Sent Lisi Program in St. Lucia, which departs from a traditional approach to poverty reduction through a variety of individual sectoral programs and instead uses a multidimensional approach combining social protection interventions accompanied by integrated psychosocial support addressing issues related to personal identification, health, education, family dynamics, housing, employment, and income. Using mixed methods, they conclude that this more integrated approach to poverty had good results in terms of relevance, effectiveness, efficiency, impacts, and sustainability. This is consistent with other research, most recently the analysis of six randomized trials in Ethiopia, Ghana, Honduras, India, Pakistan, and Peru, with a total of 10,495 participants (Banerjee et al. 2015).

Chapter 7 by Kazienga, Kouanda, Ouedraogo, Rothenbuhler, Over, and de Walque analyzes output and indicators of immediate outcome related to health care received by patients seeking services related to human immunodeficiency virus (HIV)/acquired immune deficiency syndrome (AIDS) in Burkina Faso. Quality of care was measured based on structured interviews with outpatients, and multivariate regressions were used to explore the determinants of the quality of care. The authors found that consulting for HIV-related services, while not more costly to patients, significantly increased the quality of care received. Consulting for HIV/AIDS also increased substantially the time spent waiting to be served. The wealth of patients was not found to affect quality of care, but did help to reduce waiting time, in particular, for HIV patients.

Chapter 8 by Rodriguez-García uses an evaluation portfolio approach to assess the community response to HIV/AIDS. It comprised 17 studies, including country-specific evaluations (Burkina Faso, India, Kenya, Lesotho, Nigeria, Senegal, South Africa, and Zimbabwe), secondary analysis of data, desk surveys, and desk studies. It argues forcefully that this approach enabled the evaluation to identify commonalities and corroborate differences across interventions, providing a more integrated assessment of the overall effectiveness of such a broad intervention.

Third Contribution: Assessing How Public Management Systems Can Contribute to Poverty and Inequality Reduction

Chapter 9 by Fernandez, Garcia-Lopez, Tuon, and Martin looks at ways to assess the contribution of a national development plan (NDP) to reducing poverty and inequality through better elaboration, implementation, and monitoring and evaluation. The two case studies of Cambodia and Costa Rica conclude that NDP evaluations are more complex than project or program evaluations, since they require a combination of macro, meso, and micro approaches, a grasp of technical and institutional issues, a knowledge of a variety of sectors, and an ability to deal with cross-cutting issues. They also point to the positioning of the NDP within the results-based management cycle, linking it to programming and budgeting of concrete poverty and inequality reduction policies and programs at the elaboration phase (top down) and articulating monitoring and evaluation at the operational, programmatic, and strategic levels at the M&E phase (bottom up).

Chapter 10 by Martin, Boily, and Lariviere analyzes a large range of poverty reduction programs in Malaysia at the central level and in two states chosen for their high poverty incidence, Sabah and Sarawak. Evaluation methods included a variety of qualitative and quantitative methods, including a survey of program and project managers. Malaysia is an emerging country that has made great progress in reducing mass poverty, but is faced with the more difficult challenge of addressing poverty pockets. The programs designed for tackling mass poverty are not well equipped to handle poverty pockets, which requires much finer targeting and efforts to link sector strategic objectives and targets to program outputs and costs and to design multiservice packages to address a web of constraints facing the hard-core poor. The chapter formulates several recommendations with regard to planning, budgeting, and monitoring processes at the national and, even more, at the state levels.

Chapter 11 by Lahey focuses on the importance of building a national monitoring and evaluation system to be able to measure the implementation of poverty and inequality reduction strategies and programs. Building country capacity for M&E in the form of a national M&E system requires (1) recognizing and addressing capacity gaps inhibiting development of a national M&E system, (2) developing key components of infrastructure, and (3) sorting out roles and responsibilities of the main players implicated.

Chapter 12 by Ling outlines the conflicting pressures faced by aid agencies and international nongovernmental organizations (NGOs). On the one hand, they are accountable for money they receive and have to demonstrate results during the project's life cycle according to a results-based management approach and, for example, use of a logical framework analysis. On the other hand, they are asked to address underlying constraints in income, wealth, social, and cultural power and to induce in-depth behavioral change, which is complex, takes time, and is dynamic. The confusion has recently become more intense as a result of changes in the aidscape, among others the arrival of new players and the decrease in traditional funding sources. Aid organizations have to address underlying drivers of inequality—what Ling calls structural, underlying, and proximal binding constraints.

Getting the Evaluation Community to Address Inequality

Beyond the contribution of evaluation to poverty and inequality analysis, the authors of the chapters in this book also demonstrate that the evaluation community is starting to address inequality. Chapter 13 by Picciotto advocates eloquently for a more progressive evaluation model in which (a) greater weight is given to ethical values and social justice, (b) greater use is made of contemporary policy research findings about inequality to design new metrics and give higher priority to the global dynamics that have contributed to growing economic and social disparities, and (c) evaluation is perceived as a morally engaged, value-driven occupation with an emphasis on results in terms of social justice and democratic process.

Conclusion

The various chapters of this book illustrate the contributions that evaluation can make to reducing poverty and inequality by improving the analytical framework, analyzing the performance and results of specific programs and projects, as well as assessing and designing better public management systems. They demonstrate that poverty and inequality are complex issues and that the effects of policies and programs will change depending on the specifics of the target group. Advocates of miracle cures and marketers of the latest intellectual fashion, beware! The world is too complex for one-size-fits-all solutions.

Beyond the specific contributions presented, three characteristics of evaluations are relevant for poverty and inequality analysis:

- *A global-local approach.* The approach has to be global to move beyond disciplinary boundaries and consider cross-cutting issues and has to be local to account for the diversity of countries, sectors, institutions, and cultures considered.
- *A problem-solving orientation.* The issue evaluated is the core focus and determines the choice of evaluation methods, which analyze the issue from a variety of angles.
- *An evolutionary approach.* The chapter authors are iconoclasts who do not have any preestablished theory or school of thought to defend. This gives rise to an openness of mind and ability to adapt the analytical framework, the evaluation methods, and the interpretation of results in constant interaction with the stakeholders.

Such characteristics make evaluation a domain that can help us to understand complex issues like poverty, inequality, vulnerability, and their interactions as well as to propose a relevant and useful theory of change for public policies and projects to improve the plight of a large part of the world's population in industrial and developing countries alike.

Notes

1. Some developing countries prefer to rely on an income variable, but this has been shown to be more prone to declaration and measurement errors, as well as variations over time.
2. Even the concept of absolute poverty incorporates relative aspects. For example, the food and nonfood shares assign weights to items in the consumption basket relative to consumption patterns of a population reference group.
3. Incidence is the proportion of the poor in the population. Depth is the gap between the average expenditure level of the poor and the poverty line. Severity is the distribution of the poor below the poverty line. See also Foster, Greer, and Thorbeck (2010).
4. Equity is about fair or just treatment of everyone. Some inequality can be equitable. In most societies, it is considered equitable that someone having and using more complex and scarcer skills, working longer hours, or having more dangerous jobs should earn more than others. As economists say, marginal cost should equal the value of the marginal product at equilibrium.
5. Even if those three sectors are subject to significant fluctuations in the short run, as exemplified by the subprime crisis in the United States around 2008–10 and the oil market glut of 2014–15.

References

Atkinson, A. B., and F. Bourguignon. 2000. *Handbook on Income Distribution*. Amsterdam: North-Holland.

———. 2007. *Handbook on Income Distribution*. Amsterdam: North-Holland.

Banerjee, A., E. Duflo, N. Goldberg, D. Karlan, R. Osei, W. Parienté, J. Shapiro, B. Thuysbaert, and C. Udry. 2015. "A Multifaceted Program Causes Lasting Progress for the Very Poor: Evidence from Six Countries." *Science* 348 (6236). doi: 10.1126/science.1260799.

Boily, M-H., S. Lariviere, F. Martin, L. Traoré, and M. W. Cissé. 2000. "Etude d'évaluation d'impact de la microfinance: Le cas du Réseau Nyesigiso au Mali." Chaire en Développement International, Université Laval, Québec.

Chambers, R. 1997. *Whose Reality Counts: Putting the First Last*. London: Intermediate Technology.

Cingano, F. 2014. "Trends in Income Inequality and Its Impact on Economic Growth." Social, Employment, and Migration Working Paper 163, OECD Publishing, Paris. http://dx.doi.org/10.1787/5jxrjncwxv6j-en.

Dabla-Norris, E., K. Kochhar, F. Ricka, N. Suphaphiphat, and E. Tsounta. 2015. "Causes and Consequences of Income Inequality: A Global Perspective." IMF Staff Discussion Note 15/13, International Monetary Fund, Washington, DC.

Foster, J., J. Greer, and E. Thorbecke. 1984. "A Class of Decomposable Poverty Measures." *Econometrica* 52 (3): 761–76.

———. 2010. "The Foster-Greer-Thorbecke (FGT) Poverty Measures: Twenty-Five Years Later." *Journal of Economic Inequality* 8 (4): 491–524.

Goldin, C., and L. Katz. 2011. *The Race between Education and Technology*. Cambridge, MA: Harvard University Press.

Haughton, J., and S. Khandker. 2009. *Handbook on Poverty and Inequality*. Washington, DC: World Bank.

Lustig, N., L. F. Lopez-Calva, and E. Ortiz-Juarez. 2012. "Declining Inequality in Latin America in the 2000s: The Cases of Argentina, Brazil, and Mexico." Working Paper 307, Center for Global Development, Washington, DC; OECD, Paris.

MEPI (Ministère de l'Economie, du Plan et de l'Intégration). 1997. *Stratégie nationale de lutte contre la pauvreté*. Bamako, Mali: MEPI.

Milanovic, B. 2011. "Global Income Inequality: The Past Two Centuries and Implications for 21st Century." Powerpoint presentation, World Bank, Washington, DC.

Mora, L., and R. Rist. 2009. *The Road to Results: Designing and Conducting Effective Development Evaluations*. Washington, DC: World Bank.

Narayan, D., with R. Patel, K. Schafft, A. Rademacher, and S. Koch-Schulte. 1999. "Can Anyone Hear Us? Voices from 47 Countries." Poverty Group, PREM, World Bank, Washington, DC.

Piketty, T. 2013. *Le capital au XXIe siècle*. Paris: Editions du Seuil. English translation: *Capital in the Twenty-First Century*. Cambridge, MA: Harvard University Press, 2014.

Ravallion, M. 2008. "Evaluating Anti-Poverty Programs." In *Handbook of Development Economics*, vol. 4. Amsterdam: North-Holland-Elsevier.

Sen, A. 1995. *Inequality Reexamined*. Cambridge, MA: Harvard University Press.

Silber, J. 1999. *Handbook on Income Inequality Measurement*. Northwell, MA: Kluwer.

UNDP (United Nations Development Programme). 2014. *The 2014 Millennium Development Goals Report*. New York: UNDP.

United Nations Statistic Division. 2005. *United Nations Handbook on Poverty Statistics: Concepts, Methods, and Policy Use*. New York: United Nations Statistic Division.

World Bank. 2009. *Handbook on Poverty and Inequality*. Washington, DC: World Bank.

green
press
INITIATIVE

www.ingramcontent.com/pod-product-compliance
Lightning Source LLC
Chambersburg PA
CBHW080413270326
41929CB00018B/3008